CW00801543

HEGEL'S *ELEMENT*
PHILOSOPHY OF

A Critical Guide

Hegel's *Elements of the Philosophy of Right*, one of the classic texts of German Idealism, is a seminal work of legal, social and political philosophy that has generated very different interpretations since its publication in 1821. Written with the advantage of historical distance, the essays in this volume adopt a fresh perspective to make readers aware of the breadth and depth of this classic work. Their themes reflect the continuing relevance of the text to modern-day concerns, and include the concept of property, Hegel's view of morality, the concept of *Sittlichkeit*, the modern family, and the nature and tensions of civil society, together with its relation to the state. The volume will be of interest to all scholars and students of German Idealism.

DAVID JAMES is Associate Professor of Philosophy at the University of Warwick. His publications include *Fichte's Republic: Idealism, History and Nationalism* (Cambridge University Press, 2015); *Rousseau and German Idealism: Freedom, Dependence and Necessity* (Cambridge University Press, 2013); and *Fichte's Social and Political Philosophy: Property and Virtue* (Cambridge University Press, 2011). He is co-editor (with Günter Zöller) of *The Cambridge Companion to Fichte* (Cambridge University Press, 2016).

CAMBRIDGE CRITICAL GUIDES

Titles published in this series:

Hegel's *Phenomenology of Spirit*
EDITED BY DEAN MOYAR AND MICHAEL QUANTE

Mill's *On Liberty*
EDITED BY C. L. TEN

Kant's *Idea for a Universal History with a Cosmopolitan Aim*
EDITED BY AMÉLIE OKSENBERG RORTY AND JAMES SCHMIDT

Kant's *Groundwork of the Metaphysics of Morals*
EDITED BY JENS TIMMERMANN

Kant's *Critique of Practical Reason*
EDITED BY ANDREWS REATH AND JENS TIMMERMANN

Wittgenstein's *Philosophical Investigations*
EDITED BY ARIF AHMED

Kierkegaard's *Concluding Unscientific Postscript*
EDITED BY RICK ANTHONY FURTAK

Plato's *Republic*
EDITED BY MARK L. MCPHERRAN

Plato's *Laws*
EDITED BY CHRISTOPHER BOBONICH

Spinoza's *Theological–Political Treatise*
EDITED BY YITZHAK Y. MELAMED AND MICHAEL A. ROSENTHAL

Aristotle's *Nicomachean Ethics*
EDITED BY JON MILLER

Kant's *Metaphysics of Morals*
EDITED BY LARA DENIS

Nietzsche's *On the Genealogy of Morality*
EDITED BY SIMON MAY

Kant's *Observations and Remarks*
EDITED BY RICHARD VELKLEY AND SUSAN SHELL

Augustine's *City of God*
EDITED BY JAMES WETZEL

Descartes' *Meditations*
EDITED BY KAREN DETLEFSEN

Kant's *Religion within the Boundaries of Mere Reason*
EDITED BY GORDON MICHALSON

Kant's *Lectures on Anthropology*
EDITED BY ALIX COHEN

Kierkegaard's *Fear and Trembling*
EDITED BY DANIEL CONWAY

Kant's *Lectures on Ethics*
EDITED BY LARA DENIS AND OLIVER SENSEN

Aristotle's *Physics*
EDITED BY MARISKA LEUNISSEN

Aristotle's *Politics*
EDITED BY THORNTON LOCKWOOD AND THANASSIS SAMARAS

Aquinas's *Disputed Questions on Evil*
EDITED BY M. V. DOUGHERTY

Fichte's *Foundations of Natural Right*
EDITED BY GABRIEL GOTTLIEB

HEGEL'S *ELEMENTS OF THE PHILOSOPHY OF RIGHT*

A Critical Guide

EDITED BY

DAVID JAMES

University of Warwick

CAMBRIDGE
UNIVERSITY PRESS

University Printing House, Cambridge CB2 8BS, United Kingdom

One Liberty Plaza, 20th Floor, New York, NY 10006, USA

477 Williamstown Road, Port Melbourne, VIC 3207, Australia

314-321, 3rd Floor, Plot 3, Splendor Forum, Jasola District Centre, New Delhi - 110025, India

79 Anson Road, #06-04/06, Singapore 079906

Cambridge University Press is part of the University of Cambridge.

It furthers the University's mission by disseminating knowledge in the pursuit of education, learning and research at the highest international levels of excellence.

www.cambridge.org
Information on this title: www.cambridge.org/9781107434929
10.1017/ 9781139939560

© Cambridge University Press 2017

This publication is in copyright. Subject to statutory exception and to the provisions of relevant collective licensing agreements, no reproduction of any part may take place without the written permission of Cambridge University Press.

First published 2017
First paperback edition 2018

A catalogue record for this publication is available from the British Library

Library of Congress Cataloging in Publication data
Names: James, David, 1966– editor.
Title: Hegel's 'Elements of the philosophy of right' : a critical guide / [edited by] David James, University of Warwick.
Description: New York : Cambridge University Press, 2017. |
Series: Cambridge critical guides | Includes bibliographical references and index.
Identifiers: LCCN 2016050460 | ISBN 9781107077928 (hardback : alk. paper)
Subjects: LCSH: Hegel, Georg Wilhelm Friedrich, 1770–1831. Grundlinien der Philosophie des Rechts. | Law–Philosophy. | Natural law.
Classification: LCC K230.H43 A3116 2017 | DDC 320.01/1–dc23
LC record available at https://lccn.loc.gov/2016050460

ISBN 978-1-107-07792-8 Hardback
ISBN 978-1-107-43492-9 Paperback

Cambridge University Press has no responsibility for the persistence or accuracy of URLs for external or third-party internet websites referred to in this publication, and does not guarantee that any content on such websites is, or will remain, accurate or appropriate.

Contents

Contributors

Andrew Buchwalter is Presidential Professor at the University of North Florida. He is the author of *Dialectics, Politics, and the Contemporary Value of Hegel's Practical Philosophy* (Routledge, 2011) and the edited volumes *Hegel and Global Justice* (Springer, 2012) and *Hegel and Capitalism* (SUNY Press, 2015).

Stephen Houlgate is Professor of Philosophy at the University of Warwick. He is the author of *Hegel, Nietzsche and the Criticism of Metaphysics* (1986), *An Introduction to Hegel: Freedom, Truth and History* (1991; 2nd edn, 2005), *The Opening of Hegel's Logic* (2006) and *Hegel's Phenomenology of Spirit* (2013), and he has also published numerous articles on Hegel, as well as on Kant, Schiller, Schelling, Nietzsche, Derrida, Danto, Rawls, Brandom and McDowell. He is the editor of *Hegel and the Philosophy of Nature* and *The Hegel Reader* (both 1998), *Hegel and the Arts* (2007) and *G. W. F. Hegel: Elements of the Philosophy of Right* (2008), and co-editor with Michael Baur of *A Companion to Hegel* (2011).

Kimberly Hutchings is Professor of Politics and International Relations at Queen Mary University of London. She is the author of several books, including *Kant, Critique and Politics* (1996), *Hegel and Feminist Philosophy* (2003) and *Time and World Politics: Thinking the Present* (2008), and co-editor (with Tuija Pulkkinen) of *Beyond Antigone: Hegel's Philosophy and Feminist Thought* (2010).

David James is Associate Professor of Philosophy at the University of Warwick. His publications include *Fichte's Republic: Idealism, History and Nationalism* (Cambridge University Press, 2015), *Rousseau and German Idealism: Freedom, Dependence and Necessity* (Cambridge University Press, 2013) and *Fichte's Social and Political Philosophy: Property and Virtue* (Cambridge University Press, 2011).

Dean Moyar is Associate Professor in the Department of Philosophy at Johns Hopkins University. He is the author of *Hegel's Conscience* (Oxford University Press, 2011). He is co-editor (with Michael Quante) of *Hegel's Phenomenology of Spirit: A Critical Guide* (Cambridge University Press, 2008) and the editor of the *Routledge Companion to Nineteenth Century Philosophy* (2010).

Frederick Neuhouser is Professor of Philosophy at Barnard College, Columbia University. He is the author of four books: *Rousseau's Critique of Inequality* (2014); *Rousseau's Theodicy of Self-Love: Evil, Rationality, and the Drive for Recognition* (2008); *Actualizing Freedom: Foundations of Hegel's Social Theory* (2000); and *Fichte's Theory of Subjectivity* (1990).

Frank Ruda is Interim Professor for Philosophy of Audiovisual Media at the Bauhaus University of Weimar. His publications include *Hegel's Rabble: An Investigation into Hegel's Philosophy of Right* (Continuum, 2011), *For Badiou: Idealism without Idealism* (Northwestern University Press, 2015) and *Abolishing Freedom: A Plea for a Contemporary Use of Fatalism* (Nebraska University Press, 2016).

Hans-Christoph Schmidt am Busch is Professor of Philosophy at the Technische Universität Braunschweig. His recent books include *La 'reconnaissance' comme principe de la Théorie critique* (Éditions de l'école normale supérieure, 2015) and *Hegel et le saint-simonisme* (Presses Universitaires du Mirail, 2012). He is the editor of Charles Fourier, *Über das weltweite soziale Chaos. Ausgewählte Schriften zur Philosophie und Gesellschaftstheorie* (Akademie Verlag, 2012) and co-editor (with C. F. Zurn) of *The Philosophy of Recognition: Historical and Contemporary Perspectives* (Rowman & Littlefield, 2010). He has also edited a special issue of *Ethical Theory and Moral Practice* on 'Karl Marx and the philosophy of recognition' (2013).

Ludwig Siep is Professor Emeritus at the University of Münster. His books include *Hegels Fichtekritik und die Wissenschaftslehre von 1804* (1970), *Anerkennung als Prinzip der praktischen Philosophie* (2nd edn, 2014), *Praktische Philosophie im Deutschen Idealismus* (1992), *Der Weg der Phänomenologie des Geistes* (2000, English translation: *Hegel's Phenomenology of Spirit*, Cambridge University Press, 2014), *Aktualität und Grenzen der praktischen Philosophie Hegels* (2010) and *Der Staat als irdischer Gott. Genesis und Relevanz einer Hegelschen Idee* (2015). He is the editor of *G. W. F. Hegel: Grundlinien der Philosophie des Rechts* (3rd edn, 2014).

Allen W. Wood is Ruth Norman Halls Professor at Indiana University and Ward W. and Priscilla B. Woods Professor emeritus at Stanford University. He is the author of numerous articles and author or editor of over twenty books, including *Karl Marx* (1981; 2nd edn, 2004), *Hegel's Ethical Thought* (1990), *Kant's Ethical Thought* (1999), *The Free Development of Each: Studies on Freedom Right and Ethics in Classical German Philosophy* (2014) and *Fichte's Ethical Thought* (2016).

Abbreviations

Writings of Hegel

Werke	*Werke*, ed. Eva Moldenhauer and Karl Markus Michel, 20 vols. (Suhrkamp: Frankfurt am Main, 1969–1971). Cited by volume and page number.
EL	*The Encyclopaedia Logic* (Part I of the *Encyclopaedia of the Philosophical Sciences*), trans. T. F. Geraets, W. A. Suchting and H. S. Harris (Indianapolis: Hackett, 1991). Cited according to paragraph (§) numbers. R indicates a remark which Hegel himself added to the paragraph, while A indicates an addition deriving from student lecture notes.
GW	*Gesammelte Werke*, ed. Nordrhein-Westfälischen Akademie der Wissenschaften in association with the Deutsche Forschungsgemeinschaft (Hamburg: Felix Meiner, 1968–). Cited by volume and page number.
HPW	*Political Writings*, ed. Laurence Dickey and H. B. Nisbet (Cambridge: Cambridge University Press, 1999)
LNR	*Lectures on Natural Right and Political Science: The First Philosophy of Right, Heidelberg 1817–1818 with Additions from the Lectures of 1818–1819*, trans. J. Michael Stewart and Peter C. Hodgson (Berkeley: University of California Press, 1995). Cited by paragraph (§) numbers. R indicates a remark.
JR	*Jenaer Realphilosophie. Vorlesungsmanuskripte zur Philosophie der Natur und des Geistes von 1805–1806*, ed. Johannes Hoffmeister (Hamburg: Meiner, 1969)
NL	*Natural Law*, trans. T. M. Knox (Philadelphia: University of Pennsylvania Press, 1975)
PhG	*Phenomenology of Spirit*, trans. A. V. Miller (Oxford: Oxford University Press, 1977)
PM	*Philosophy of Mind*, trans. W. Wallace and A. V. Miller, rev. Michael J. Inwood (Oxford: Oxford University Press, 2007).

	Cited according to paragraph (§) numbers. R indicates a remark which Hegel himself added to the paragraph, while A indicates an addition deriving from student lecture notes.
PR	*Elements of the Philosophy of Right*, ed. Allen W. Wood, trans. H. B. Nisbet (Cambridge: Cambridge University Press, 1991). Translation of *Grundlinien der Philosophie des Rechts oder Naturrecht und Staatswissenschaft im Grundrisse*, in *Werke*, vol. 7. Cited according to paragraph (§) numbers. R indicates a remark which Hegel himself added to the paragraph, while A indicates an addition deriving from student lecture notes. The only exceptions are the Preface, which is cited by the page number of the English translation followed by that of the German edition, and Hegel's marginal notes, which are cited by the German edition page number only.
PR 1819/20	*Philosophie des Rechts. Die Vorlesung von 1819/20 in einer Nachschrift*, ed. Dieter Henrich (Frankfurt am Main: Suhrkamp, 1983).
PR 1819/20 Ringier	*Vorlesungen über die Philosophie des Rechts. Berlin 1819/1820*, transcribed by Johann Rudolf Ringier, in *G. W. F. Hegel. Vorlesungen. Ausgewählte Nachschriften und Manuskripte*, vol. 14, ed. Emil Angehrn, Martin Bondeli and Hoo Nam Seelmann (Hamburg: Felix Meiner, 2000).
PR 1821/22	*Die Philosophie des Rechts. Vorlesung von 1821/22*, ed. Hansgeorg Hoppe (Frankfurt am Main: Suhrkamp, 2005). Cited by paragraph (§) number.
PW	*Political Writings*, trans. T. M. Knox, ed. Z. A. Pelczynski (Oxford: Oxford University Press, 1964)
SEL	*System of Ethical Life (1802/03) and First Philosophy of Spirit*, ed. and trans. H. S. Harris and T. M. Knox (Albany, NY: SUNY Press, 1979).
SL	*Science of Logic*, trans. A. V. Miller (Amherst: Humanity Books, 1999).
VNS	*Vorlesungen über Naturrecht und Staatswissenschaft*, transcribed by Peter Wannenmann, in *G. W. F. Hegel. Vorlesungen. Ausgewählte Nachschriften und Manuskripte*, vol. 1, ed. Claudia Becker, Wolfgang Bonsiepen, Annemarie Gethmann-Siefert, Friedrich Hogemann, Walter Jaeschke, Christoph Jamme, Hans Christian Lucas, Kurt Rainer Meist and Hans Josef Schneider (Hamburg: Felix Meiner, 1983). Cited by paragraph (§) number.

VRP *Vorlesungen über Rechtsphilosophie 1818–1831*, ed. Karl-Heinz Ilting, 4 vols. (Stuttgart: Frommann-Holzboog, 1973–1974). Cited by volume and page number.

Writings of Kant

AA *Kant's gesammelte Schriften*, ed. Königliche Preußische (later Deutsche) Akademie der Wissenschaften (Berlin: Reimer/de Gruyter, 1900–).

G *Grundlegung zur Metaphysik der Sitten* (AA 4). *Groundwork of the Metaphysics of Morals*, in *Practical Philosophy*, trans. and ed. Mary J. Gregor (Cambridge: Cambridge University Press, 1996). Cited by AA page number.

KrV *Critique of Pure Reason*, trans. and ed. Paul Guyer and Allen W. Wood (Cambridge: Cambridge University Press, 1998). Cited by A/B pagination.

KpV *Kritik der praktischen Vernunft* (AA 5). *Critique of Practical Reason*, in *Practical Philosophy*. Cited by AA page number.

KU *Kritik der Urteilskraft* (AA 5). *Critique of the Power of Judgment*, ed. Paul Guyer, trans. Paul Guyer and Eric Matthews (Cambridge: Cambridge University Press, 2000). Cited by AA page number.

MS *Metaphysik der Sitten* (AA 6). *The Metaphysics of Morals*, in *Practical Philosophy*. Cited by AA page number.

R *Religion innerhalb der Grenzen der bloßen Vernunft* (AA 6). *Religion within the Boundaries of Mere Reason*, in *Religion and Rational Theology*, ed. and trans. Allen W. Wood and George di Giovanni (Cambridge: Cambridge University Press, 1996). Cited by AA page number.

TP *Über den Gemeinspruch: Das mag in der Theorie richtig sein, taugt aber nicht für die Praxis* (AA 8). *On the common saying: That may be correct in theory but it is of no use in practice*, in *Practical Philosophy*. Cited by AA page number.

Writings of Fichte

SW *Fichtes sämmtliche Werke*, ed. I. H. Fichte (Berlin: de Gruyter, 1970). Cited by volume and page number.

EPW *Fichte: Early Philosophical Writings*, ed. Daniel Breazeale (Ithaca, NY: Cornell University Press, 1988). Cited by page number.

SE *The System of Ethics* (1798), trans. and ed. Daniel Breazeale and Günter Zöller (Cambridge: Cambridge University Press, 2005).

Introduction: Freedom and History in Hegel's Philosophy of Right

David James

G. W. F. Hegel's *Elements of the Philosophy of Right or Natural Law and Political Science in Outline* (*Grundlinien der Philosophie des Rechts oder Naturrecht und Staatswissenschaft im Grundrisse*), to give the work its full title, was, according to its title page, published in 1821, though the actual year of publication appears to have been 1820.[1] This work was conceived as a 'textbook' (*Lehrbuch*) designed by Hegel to fulfil 'the need to provide my audience with an introduction to the lectures on the *Philosophy of Right* which I deliver in the course of my official duties' (PR *Preface*, 9[11]). The audience in question was made up of Hegel's students at the University of Berlin, where he had already begun to lecture on the same topic in the winter semesters of 1818–19 and 1819–20, and would do so another three times, in 1821–22, 1822–23 and 1824–25, if one excludes the series of lectures he began to deliver in the winter of 1831 that was soon cut short by his death in the same year. Hegel had also lectured on the same topic at the University of Heidelberg in the winter semester of 1817–18, by which time he had published the first edition of his *Encyclopaedia of the Philosophical Sciences in Outline* (*Enzyklopädie der philosophischen Wissenschaften im Grundrisse*), which introduces some of the central concepts developed in the published version of the *Philosophy of Right*. The latter is, in fact, described as 'a more extensive, and in particular a more systematic, exposition of the same basic concepts' found in the *Encyclopaedia* in the section on 'objective' spirit (PR *Preface*, 9[11]). It consists of consecutively numbered paragraphs to which in many cases Hegel has added remarks 'so as to clarify on occasion the more abstract contents of the text and to take fuller account of related ideas [*Vorstellungen*] which are current at the present time' (PR *Preface*, 9[11]),

[1] See Hans-Christian Lucas and Udo Rameil, 'Furcht vor der Zensur? Zur Entstehungs- und Druckgeschichte von Hegels Grundlinien der Philosophie des Rechts', *Hegel-Studien* 15 (1980), 91–92.

together with a preface and an introduction. Additions drawn from student notes were subsequently added to the edition of the *Philosophy of Right* that formed part of the edition of Hegel's works undertaken after his death by some of his students.

Although Hegel regarded the function of the Preface to the *Philosophy of Right* as 'merely to make external and subjective comments on the point of view of the work to which it is prefaced' (PR *Preface*, 23[28]), this preface and some claims found in the additions to the main paragraphs of the *Philosophy of Right* derived from student notes of the lectures have played a major role in the reception of the work. Already in 1857 Hegel was said to deserve the title of 'the official Prussian philosopher of the Restoration and of the state',[2] in particular on the basis of the following claim made in the Preface: 'What is rational is actual; and what is actual is rational' (PR *Preface*, 20[24]). This so-called *Doppelsatz* is here interpreted to mean that whatever exists must, merely in virtue of the fact that it exists, be considered rational and in this respect good. Thus, the Prussian state, in which Hegel happened to be living at the time, must be considered rational and good in virtue of its mere existence. Although this type of interpretation of the *Doppelsatz* ignores Hegel's technical use of the term 'actual' (*wirklich*) or 'actuality' (*Wirklichkeit*), and the way in which he carefully distinguishes it from the notions of factual being (*Dasein*) and existence (*Existenz*) (EL § 6R),[3] it came, in the wake of two world wars, to characterize the twentieth-century Anglophone reception of Hegel's political philosophy. Hegel became, in fact, more than simply a reactionary figure and apologist for the Prussian state: he was even held to be an advocate of unlimited state power and the historicist doctrine that the rightness of something is determined by its historical success, making him a forerunner of modern totalitarianism.[4] It took until the early 1970s

[2] Rudolf Haym, 'Extract from *Hegel and his Times* (1857)', in Robert Stern (ed.), *G. W. F. Hegel Critical Assessments*, Vol. I, trans. Julius Kraft, (London: Routledge, 1993), 221.

[3] This distinction opens the way for a reading of the *Doppelsatz* that stresses its progressive nature, in the sense of demanding the transformation of existing states whenever they do not measure up to the demands of reason. See Michael O. Hardimon, *Hegel's Social Philosophy: The Project of Reconciliation* (Cambridge: Cambridge University Press, 1994), 52–83. Insofar as it emphasizes the dynamic nature of Hegel's notion of reason, and the need for reason to be actualized in the world, this type of interpretation of the *Doppelsatz* finds support in an alternative formulation of it which Hegel is recorded as having offered: 'What is rational becomes actual, and the actual becomes rational' (VRP 1819/20, 51).

[4] This tendency culminates in Karl Popper's denunciation of Hegel's philosophy published in the final year of the Second World War, which also charges Hegel with being a nationalist. See K. R. Popper, *The Open Society and Its Enemies, Volume II, The High Tide of Prophecy: Hegel, Marx, and the Aftermath* (London: Routledge & Kegan Paul, 1945), 25–76.

for a full-length study that provided a corrective to this one-sided picture of Hegel's political philosophy to be published in English.[5]

More recently, the tendency has been to discuss Hegel's *Philosophy of Right* in terms of a concept that forms a central liberal value and is typically assumed to be strictly opposed to totalitarianism, namely freedom.[6] It appears difficult, in fact, to explain how any serious engagement with the text could arrive at the conclusion that Hegel was an enemy of freedom, as is implied by the view of the *Philosophy of Right* as the model of a proto-totalitarian state, when he himself makes clear in the Introduction that freedom is both the subject and the object of this work, by defining right as 'any existence [*Dasein*] in general which is the *existence* of the *free will*' (PR § 29). There is also the following statement:

> The basis of right is the *realm of spirit* in general and its precise location and point of departure is the *will*; the will is *free*, so that freedom constitutes its substance and destiny and the system of right is the realm of actualized freedom, the world of spirit produced from within itself as a second nature. (PR § 4)

Hegel clearly thinks, then, that for a law, social practice or institution to count as an instance of right in the strict sense of an object of the 'philosophical science of right' (PR § 1), it must somehow represent a way in which the free will gives itself existence and thereby actualizes itself. In this respect, the concept of right has for Hegel a normative dimension: for something to count as an instance of right it must meet certain standards. Right cannot, therefore, be identified simply with whatever happens to exist. Rather, if any law, social practice or institution is to count as a legitimate one which imposes genuine obligations on individual or collective social or political agents, it must meet the condition of being a way in which the free will gives itself existence, in the sense that such a will is able to actualize itself through this law, social practice or institution, making the law, social practice or institution in question into an enabling condition of freedom. One must assume, then, that Hegel's *Philosophy of Right*, as a 'system' of right, aims to present all such legal, social and political conditions of freedom as forming a unified whole, a task that will demand showing how each sphere of right necessarily relates to the other ones.

[5] Shlomo Avineri, *Hegel's Theory of the Modern State* (Cambridge: Cambridge University Press, 1972).

[6] Paul Franco, *Hegel's Philosophy of Freedom* (New Haven: Yale University Press, 1999); Frederick Neuhouser, *Foundations of Hegel's Social Theory: Actualizing Freedom* (Cambridge, MA: Harvard University Press, 2000); and Alan Patten, *Hegel's Idea of Freedom* (Oxford: Oxford University Press, 1999).

The importance Hegel clearly attaches to the concept of freedom promises to provide a corrective to accounts of his social and political philosophy that emphasize certain claims that feature in what is, after all, only a preface or in some of the additions that derive from student notes of Hegel's lectures, rather than from a text that Hegel himself intended for publication. These include claims that suggest the existence of an all-powerful state with a quasi-divine status, such as the one that '[t]he state consists in the march of God in the world' (PR § 258A) and the one that we should 'venerate the state as an earthly divinity' (PR § 272A). The centrality of the concept of freedom to Hegel's *Philosophy of Right* is not by itself sufficient, however, to counter the view of Hegel as an essentially anti-liberal or even proto-totalitarian political philosopher, for it is precisely his 'positive' notion of freedom that has been claimed to justify this view of his philosophy. According to Isaiah Berlin, this notion of freedom involves ideas of self-mastery and self-direction that entail the existence of a real and higher rational self, on the one hand, and an inauthentic and lower irrational self, on the other. This in turn allegedly justifies coercing others into doing what they would have done if they had obeyed their real and higher self instead of obeying commands prompted by the mistaken beliefs and desires of their lower self.[7] According to Berlin, it is, moreover, natural to view this task of coercing others as one that is performed by an authoritarian state. When applied to Hegel, however, this account of the alleged perils of a positive concept of freedom confronts at least two major difficulties, leaving aside the question as to whether Berlin's characterization of positive freedom is even a fair one.[8] First of all, Hegel identifies certain spheres of right in which something very much like Berlin's preferred negative concept of freedom, insofar as it involves freedom from coercion, including state coercion, is recognized and protected. Secondly, Hegel arguably has good reasons for seeking to develop a concept of freedom which complements, rather than displaces altogether, this negative concept of freedom.

Regarding the first point, the spheres of right in which negative freedom is recognized and protected are abstract right and civil society especially, whereas Hegel's 'positive' concept of freedom is present in the sphere of morality and is then given a social and political content in some

[7] Isaiah Berlin, *Two Concepts of Liberty* (Oxford: Clarendon Press, 1958).

[8] Arguably, however, it is not a fair one, because in order to establish a connection between totalitarianism and the positive concept of freedom Berlin can be seen to introduce ideas that are wholly independent of the latter. See Allen W. Wood, *Hegel's Ethical Thought* (Cambridge: Cambridge University Press, 1990), 42 and Raymond Geuss, *Outside Ethics* (Princeton, NJ: Princeton University Press, 2005), 69–70.

of the institutions of civil society and in the state, or, to be more precise, through the relation in which individuals stand to these institutions and to the state. Abstract right is 'abstract' or 'formal' because 'it is not a question of particular interests, of my advantage or welfare, and just as little of the particular ground by which my will is determined, i.e. of my insight and intention' (PR § 37). Rather, all 'particularity' is ignored, making it possible to conceive of individuals as equal and identical legal subjects, each of which has the right to be treated as a person, that is to say, as an 'abstract and free "I"' (PR § 35R), and is the bearer of a set of rights, each of which follows from the concept of personality. These rights include the right of private property and the right to enter freely into contractual relations with other persons. Given this abstraction from all concrete ends and interests, the obligations that persons have towards each other and the obligations that the state has towards each and every person are purely negative in character, assuming as they do the form of the general prohibition '*not to violate* personality and what ensues from personality' (PR § 38). The actualization of this form of right presupposes a legal system, which applies laws and judges individual cases of alleged violations of right, an agency concerned with law enforcement and the detection, investigation and prevention of crime, and other administrative and legislative bodies that operate at the level of the political state. These institutions, as essential parts of Hegel's account of civil society and the state, form moments of that which he terms 'ethical life' (*Sittlichkeit*).

Negative freedom is therefore respected within Hegel's state, in that the latter recognizes the legitimacy of a legally and institutionally guaranteed sphere of personal freedom in which individuals are free from coercive acts on the part of others and also on the part of the state, at least so long as they do not violate the rights of others to enjoy their own sphere of personal freedom. Although Hegel regards abstract right and the institutions that actualize it at the level of ethical life as negative conditions of freedom, in the sense that one could not be free in an external sense if one's actions were subject to arbitrary interference, whether it be actual or potential interference, on the part of others, he criticizes this negative concept of freedom on account of its one-sidedness. On reflection, this concept of freedom can, in fact, be understood as in some sense incompatible with the notion of freedom itself.

When the negative concept of freedom is taken to be the only genuine form of freedom and the need for it to be protected by means of law and by the state is also granted, we would appear to have a scenario in which freedom is limited for the sake of freedom, in the sense that each person's freedom from constraint, and thus the opportunity to act according to his or her own desires, whatever they happen to be, requires the real or potential limitation of the freedom of others to act according to certain desires that they might have. The purely negative character of this form of limitation means that what is rational (i.e. law understood as something to which all rational agents could agree insofar as they are concerned with securing their personal freedom) can 'appear only as a limitation on … freedom … and not as an immanent rationality, but only as an external and formal universal' (PR § 29R). This purely external form of limitation contradicts the notion of freedom in the sense that it implies that one is limited by something purely external to oneself at the same time as one takes oneself to be free in the negative sense of not being subject to constraint. In this way, Hegel appears to want to argue that direct forms of coercion, especially the application of physical force, are only the most obvious forms of a lack of freedom. Is there, then, a form of freedom in which the idea that freedom is limited can be thought together with the idea that one remains free despite this limitation of one's freedom in a purely negative sense? Hegel thinks that it is possible to conceive of such a form of freedom only if that which is rational, and in virtue of its rationality of general validity ('universal'), can be understood not as an 'external' limitation on one's freedom but, rather, as in some sense a matter of *self*-limitation or *self*-determination.

This type of freedom is found at the individual level in morality, where we have a series of forms of agency in which freedom in the negative sense is limited through an act of self-limitation or self-determination. One example of this is when a moral agent restricts itself in the sense of ruling out other possible courses of action through the act of willing one end (and thus the means to it) rather than other possible ends. Through such an act this agent becomes, moreover, responsible for one set of consequences rather than another set of possible consequences. There is also an act of self-determination or self-limitation when an agent subjects itself to a set of norms that obliges it to act (or not to act) in certain ways rather than in other ones. In both cases, a fundamental right of the subject is satisfied insofar as the agent is genuinely able to recognize itself in its actions and their consequences, or in the norms which it obeys, in the sense that it can view them as products of its own will. This is to honour 'the *right of the subjective will*' and the idea that 'the will can *recognize* something or *be* something only in so far as that thing is *its own*, and in so far as the will is present to itself in it as subjectivity' (PR § 107). Hegel's recognition of this right of the subjective will leads him to stress the importance of the subjective dimension of freedom, as when he speaks of 'the right of subjective freedom', which consists in finding satisfaction in an action through being able to recognize it as expressive of one's own particular self (PR §§ 121, 124, 124R). Although the notion of self-determination is clearly present in Hegel's account of the moral standpoint, *pace* Berlin nothing I have said so far suggests a justification of state coercion based on the idea of making individuals do what they would have done if they had obeyed their real and higher self instead of obeying the commands prompted by the mistaken beliefs and desires of their lower self. Rather, Hegel develops what can be seen as a much richer concept of freedom in comparison with Berlin's reductive notion of freedom, which identifies genuine freedom as nothing more than being able to act in accordance with one's given desires in the absence of external constraints, by drawing attention to the importance of the subjective aspect of free agency and by seeking to explain how individuals can remain free even when their freedom is at the same time limited or subject to constraint.

Hegel makes claims that nevertheless support the idea that in order to be truly free the subjective aspect of free agency must have as its object something that conforms to certain objectively valid standards. He does not, therefore, treat existing desires or beliefs as in themselves authoritative. The sheer givenness of these desires and beliefs means, in fact, that the content of the will 'is not derived from its own self-determining activity as such' (PR § 15R). Here we can see the importance of the idea of a free will which is not immediately determined by the desires and beliefs that it just happens to have, as well as the importance of the idea that being truly free requires willing the right kind of content. The correspondence between the subjectivity of the free, undetermined will and the objectivity of the content of its willing forms the 'abstract concept of the Idea of the will' which 'is in general *the free will which wills the free will*' (PR § 27). It is only, however, when 'the will has universality, or itself as infinite form, as its content, object, and end' that 'it is free not only *in itself* but also *for itself*' (PR § 21). In the same paragraph, moreover, Hegel appears to treat the notions of 'self-determining universality', the will and freedom as different expressions of what is essentially the same idea. It is only when its content is of a universal kind, then, that the willing agent can become fully conscious of its freedom, in the sense of being able to recognize itself in that which limits its will. This demand for the will to be able to recognize itself in a content of a universal kind signals a clear way in which existing desires and beliefs can be measured against a standard that is independent of them: they must in some sense be compatible with, or correspond to, that which has a universal status.

In the later paragraphs on morality, Hegel argues with reference to the alleged failures of Kant's moral theory and the moral subjectivism of appeals to conscience alone to determine the content of duty that it is only at the level of ethical life and in the state that 'substantial' freedom becomes genuinely possible (PR § 149, § 149A, § 257). While both abstract right and morality adopt the perspective of individuals and abstract from the determinate social context which forms the implicit background to their views of themselves, of others and of the world in which they act, this social context is made explicit at the level of ethical life. Here the individual is in each case viewed as part of a larger whole, whether as family member, as an economic and social agent in a condition of mutual dependence or as a citizen. As the member of a larger whole, the individual not only stands in essential relations to others but also is dependent on them, regardless of whether or not he or she recognizes this fact, so that once again the will is limited or constrained.

Given this social context, the claim that Hegel's *Philosophy of Right* opens the way to forms of state coercion justified on the basis of making individuals do what they would have done if they had obeyed their real and higher self is surely both an exaggerated and a misguided one. First of all, as we have seen, Hegel allows some space for acting on the basis of given beliefs and desires, irrespective of their precise nature, so long as doing so does not violate the personal freedom of others. Secondly, this area of negative freedom itself presupposes constraints on what individuals may or may not do, and it must, if necessary, be maintained by means of coercion exercised by the state or an alternative body capable of fulfilling this function. Here Hegel is not self-evidently wrong to think that individuals would be freer if they did not experience such necessary constraints on their freedom in the negative sense of the term as limitations with which they cannot identify themselves as free agents. These constraints on their wills can be regarded as universal not only in the sense of deriving from laws that are valid for and apply to all individuals, but also in the sense of being constraints imposed on social agents by the demands of social cooperation and the need to live peaceably together within the same legal and political community. Thus explaining how the will can remain free at the same time as it is subject to constraints will require providing an account of how individuals can identify themselves with, and for this reason freely endorse, these social constraints as well as any formal legal ones. Otherwise essential features of their social world will remain purely external forms of constraint.

Among such social constraints on freedom understood in a purely negative sense, Hegel includes practices, norms and forms of association that arise largely spontaneously in civil society as a result of individuals seeking to satisfy their needs by means of acts of production and acts of exchange with others. This shows that for him the fact of human interdependence by itself means that the extent to which human beings are not subject to constraints of one kind or another, and are therefore able to act on the basis of given desires and beliefs without suffering any form of interference, must be thought to be very limited indeed. Thus, one restricts the realm of freedom to a severely limited sphere of human existence and actions when one reduces the idea of freedom to the negative concept of it. Hegel, in contrast, endeavours to understand how such constraints can be understood as compatible with the idea of freedom. Moreover, Hegel views both human needs and their objects as social in character (and in this respect 'universal') and for this reason as not being fixed (PR §§ 190–192). It is therefore not clear how being able to act on the basis of given desires or beliefs in the absence of constraint is sufficient to explain the possibility of freedom. Rather, these desires or beliefs are themselves determined by society, and thus by factors beyond an individual's immediate control; and if society were organized differently from how it happens to be organized, people's beliefs and desires could in some significant cases turn out to be very different from what they currently happen to be. The acceptance of the authority and incorrigibility of given desires and beliefs in any statement of what freedom essentially is – such as being able to act in accordance with these desires or beliefs, given the absence of any external impediments to doing so – in this respect begins to look questionable.

Hegel has some good reasons, then, for seeking to develop an alternative concept of freedom which complements, rather than displaces altogether, the negative concept of freedom favoured by Berlin. This concept of freedom is one that Hegel associates with the idea that the object of the will is in some way the will itself 'and therefore not something which it sees as *other* or as a *limitation*' (PR § 22). With this form of freedom 'the will is completely *with itself* [*bei sich*], because it has reference to nothing but itself, so that every relationship of *dependence* on something *other* than itself is thereby eliminated' (PR § 23). The object of the will is not literally itself, however, and it is not the case that there is no dependence whatsoever on its object. A careful reading of the first passage suggests, in fact, that the object is the will itself only in the sense that something independent of the will can be viewed in such a way that the subject or agent can in some sense recognize itself in this object, even though it constitutes a limit to its act of willing and thus constrains it.

As we have seen, the particular form that any such constraint on willing assumes in a collective and communal body made up of members of the same society and the same state includes practices, norms and forms of association connected with the generation and satisfaction of needs in a condition of interdependence, as well as laws and the institutions of the state. The way in which individuals may recognize themselves in that which at the same time acts as a constraint on their wills may therefore vary, assuming such forms as the following ones: an emotional identification with other individuals, as in the family; treating with respect others with whom one shares the same legal or social space because one recognizes one's own status and character as a person in them; the sense that one's particular ends are best realized by acting in conformity with generally recognized norms and through participation in certain forms of human association; and insight into the essentially rational character of certain laws and institutions. Thus, although the objective 'ethical substance and its laws and powers are … an object, inasmuch as *they are*, in the supreme sense of self-sufficiency' (PR § 146), making them in this respect independent of the wills of individuals,[9] they are not 'something *alien* to the subject' in the case of genuine ethical life; rather, 'the subject bears *spiritual witness* to them as to *its own essence*, in which it has its *self-awareness* and lives as in its element which is not distinct from itself' (PR § 147). For Hegel, it is not, however, simply a matter of understanding *how* relations between individuals, whether direct relations or institutionally mediated ones, can be thought in such a way that the constraints generated by these relations are compatible with the idea of freedom. Given the role of institutions and the state in particular in Hegel's *Philosophy of Right*, it is also a matter of demonstrating *what* institutions and what *kind* of state could explain the possibility of this compatibility of freedom and constraint. Moreover, the role of institutions and the state shifts the question from one concerning relations between individuals to one concerning the relation between individuals and the institutions of the state.

[9] This independence is not absolute, however, since ethical life 'has its knowledge and volition in self-consciousness, and its actuality through self-conscious action' (PR § 142). Yet, even if the institutions of ethical life depend on individuals when it comes to their existence and effective functioning, they do not depend on any particular individual, and in this sense individuals remain 'accidental to them' at the same time as 'these powers have their representation, phenomenal shape, and actuality' in individuals in the way indicated above (PR § 145).

Hegel claims that the state constitutes the 'ultimate' end that 'possesses the highest right in relation to individuals, whose *highest duty* is to be members of the state' (PR § 258). It is, in fact, 'only through being a member of the state that the individual himself has objectivity, truth, and ethical life' (PR § 258R). Given the importance of this essentially *political* relation, any attempt to 'reactualize' Hegel's *Philosophy of Right* as a normative *social* theory, based on 'our own post-metaphysical standards of rationality',[10] must be taken to mark a significant departure from Hegel's own understanding of his *Philosophy of Right*, in which the social sphere is ultimately subordinate to the 'higher' sphere of the political. The advantages of such an attempt to recast Hegel's *Philosophy of Right* as a normative social theory are nevertheless clear. One would avoid not only having to invoke the 'speculative' form of reason that Hegel seeks to articulate in its purest form in his works on logic, but also having to accord the political state the same status and ultimate authority that Hegel himself accords it. Even philosophers who in some sense identify themselves as Hegelians have attacked his *Philosophy of Right* from precisely this direction, as with Adorno's claim that

> it was in the philosophy of right [*Rechtsphilosophie*] that Hegel, following the phenomenology and logic, drove the cult of the world's course to extremes. In large measure, legality is the medium in which evil proves to be right on account of its objectivity and acquires the appearance of good. Positively it admittedly secures the reproduction of life; but, in its existing forms, its destructiveness shows itself undiminished, thanks to the destructive principle of violence. While the lawless society [*die Gesellschaft ohne Recht*] becomes the prey of pure arbitrariness, as it did in the Third Reich, the law [*Recht*] in society preserves the terror to which it is always ready to resort with the aid of quotable statutes. Hegel furnished the ideology of positive law [*die Ideologie des positiven Rechts*] because the need for it was most pressing in a society that was already visibly antagonistic.[11]

This characterization of Hegel's *Philosophy of Right* may appear to mark a return to the view of Hegel as an apologist of the existing Prussian state of his own time, whose laws are deemed valid simply in virtue of their existence, and which achieves a semblance of goodness by guaranteeing social order, despite the injustices that it helps perpetuate. This uncritical attitude towards the existing state is accompanied, moreover, by a misplaced

[10] Axel Honneth, *The Pathologies of Individual Freedom: Hegel's Social Theory*, trans. Ladislaus Löb (Princeton, NJ: Princeton University Press, 2010), 5.

[11] Theodor W. Adorno, *Negative Dialektik* (Frankfurt am Main: Suhrkamp, 2003), 303/*Negative Dialectics*, trans. E. B. Ashton (London: Continuum, 1973), 309; translation modified.

optimism which views human history in progressive terms, with the modern coercive state being held to represent the flower of a historical process. There is, however, an important difference this time, because the need for law itself is explained specifically in terms of social antagonisms based on class conflict that threaten social order, and therefore even the modern *Rechtsstaat*, which many take to be a sign of progress, is viewed as founded on and sustained by the violence needed to maintain social order in the face of tensions generated by the capitalist mode of production. Thus, the ideological function of Hegel's *Philosophy of Right* is not to be identified with an attempt to foster acceptance of any particular existing modern state, such as the Prussian one. It is instead to be identified with an attempt to foster acceptance of the modern state as such, which in Hegel's own time was being increasingly determined by the capitalist mode of production and the antagonistic relations of production generated by it. It is not, therefore, simply a question of whether or not the political state as described by Hegel, with its constitutional monarchy, legislative role for the landed nobility and absence of direct universal suffrage, is compatible with a concept of freedom that demands that individuals do not experience the constraints to which they are subject as purely external, alien ones. Rather, it is just as much a question of the state's relation to society insofar as the latter is an economic sphere with its own set of relations.

The nature of the state together with its relation to society as set out in the *Philosophy of Right* can in fact be partly explained in terms of the limits of the claims that Hegel considers himself entitled to make, given his own historical standpoint. He claims that

> To comprehend *what is* is the task of philosophy, for *what is* is reason. As far as the individual is concerned, each individual is in any case a *child of his time*; thus philosophy, too, is *its own time comprehended in thoughts*. It is just as foolish to imagine that any philosophy can transcend its contemporary world as that an individual can overleap his own time or leap over Rhodes. (PR *Preface*, 21–22[26])

Although the emphasis that Hegel places on comprehending the rationality of what already is in a historical sense might be seen to support a conservative reading of the *Philosophy of Right*, it could alternatively be viewed simply as a reflection of his belief that the modern state is generally rational and rational to a greater extent than any other previous forms of social and political organization. This position would not be a conservative one in a strict sense, since it does not exclude the possibility that a particular existing state, including the Prussian state of Hegel's own time, will lack some of the fundamental features of a truly rational state and will in this sense require reform. Moreover, tradition and past practices are not accorded any kind of intrinsic value, as they would be if broad acceptance of them were held to be a sufficient reason for rejecting any reforms that threatened their existence or authority.

The emphasis on comprehending the rationality of what is nevertheless limits the authority of philosophical claims, and, in particular, the claims of philosophical critique, in that philosophy is not entitled to make prescriptive claims concerning how things ought to be that dogmatically assert or imply the irrationality and injustice of the modern state at the same time as it constructs the ideal of a completely different form of social and political organization. Yet even if the rights of philosophical critique are in this way limited, this does not entail that a philosopher who finds him- or herself at a very different historical standpoint from the one occupied by Hegel will not be justified in asking whether the form of ethical life described by Hegel is actually the best form of social and political organization currently available to humankind, given the fundamental aims of his *Philosophy of Right* and the new historical conditions. After all, in the intervening time humankind could have become aware of possibilities that were simply unthinkable to someone in Hegel's position, or it may have come to confront problems that Hegel could not reasonably have been expected to identify, let alone solve.

In relation to the last possibility, the social tensions which – or so Adorno implies – Hegel's *Philosophy of Right* attempts either to conceal or to suppress were, in fact, acknowledged by Hegel himself. He speaks of the normal workings of a market economy as generating considerable material inequality and bringing about economic crises that lead to the creation of a class of people who are unable 'to feel and enjoy the wider freedoms, and particularly the spiritual advantages, of civil society' (PR § 243), while the creation of such a class of people is said to facilitate the concentration of wealth in the hands of a small group of people (PR § 244). Hegel is not blind, then, to the existence of social tensions with which the modern state must contend. It can be argued, however, that the existence of such tensions means that he ultimately fails to explain, in the case of those people who are denied 'the wider freedoms' that society has to offer by the normal workings of a market economy, the possibility of a form of social and political freedom which consists in being able to recognize oneself in that which limits one's own will, so that one does not experience it as a purely external and alien form of constraint. These people will arguably instead experience the state and its institutions as alien to their own wills, in the sense of constraints on their freedom with which they cannot identify themselves as free and rational agents.

Any attempt to demonstrate the relevance of the *Philosophy of Right* by recasting it in some way will have to confront the problem of how its basic intentions can be realized without ignoring, downplaying or masking those social tensions of which Hegel was himself aware and whose nature he was in large part able to explain. To meet this challenge one would, moreover, need to take into account the different historical context in which the problem poses itself if the attempt to demonstrate the continued relevance of the *Philosophy of Right* is to attain the level of reflection achieved by Hegel's philosophy, which demands reflection on its own historical conditions and presuppositions. Among the distinctive features of this different historical context today one might include the considerable power enjoyed by large modern corporations and financial institutions both at a national and at a global level. It can be argued that this power results in forms of influence that reduce the modern political state to little more than an instrument of global capital, with the interests of the latter being furthered at the expense of, and with no regard for, the interests of many citizens of the modern state. For Hegel, this would represent a fundamental reversal of the 'logical' structure of modern ethical life, in that a subordinate moment of the latter, namely the moment of civil society that he associates with labour, production and exchange – the 'system of needs', as he calls it – dominates the ethically higher moment of the state, which is concerned with the general interest or the 'universal'. This would amount to the existence of a divergence between two different orders of things which for Hegel are meant to proceed more or less in tandem: the ethical order made up of the moments of right as set out in the *Philosophy of Right* and the historical order of things.

Although Hegel warns us not to confuse these two orders, since, for example, abstract right cannot be thought to be prior to the family nor civil society prior to the state in terms of their historical order (PR § 32R, 32A), the modern state would have had to develop in such a way that it roughly conforms to the ethical order of things set out in the *Philosophy of Right* for Hegel to have been genuinely in a position to comprehend the *rationality* of what is at the point in human history which he himself occupied. There could not, for example, be a situation in which the state was at this point in history subordinate to what is only one moment of civil society in the way that it arguably is today. The fact that a subordinate moment of right may today be said to have achieved dominance over what is, for Hegel, a higher moment of right implies that the modern state as we, rather than Hegel, experience it is, in fact, less rational from a Hegelian perspective than a nineteenth-century *Rechtsstaat*. If for the sake of argument one accepts the claim that the political state has become subordinate to one moment of civil society in the way indicated above, the only way to avoid this conclusion without completely departing from Hegel's own approach would be to show that this reversal of the ethical order of things in reality accords more fully with the genuine enabling conditions of human freedom than does the ethical order that Hegel argued for. This is a very big challenge indeed, given the way in which Hegel himself shows how the power of markets can be seen to undermine the freedom (in the 'positive' sense) of social agents, by subjecting them to an impersonal form of necessity which has a wholly alien quality.[12]

In this introduction I have attempted to give a sense of the complexity and the achievements of Hegel's *Philosophy of Right*, and to show thereby how misguided it is to pigeonhole it with crude political labels, as has unfortunately often been done in the past. It is hoped that this book will contribute to the different, more nuanced reception of this work that has characterized some more recent accounts of it. The book is not intended to be comprehensive. Rather, each contributor focuses on what he or she finds to be of particular interest in Hegel's *Philosophy of Right*. If this has to some extent reduced the scope of the book, particularly by allowing Hegel's theory of civil society to receive more attention than the other aspects of his account of *Sittlichkeit*, especially that of the structure of the political state, this approach can be defended, I believe, on the grounds of Hegel's own understanding of the relationship between right and history. Indeed, this relationship between right and history makes the question of the extent of the Hegelian state's modernity a fitting end to the book.

[12] See David James, *Rousseau and German Idealism: Freedom, Dependence and Necessity* (Cambridge: Cambridge University Press, 2013), 179–186.

CHAPTER I

The Method of the Philosophy of Right

Frederick Neuhouser

The aim of the *Philosophy of Right* is to comprehend the modern social world so as to reveal it as rational, and its demands on us as justified, by demonstrating how its principal institutions work together to realize 'practical freedom', the species of *self-determination* that Hegel associates with will or free agency. Right (*Recht*),[1] as Hegel employs the term, is defined in relation to practical freedom: it is what he calls freedom as 'Idea' (*Idee*) or, equivalently, the '*existence* [*Dasein*] of the *free will*' (PR § 29). Both of these expressions refer, more colloquially, to any respect in which practical freedom is realized[2] in the world (PR § 4), but, as is fitting for social and political philosophy, most instances of Right will be ways in which practical freedom finds an existence (is realized) in institutions and practices of social life. The *Philosophy of Right*'s goal is not to prescribe new institutions but to bring individuals, through the comprehension of their social world, to regard the demands their social life places on them as rationally justified, in large part[3] because fulfilling them is necessary for their own freedom to be realized. It is because philosophical comprehension involves seeing 'what is' (PR *Preface*, 21[26]) as essential to the realization of freedom that such comprehension *reconciles* individuals to the social world they inhabit and sustain through their own activity: what can otherwise appear as external *constraints* on their activity is shown by philosophy to

[1] I capitalize 'Right' in order to emphasize that the term has no single equivalent in English. Hegel's *Philosophy of Right* treats a variety of topics named by distinct terms in English, including individual rights, law, justice, political philosophy, morality and social theory.

[2] I will use the more colloquial term 'realization' to translate *Verwirklichung* rather than the more awkward 'actualization'. For an account of the role played by *Verwirklichung* in Hegel's method, see Robert Pippin, 'Hegel's Political Argument and the Role of "Verwirklichung"', *Political Theory* 9 (1981), 509–532.

[3] As I note in the antepenultimate paragraph of this essay, the freedom realized in the rational social order is not exhausted by the freedoms enjoyed by its individual members; that freedom also includes a type of freedom (a self-determined reproduction of itself) that Hegel ascribes only to the social order as a whole. See Frederick Neuhouser, *Foundations of Hegel's Social Theory: Actualizing Freedom* (Cambridge, MA: Harvard University Press, 2000), 114–144.

be instead the conditions of their freedom. It is relevant to grasping the method of the *Philosophy of Right* that Hegel describes philosophical comprehension as a process of giving rational *form* to an existing content that is already 'in itself', or, implicitly, rational (PR *Preface*, 11[13–14]). Hence, whatever else is involved in seeing existing institutions as rational, part of philosophical comprehension consists in regarding them as systematically ordered – as constituted, both internally and in their interrelations, in accordance with the complex requirements of their overarching end, the realization of freedom.

My aim in this essay is to illuminate some aspects of the distinctive method by means of which the *Philosophy of Right* claims to achieve the goals just described.[4] Although questions of methodology are extremely important to Hegel, his scattered remarks on the topic in this text are difficult to piece together into a coherent account. If we add to this the problem that Hegel's method is very different from those employed by more familiar approaches to social and political philosophy, the urgency of attending to the text's method before attempting to interpret or evaluate its claims becomes apparent. Already in the Preface Hegel tells us that the *Philosophy of Right*'s method is the method of philosophy, or of 'Science', more generally (PR *Preface*, 10[12–13]). This immediately raises the question of the extent to which understanding the method of the *Philosophy of Right* depends on a familiarity with other parts of Hegel's system. I address this question immediately below, in discussing what the *Philosophy of Right* presupposes from the parts of Science that precede it in Hegel's system. After this, I turn to the essay's main concern, explicating the method Hegel relies on in showing that the basic institutions of the modern social world are rational, or necessary for practical freedom to be realized. Crucial to this is understanding the *movement* of the *Philosophy of Right*, the way in which it proceeds systematically from one claim about Right, and from one *domain* of Right, to another. Hegel describes philosophy's way of proceeding as a 'development of the concept' (of practical freedom) (PR § 32), but understanding what this means requires attending carefully to what the *Philosophy of Right* actually does and to the kinds of arguments it invokes. As we shall see, *developing* the concept of practical freedom involves more than conceptual analysis in a straightforward sense of that term. For Hegel, developing the concept of practical freedom

[4] For another helpful article on Hegel's method, see Kenneth Westphal, 'The Basic Context and Structure of Hegel's "Philosophy of Right"', in Frederick C. Beiser (ed.), *The Cambridge Companion to Hegel* (Cambridge: Cambridge University Press, 1993), 234–269.

requires operating on, and moving back and forth between, two planes of analysis: it involves 'deducing' a complete ensemble of (three) distinguishable but related *conceptions* of practical freedom and, intertwined with that, systematic reflection on the institutions and practices that *realize* practical freedom in all its guises.[5] It is the way in which Hegel combines logical reflection on the concept of practical freedom with questions concerning its institutional realization that accounts for the distinctiveness of the *Philosophy of Right*'s method.

Presuppositions of the *Philosophy of Right*

Commentators on this text tend to fall into two camps: those who regard its arguments as fully intelligible independently of the rest of Hegel's system and those who insist that those arguments cannot be divorced from claims established elsewhere, above all, in the *Logic*.[6] Not surprisingly, both camps can point to passages in the text that support their respective positions. In this section I survey those passages with a view to uncovering what Hegel means when referring to what the *Philosophy of Right* 'presupposes' (*setzt voraus*) (PR *Preface*, 10[12]). Ultimately, my interpretation shares more with those of the first of these two camps, but it attempts to do justice to the legitimate claims of the second as well.

A careful reading of Hegel's remarks on the relation between the *Philosophy of Right* and his system as a whole reveals three claims regarding what the former 'presupposes' when detached from the latter. (Of course, whatever appears as a presupposition from the perspective of the *Philosophy of Right* alone is supposed to be established in earlier parts of the system.) The first presupposition is simply the recognition that philosophy – the 'speculative mode of cognition' – differs from ordinary ways of knowing; moreover, the distinctive aspect of philosophical knowledge that Hegel mentions here is clearly relevant to questions of method: it is the way in which philosophy 'progresses from one topic to another' (PR *Preface*, 10[12]).

The second presupposition is bound up with the first. It concerns not merely *that* philosophy differs from other modes of knowledge but *how*

5 Hegel describes these two planes as follows: when we 'observe how the concept determines itself … what we obtain … is a series of thoughts [or conceptions of freedom] and another series of existing configurations [or realizations of those conceptions]' (PR § 32A; translation modified).

6 To the first camp belongs, for example, Allen W. Wood, *Hegel's Ethical Thought* (Cambridge: Cambridge University Press), 1990, 1–8; to the second, Eric Lee Goodfield, *Hegel and the Metaphysical Frontiers of Political Theory* (London: Routledge, 2014).

they differ. In this context Hegel explicitly notes that the *Philosophy of Right* presupposes a familiarity with 'the nature of speculative knowledge', which he claims to have set out in his *Science of Logic* (PR *Preface*, 10[12]). It is significant, however, that whenever Hegel refers to how the *Philosophy of Right* depends on the *Logic*, he points not to any specific philosophical doctrine but to the nature of philosophical knowledge in general – more precisely, to the method by means of which 'the concept ... develops out of itself', making it a purely '*immanent* progression and production of its own determinations' (PR § 31). Applied to the present case, this implies that understanding the method of the *Philosophy of Right* requires being able to show how the initially bare concept of practical freedom (or self-determination of the will) develops into a more determinate concept – into a systematically interrelated set of conceptions of freedom – through a procedure that (in a sense to be clarified below) is immanent. This means that understanding how the *Philosophy of Right* proceeds in the distinctive way that makes it philosophy does not require invoking specific concepts or claims that appear in the *Logic*; what is required, rather, is that the development of the concept of freedom as followed by the text's readers be of the same general type, and possess the same type of necessity, as exhibited by the development of concepts in the *Logic*. More precisely, readers of the *Philosophy of Right* who comprehend the necessity of its conceptual progression – from personal to moral to social (or *sittliche*) freedom – are in need of no further instruction in philosophical method to be had from the *Logic*. One of the challenges I take up here is showing that the rigour of the *Philosophy of Right*'s development of the concept of practical freedom can be reconstructed even for readers unfamiliar with the *Logic* (as Hegel himself must have believed since he explicitly welcomed such readers into his lectures on Right (PR § 4R)).

The *Philosophy of Right*'s third presupposition is metaphysical rather than epistemological. It consists in a small number of philosophical claims, namely, '*that* the will is free and of *what* the will and freedom are' (PR § 4R). These claims Hegel takes to be established not in the *Logic* but in the *Encyclopaedia*'s chapter on subjective spirit (PM §§ 363–399), immediately preceding his treatment of Right in the chapter on objective spirit. In other words, much of the *Philosophy of Right*'s Introduction – its account of the will and the basic nature of practical freedom, as well as its definition of Right – is not argued for within that text itself. These doctrines, rather, are simply taken over as results that find their proof elsewhere in Hegel's system (PR § 2). Yet Hegel is quick to point out – again to readers who have not mastered the system as a whole – that the presupposed character of these doctrines does not imply that reading the *Philosophy of Right* on its own rules out discovering in it most of the philosophical rigour appropriate to science. For all readers, he claims, will be able to picture (*vorstellen*), and to find plausible, what the Introduction asserts about the will. As long they are willing to inspect their own 'self-consciousness', they can acquire a serviceable grasp of the three fundamental moments of the will articulated in §§ 5–7, as well as the 'further determinations' of the will set out in the Introduction (PR § 4R). This means that, if we restrict ourselves to the *Philosophy of Right* alone, we will be able to understand and find compelling (though not prove philosophically) the concepts of will, freedom and Right with which the text begins. Moreover, even without referring to the *Logic* we will be able to grasp the necessity of the movement by which we arrive at the three specific conceptions of freedom relevant to Right, as well as the accounts of the institutions and practices of Right that realize those conceptions. In other words, even if the *Philosophy of Right* is read in abstraction from the rest of Hegel's system, the philosophical task it claims to carry out is very robust indeed.

Thus far, I have mentioned only the three aspects of the *Philosophy of Right*'s project that Hegel himself considers 'presupposed' when the text is separated from the rest of his system. In truth, there is a more substantive and more controversial assumption at work in the text – and in any part of the philosophy of nature or spirit when detached from the system. The importance of this assumption will become evident below, when examining the part of Hegel's method that involves looking to *experience* – to already existing institutions – in order to give determinacy to philosophy's account of the rational social order. The assumption in question is implicit in the claims, also discussed below, that philosophy's task is to comprehend the present (PR *Preface*, 20[24]) and 'to comprehend *what is*' (PR *Preface*, 21[26]). The idea that – after Napoleon, at least – *what is* is already implicitly rational and requires only the rational form that philosophical comprehension can bestow on it in order to become *completely* rational is fundamental to the *Philosophy of Right*'s project. It is expressed in the most famous of the Preface's declarations, that 'what is rational is actual [*wirklich*]; and what is actual is rational' (PR *Preface*, 20[24]). When Hegel announces this doctrine here, however, he refers to it not as a presupposition but as a 'conviction' (*Überzeugung*) or 'insight' (*Einsicht*) that the *Philosophy of Right* 'takes as its point of departure', which I take to mean that this conviction defines the very standpoint philosophy must take up if it is to be philosophy at all: to start off from the conviction that *what is* is rational,[7] even if still imperfectly or implicitly so, is constitutive for Hegel of the stance philosophy must take up if it is to comprehend reality.

Hegel's understanding of the standpoint appropriate to philosophy rests on a complex conception of reason as a goal-directed activity, driven to achieve only its own self-posited ends, as well as on (related) theses concerning the teleological character of human history. These fundamental claims are not justified in the *Philosophy of Right*, nor can they be here. (It is not even entirely clear where one should look to find Hegel's justification of the standpoint of philosophy: in the *Phenomenology of Spirit*? in the *Logic*? in some composite of the two?) For our purposes, however, it is important to note that lacking an adequate proof of the standpoint that the *Philosophy of Right* begins from does not rid its method of all philosophical rigour, as if Hegel's understanding of what it is to give rational form to an already implicitly rational content were so loose as to allow anything to be made to fit reason's form. (If this were so, Hegel would have considerably less squirming to do later in the text, when – to mention the most obvious example – he struggles mightily to reconcile the reality of poverty with the rationality of civil society (PR §§ 241–245).) The two features of the *Philosophy of Right*'s method that account for its ability to judge certain aspects of reality as less than fully rational – its ability, in Hegelian jargon, to distinguish actuality (*Wirklichkeit*) from mere reality (*Realität*) or existence (*Existenz*)[8] – are precisely the two aspects of that method I emphasize here: its resources for giving determinate content to the abstract idea of practical freedom (by developing three specific conceptions of it) and its ability to detect 'contradictions' in the ways in which those conceptions of freedom are realized in institutions of Right.

Will and Three Conceptions of Practical Freedom

As indicated above, the *Philosophy of Right*'s Introduction can be regarded as a summary of claims about the nature of will, practical freedom and Right that Hegel thinks have been proved earlier in his system. These introductory claims should be understood as abstract definitions of the will and its essential characteristic, practical freedom, which, precisely because they are abstract, tell us nothing yet about what a social world

[7] It is not only *Wirklichkeit* that Hegel calls rational: '*what is* is reason' (PR *Preface*, 21[26]).

[8] As many have pointed out, even if 'nothing is *actual* except the Idea' (PR *Preface*, 20[25]; emphasis added), much of *Realität* falls short of being a manifestation of reason.

in which freedom were realized would look like. In truth, there is more argumentation in even this part of the text than calling its doctrines 'presuppositions' implies. Most notably, there is a logical progression in the development of the three moments that define the will (PR §§ 5–7), and the necessity of that progression can be reconstructed without appealing to the *Logic* or to other parts of the system. (Very briefly: the three moments of the will are derived by reflecting on the bare concept of practical *self-determination*, where the idea of having determinations, or specific properties, must be brought together with the idea that those determinations have their source in the will itself.[9]) Because the distinctive method of the *Philosophy of Right* – developing the concept of practical freedom in interplay with thinking about how it is realized in the social world – gets under way only in 'Abstract Right', I will provide here only a brief summary of the Introduction's relevant claims.

The most prominent of these is that any instance of the free will must incorporate three moments: (a) the capacity to abstract from given determinations of the will – 'needs, desires, and drives' (PR § 5) – rather than letting one's actions simply be determined by those determinations; (b) the positing of some determinate, particular content that makes the will more than the content-eschewing, purely universal capacity to abstract from all determinations that is at issue in the first moment (PR § 6); and (c) the bringing together of *determinacy* and *self*-determination, resulting in what Hegel calls 'being-with-oneself in an other' (*Beisichselbstsein in einem Anderen*),[10] conceived of as a form of *appropriating* the particular content of one's will – making it 'one's own' as opposed to foreign, external, or merely given (PR § 7A). A determination of the will that incorporates all three of these moments in some way is an end (*Zweck*), which has both a subjective and an objective aspect: an end belongs to the domain of ('inner') consciousness, but it also makes reference to the ('outer') world by presenting itself as 'something to be achieved' through action (PR § 9). This means that practical freedom remains incomplete until a will translates its internally self-determined ends into successful action in the world. Finally, full self-determination requires that the ends one espouses and

[9] An excellent treatment of Hegel's conception of freedom can be found in Alan Patten, *Hegel's Idea of Freedom* (Oxford: Oxford University Press, 1999), 43–81. See also David James, *Rousseau and German Idealism: Freedom, Dependence and Necessity* (Cambridge: Cambridge University Press, 2013), 145–147; and Robert Pippin, 'Hegel, Freedom, the Will', in Ludwig Siep (ed.), *Grundlinien der Philosophie des Rechts* (Berlin: Akademie Verlag, 1997), 31–54.

[10] For more on this term, see Wood, *Hegel's Ethical Thought*, 45–51 and Neuhouser, *Foundations of Hegel's Social Theory*, 19–25.

realizes in action be self-determined in the robust sense that their particular content be consonant with the will's essential nature (its freedom). The will that is fully free, then – free 'in and for itself' (PR § 22) – determines its ends not randomly, nor merely with a view to maximizing pleasure, but in accordance with its essence as free, and it makes these robustly self-determined ends real through successful action in the world. The three specific conceptions of freedom discussed below – personal, moral and social freedom – are all instances of willing that is free in and for itself. That is, each involves a will espousing ends in accordance with a specific understanding of its freedom and acting to 'objectify' that conception (to make it real). What distinguishes these forms of the will that is free in and for itself is that each operates with a distinct understanding of the freedom that constitutes its essential nature and that serves as the criterion for its espousal of ends.

Before investigating the method of the *Philosophy of Right* in more detail, it will be helpful to clarify the three conceptions of practical freedom that ground its account of the institutions of Right (without yet examining the arguments that reveal the necessity of moving from one to the other). As noted above, the three conceptions are the following: personal freedom, the foundation of 'Abstract Right'; moral freedom, the foundation of 'Morality'; and social freedom, the foundation of 'Ethical Life' (*Sittlichkeit*). Of these, personal freedom is the simplest, which explains why it is the first treated in the *Philosophy of Right*. The type of self-determination at issue in personhood is the will's choosing of its ends. Persons are characterized by given drives and desires that have the capacity to motivate them to act, but they are persons in virtue of the fact that their wills are not *determined* by the drives and desires they happen to have. Rather, persons have the ability to reject some of their desires and to embrace others; their self-determination consists in 'stepping back' from given inclinations and deciding which among them to satisfy and how specifically to do so. A will qualifies as self-determined on this conception in virtue of having chosen which ends to act on, regardless of the reasons for making the choice it does. Moreover, as a will that is free in and for itself, personhood entails constraining one's choices in accordance with one's own self-conception as a free chooser of ends: choices that undermine the conditions of one's choosing agency – consenting to be a slave, for example – fail to meet personhood's criteria for free action.

The moral subject embodies a more complex conception of self-determination. Moral subjects are self-determining in that they determine what to do in accordance with self-determined *principles* – in accordance with their own understanding of what is (morally) good. Moral subjectivity is more complex than personhood, first, because it involves determining one's will in accordance with *principles* that define one's understanding of the good and, second, because those principles are 'one's own' in the sense that the moral subject is able to *reflect* on them and to affirm, reject, or revise them accordingly. Individuals realize moral freedom, then, when they subscribe to their own rationally assessable vision of the good, determine their ends in accordance with it, and bring about the good in the world through their own actions.

In contrast to personal and moral freedom, where the emphasis is on free individuals conceived of independently of others, social freedom consists in certain ways of participating in the three principal social institutions of modernity (the family, civil society and the state). The starting point for Hegel's conception of social freedom is the freedom that citizens enjoyed in the ancient Greek city-state. According to Hegel, citizens in ancient Greece had so deep an attachment to their polis that their membership in it constituted a central part of their identities: participating in the life of the polis was valuable for its own sake (not simply as a means to other ends), as well as the source of the projects and social roles that were central to their self-understandings. Hegel regards this as a kind of freedom for two reasons. First, the fact that Greek citizens regarded their community's good as convergent with their own enabled them to obey the laws governing them – laws directed at the collective good[11] – without experiencing them as external constraints. Second, the polis was the source of a distinctive and deep satisfaction for its members. It provided a social framework that gave meaning to their lives and served as the primary arena within which, by fulfilling their social roles, they achieved their 'sense of self' through the recognition of their fellow citizens. Apart from these 'subjective' aspects of social membership, social freedom as conceived of in the *Philosophy of Right* includes an 'objective' element: the institutions that individuals subjectively embrace as their own in fact promote the personal and moral freedom of social members generally; those institutions are rational (in part) because, independently of the subjective relation their members have to them, they create the *conditions* under which social members are formed as persons and moral

[11] Hence, like moral freedom, social freedom includes acting in accordance with a conception of the good. Part of *modern* social freedom involves relating to the conception of the good that animates social life in the mode of a moral subject, as an individual locus of moral authority that is rationally responsible for the conception of the good according to which it acts.

subjects and under which they realize the forms of freedom corresponding to those self-conceptions.[12]

Method

The aim of the remainder of this essay is to clarify the distinctive method of the *Philosophy of Right* and, in doing so, to reconstruct some of the moves by which Hegel demonstrates that the basic institutions of the modern social world are rational because they are necessary for the full realization of practical freedom. As already noted, one part of his procedure can be described as a development of the *concept* of practical freedom (into three systematically related conceptions of freedom), but Hegel also characterizes what the *Philosophy of Right* accomplishes as 'developing the *Idea* [*Idee*] … out of the concept [of freedom]' (PR § 2). Since, in Hegelian jargon, the Idea of *x* includes the *concept* of *x* together with its *realization* in the world (PR § 1), the *Philosophy of Right*, in developing the Idea of Right out of its concept, will derive not only a complete ensemble of conceptions of practical freedom but also the real-world configurations (*Gestaltungen*) (PR § 32) of Right corresponding to them, that is, the specific practices and institutions required for practical freedom in its various guises to be fully realized. Moreover, these two aspects of Hegel's account of Right are carried out in conjunction with each other, and grasping how they are interrelated is essential to understanding the *Philosophy of Right*'s method. In short, the movement that leads from one conception of freedom to another – the progression from personal to moral to social freedom – is possible only by attending to the 'contradictions' that come into view when one considers how a given conception of freedom would be realized in the world in the absence of the full complement of social institutions that by the end of the book have been shown to be necessary if practical freedom is to be fully realized (a condition that will require the realization and integration of all three conceptions of practical freedom). Although one can distinguish conceptual development in the *Philosophy of Right* ('development of the concept') from its claims about how the social world must be structured if practical freedom is to be realized ('development of the Idea out of the concept'), neither of these aspects of its method can proceed independently of the other; both are necessary if an *immanent* development of the Idea of freedom is to be possible.

[12] Neuhouser, *Foundations of Hegel's Social Theory*, 145–174.

This means that the three main divisions of the text – 'Abstract Right', 'Morality' and 'Ethical Life' – together with the conceptions of freedom each is based on, can be understood as stages of a single philosophical argument that aims to articulate a comprehensive, fully adequate conception of practical freedom and its realization. This argument begins with the simplest conception of a self-determined will (personal freedom) and demonstrates the necessity of supplementing that conception with a more complex conception (moral freedom) by showing how personal freedom by itself is incomplete. A specific conception of freedom is shown to be incomplete when the attempt to think a world in which it is realized reveals that such a world 'contradicts' in some way the core ideal of freedom, that of a will determined only by itself. The demonstrated incompleteness of one conception of freedom points out the need to revise that conception, where revision takes a distinctively Hegelian form: we retain rather than discard the original conception of freedom, but we regard it as incomplete – as capturing a part but not the whole of practical freedom – and as needing to be supplemented by a more complex conception of freedom whose features respond in some way to the very incompleteness that was shown to plague its predecessor. (This is what transpires in the 'transitions' that mark the text's progression from one main division to another (PR §§ 104, 141).) A similar 'dialectic' is repeated until the process yields a complete conception of practical freedom – more precisely, an ensemble of systematically related conceptions of practical freedom – the completeness of which is revealed by the fact that its realization in practices of Right reveals no further respects in which it is inadequate to the ideal of a will determined by nothing external to itself. One important feature of Hegel's argument, then, is that it does not begin with a fixed, wholly determinate conception of the freedom that a rational social order must realize. Instead, it *arrives at* such a conception only by reflecting on the achievability and adequacy of various preliminary and incomplete conceptions of freedom. The method by which the *Philosophy of Right* establishes the 'correct' conception of practical freedom and the 'correct' institutions of Right proceeds, then, not by importing and then applying concepts established in some other division of philosophy but by following out a movement of thought immanent to the barest idea of a self-determined will.

Let us now fill in some of the details of this schematic account of the *Philosophy of Right*'s method by retracing the development from the first conception of practical freedom (personal freedom) to the second (moral freedom). As I have suggested, Hegel's first step in the main body of the

Philosophy of Right is to articulate the simplest conceivable conception of a will that is free in and for itself (PR §§ 34–38). This conception is personhood, and it is the first because the free choosing central to its understanding of its freedom is the simplest conception of a self-determined will: to be free is to *not* be determined by the drives and desires one happens to have but to choose – even arbitrarily[13] – which of them to satisfy and how. Immediately after articulating this conception of freedom, Hegel turns to the second plane of analysis in the *Philosophy of Right* and asks how personal freedom is 'given existence', or realized, in the social world (PR §§ 39–46). His answer is that a person realizes her freedom as a choosing will by having at her disposal a portion of the world – made up of will-less entities, or things (*Sachen*) (PR § 42) – within which her will has unlimited sovereignty and from which other wills, as potential obstacles to achieving her ends, are excluded. The thought of an exclusive domain of activity that is subject to an individual's arbitrary will is the main idea behind Hegel's theory of Abstract Right, the principles of which define the boundaries of such a domain. They do so by ascribing to individuals a set of rights guaranteeing them the liberty to do as they please with those things that are properly regarded as subject only to their own wills – their lives, their bodies and the material things they own – which together constitute their *property* (PR § 40). Personal freedom is realized, then, when individuals inhabit a social world that secures for them a private sphere of action within which they are unhindered by other agents from pursuing the ends that, by choosing, they make 'their own'. The institutional safeguarding of the individual rights associated with property (in the extended sense that includes one's life and body) constitutes the *configuration* of Right – the *Idea* – that corresponds to freedom conceived of as personhood.

Before examining how Hegel's treatment of personal freedom gives rise to a more complex conception of practical freedom pushing us into a new domain of Right, it is worth considering more carefully what has taken place in the argument just given for the necessity of individual property rights. The argument belongs to the second of the two tasks of the *Philosophy of Right* distinguished above, that concerned with the *realization* – in institutions and practices of Right – of a specific conception of freedom. There is clearly an important conceptual component to Hegel's

[13] Persons cannot choose completely arbitrarily because they will their freedom of choice and so recognize the conditions of personhood as constraints on their choices. Such constraints, however, leave a large space for arbitrary choice.

argument in the case of personhood: if persons are to realize their freedom as free setters of ends without regard to the rational content of those ends (except that their choices may not undermine the conditions of personhood itself), then the part of the world they relate to in doing so must be such that it can be an instrument of the arbitrary wills of persons – an embodiment of their freely chosen ends – without suffering a 'violation' of their nature. This means that the worldly domain in which persons realize their freedom must be composed of will-less entities that impose no normative constraints of their own on what persons may do with them. Such will-less entities are *things*, and an institution that guarantees to persons property rights in things counts as an 'existence of the free will', or an instance of Right. To the extent that reflection on what is required for the realization of personal freedom proceeds without appeal to anything beyond the conception of personal freedom itself – to the extent that sovereignty over things can be deduced as necessary if the freedom of an arbitrarily choosing will is to be realized – one can indeed say that the Idea develops immanently out of the concept (PR § 2).

At the same time it would be absurd to pretend that Hegel's accounts of the specific practices of Abstract Right that characterize a rational society – property, contract, punishment – relied only on *a priori* arguments. That is, there is a sense in which real experience is essential to the *Philosophy of Right*'s account of the rational society. In this respect it – like all of Hegel's philosophy of nature and spirit – differs from the *Logic*. Hegel alludes to this difference in describing the project of the *Philosophy of Right* as an '*exploration of the rational*' that consists in a '*comprehension of the present and the actual*' (PR *Preface*, 20[24]). The point here is that the comprehension of the present that is essential to the *Philosophy of Right*'s account of the institutions of Right cannot be a purely *a priori* operation of reason. Hegel acknowledges this when he notes that the configurations of practical freedom – really existing institutions of Right – temporally precede philosophy's comprehension of them as such (PR § 32R). That this is essential to Hegel's conception of rational comprehension is borne out by his well-known claim that philosophy can accomplish its work only after a certain historical process has taken place: only after 'actuality has gone through its formative process and attained its completed state' (PR *Preface*, 23[28]). This is why in the same passage Hegel equates philosophy with 'the thought *of the world*' (emphasis modified) and, earlier, with '*its own time comprehended in thoughts*' (PR *Preface*, 21[26]). The same idea is expressed in the claim that 'to comprehend *what is* is the task of philosophy' (PR *Preface*, 21[26]).

If philosophy must take account of empirical reality in order to go about its business – if it depends essentially on 'what is' – then it cannot be *a priori* in the sense of providing a fully determinate account of what is rational, or how things ought to be, independently of how they in fact are. At the same time, philosophical comprehension is not merely experience's handmaiden. If reason must 'enter into external existence' (PR *Preface*, 20[25]) in order to do its work, it does so without relinquishing its sovereign status in relation to experience: 'the human being does not stop short at the existent but claims to have within himself the measure of what is right … [In] right … the thing is not valid because it exists' but because it accords with that rational criterion (PR *Preface*, 13[16]). Thus, conceptual thought that did not enter into a relation with empirical reality could not establish with sufficient determinacy what is right, but at the same time positive Right (in the existing social world) depends on philosophical comprehension to assure its normative validity. Philosophy's task is not merely to take in or describe the existing world of Right but to discern 'in the semblance of the temporal and transient the substance which is immanent and the eternal which is present' – to 'find the inner pulse' that beats in freedom's existing configurations (PR *Preface*, 20–21[25]) – and it needs reason, not merely empirical apprehension, in order to do so. How is this to be understood?

I have suggested that there is a conceptual point behind Hegel's claim that personal freedom requires rights over things in order for it to be realized. (The freedom of arbitrary, 'choosing' wills must be realized in relation to will-less entities that place no normative constraints on what their owners do with them.) This thought alone, however, does not suffice to provide a thinker who had no experience of practices that realize personal freedom with a determinate picture of what a social world in which personal freedom were realized would look like. For this determinate picture, Hegel relies on what we might call 'historical experience'. That is, he 'looks around' (PR § 2R) in the world around him – itself the outcome of centuries of humans' struggles to *make* themselves free – and finds real practices that appear to be instances of the type of realization of freedom his conceptual argument has led him to seek, in this case, various schemes of individual rights that can be interpreted as giving expression to the value of personal freedom.

Since many readers will balk at the suggestion that the argument of the *Philosophy of Right* relies on experience as a source of determinacy for the otherwise not fully determinate conceptions of freedom it 'deduces', it is worth citing Hegel himself on this issue. As he puts it, once a certain conception of practical freedom has been shown to be necessary – has been 'proved and deduced' – there remains a second step for philosophical comprehension to take:

> the second step is to look around for what corresponds to [the concept] in our ideas (*Vorstellungen*) and language … If … the representation is not … false in its content, the concept may well be shown to be … present … within it; that is, the representation may be raised to the form of the concept. But it is so far from being … the criterion of the concept which is necessary and true for itself that it must rather derive its truth from the concept, and recognize and correct itself with the help of the latter (PR § 2R).

In this passage Hegel joins two ideas encountered above: the philosophical comprehension of what is depends on 'looking around' in the real world to find determinate practices that correspond to the conceptions of freedom it has shown to be necessary; and the concept of freedom (as it develops throughout the *Philosophy of Right*) is the criterion for what among the 'infinite wealth of … appearances' is 'true' (PR *Preface*, 21[25]).

As Hegel emphasizes, it is important not to lose sight of the primacy of the Concept in relation to experience: the conceptual arguments by means of which various conceptions of practical freedom are shown to be necessary furnish the criterion of the truth of appearances. At the same time, those conceptual arguments depend on consulting experience in that they proceed by attending to – and discovering 'contradictions' in – determinate configurations of Right that the philosopher can be acquainted with only by finding them in the real world. It is time to examine more closely the claim that the method of the *Philosophy of Right* combines a conceptual reflection (on the concept of practical freedom) with 'looking around' in real experience and that progress in the former depends on the latter. This is to attempt to understand how 'dialectic' (PR § 31R) – the way in which 'the concept … develops out of itself and is merely an *immanent* progression and production of its own determinations' (PR § 31) – requires the interplay of both moments.

One illustration of how the *Philosophy of Right*'s argument depends on the interplay of these two moments can be found in the move, internal to Abstract Right, from property to contract. Here, too, Hegel begins with a conceptual argument: the idea of property involves the thought of a thing that has taken on a significance in relation to freedom. When things become implicated in realizing personal freedom, however – when they go from being mere things to being property – they are no longer merely natural entities but external depositories, or embodiments, of a person's will. But if that will now exists externally in things, and things belong to a public world shared by multiple subjects, then the will in question exists not only for itself but for other subjects as well. My relation to my property is not merely a relation between my will and the things I own but also (and more fundamentally) a relation to the wills of others. The former relation might be physical possession or control, but I *own* something only insofar as the things I take to embody my will are also regarded as such by the other wills that inhabit the same world as I. What initially (in 'property') appeared to be a relation between a will and things now appears (in 'contract') to depend on a more fundamental relation *among* wills. I exist in the world as a person – my personal freedom is realized – only to the extent that my property is recognized as such by others.

While this argument proceeds independently of any specific experience with practices of ownership, the phenomenon Hegel points to as the argument's result – contract – cannot be 'deduced' purely *a priori*. Here again Hegel 'looks around' within existing practices to find something that exhibits the structure among wills he has just shown to be necessary for personal freedom to be realized. For someone who inhabits a property-owning society the making of contracts is a familiar practice that exhibits the requisite structure. In a contract two wills come to an agreement that establishes which of the contracting parties will own what: I become the owner of what was yours, and you become the owner of what was mine, and only because we have *agreed* to that arrangement. In other words, contract is the phenomenon of Abstract Right that makes explicit the truth we have just learned about property: that one person's ownership of a particular thing depends on an agreement among a plurality of persons to treat that thing as an extension of a person's will.

Because the move from property to contract is internal to Abstract Right and therefore grounded in a single conception of practical freedom (personhood), it cannot serve to illustrate the most important aspect of Hegel's dialectic, its moving to more complex conceptions of practical freedom, and hence to new domains of Right, via 'contradictions' discovered in the ways in which an earlier conception of freedom is realized in institutions and practices of Right. Here, too, Hegel provides little explicit instruction as to the type of contradiction one should expect to find when considering the configurations of Right that realize a particular conception of freedom, though students of the *Logic* will not be surprised at his remark that progress (*Fortgang*) in the *Philosophy of Right* takes place when 'abstract forms [of practical freedom] reveal themselves to be … non-self-standing [*nicht … für sich bestehend*]' (PR § 32A; translation modified).

What this means is best elucidated by looking at specific examples of such progress.

In the transition from Abstract Right to Morality Hegel's argument takes the following form: when we investigate what is required for personal freedom to be systematically realized – realized for *all* persons – we discover that the structure of the will attributed to persons is insufficiently complex for them to be *completely* self-determined, and that, if they are to be so, the freedom of personhood must be supplemented by a more complex conception of freedom, that of moral subjectivity. The need to move beyond personal freedom comes to light in considering the practice that follows property and contract in 'Abstract Right', namely, punishment (PR § 103). Punishment is essential to Abstract Right because of the arbitrary nature of personal freedom (because it is constrained only by the requirement that one's choices not undermine one's own personhood). This means that it is a contingent matter whether my choices respect the personhood of others. Hence, if personal freedom is to be realized universally, the principles of Abstract Right must be codified in laws backed up by the threat of punishment for those who violate them.

The need to move beyond personhood to a more complex conception of freedom is demonstrated by considering how punishment can be consistent with the freedom of the punished – or, more generally, how constraint by laws that threaten punishment can be consistent with the freedom of the persons subject to them. This is possible, according to Hegel, only if 'particular' and 'universal' wills are joined within a single will: punishment reveals the requirement of 'a will which, as a particular and *subjective* will, also wills the universal as such' (PR § 103). The idea here is that, in a social world in which personal freedom is realized for all, the wills of persons must be constrained by principles that, as long as they lack a more complex will, must appear to them as external. When I am required to constrain my choices so as not to violate the personhood of others – or, if I have failed to do that, when I am punished by the law – I remain free only on the condition that I also possess a 'universal' will (that I endorse the general principles of Abstract Right). In that case I recognize the principles that constrain my actions, or the laws that punish me, as 'my own' and can regard constraint by them as *self*-constraint, that is, as self-determination in accordance with principles that come from me in the sense that I have 'insight' into their validity (PR § 132R). This, very generally, corresponds to the (internally divided) structure of the self-legislating will of a moral subject: such a subject has particular desires that may or may not accord with the demands of reason, but it also recognizes the authority of the principles that pass judgment on those desires, which means that it can regard its moral actions as 'its own' – as self-determined – even when its particular desires are overruled by universal reason.[14] The claim here – which articulates the sense in which practical freedom conceived merely as personhood fails to be self-standing – is not that a society made up of individuals who were only persons and not also moral subjects is a conceptual or practical impossibility but that such beings could not inhabit a world where personal freedom was realized and at the same time enjoy full self-determination (because their actions would be constrained by principles that were not 'their own'); as Hegel puts it, a social world of this type is not 'in keeping with freedom' (PR § 33A).

What, briefly, are the deficiencies of moral freedom that necessitate the move to 'Ethical Life' and its distinctive conception of freedom (social freedom)? As in the case of personal freedom, the deficiency of moral freedom comes to light upon envisaging the conditions of its realization, and here, too, the general character of that deficiency resides in its failure to be fully self-standing: 'morality cannot exist independently; … [it] must have the ethical [*das Sittliche*] as [its] support and foundation' (PR § 141A). The non-self-standing character of moral freedom has two aspects. First, realizing moral freedom depends on something outside the individual's will in the sense that becoming a moral subject (as well as a person) requires a formation, or *Bildung*, that can be accomplished only within social institutions of the appropriate kinds: moral subjects must be socialized so as to be able to regard their actions as constrained by normative principles, to reflect on the principles that ought to guide their actions, and to act on the principles they recognize as good. Second, moral subjects fall short of complete self-determination in that, considered on their own – apart from the places they have been socialized to occupy in the basic institutions of society – they lack the resources needed to give non-arbitrary content to the concept of the good they take to be morally authoritative. While socially detached moral subjects might sincerely desire to realize the good, without a concrete vision of the projects and forms of life that best promote the good of all, they cannot know what specific actions their allegiance to the good requires of them. In Hegel's words, moral subjectivity is 'abstract', 'empty' and 'formal' (PR §§ 134–137, 141); it fails to satisfy

[14] This argument establishes only the necessity of a will that possesses the general structure of moral subjectivity. It does not deduce every feature Hegel eventually ascribes to the moral subject, for example, its being bound by principles of the *good*, which include but also extend beyond what is required for realizing personhood.

the criteria for a fully self-determining will because it cannot by itself give sufficient determinacy to its own governing concept.

The thought that leads to the *Philosophy of Right*'s final conception of freedom – social freedom – is that the solution to both these problems lies in an account of good (or rational) social and political institutions. Thus, rational institutions are charged with the dual task of socializing their members into beings who possess the subjective capacities required to be persons and moral subjects and of providing a social framework that gives definition to the particular projects that imbue their individual lives with purpose and provide determinate content for their understanding of the good. Each of these tasks points to a respect in which the systematic realization of personal and moral freedom depends on rational institutions. That such institutions secure the conditions necessary for realizing personal and moral freedom should not, however, lead us to think that Hegel's theory values social membership for purely instrumental reasons (merely as a means to realizing the first two forms of practical freedom). On the contrary, if the problems posed by those forms of freedom are to be solved in a way that remains true to the ideal of complete self-determination, this solution must give rise to a new and more substantive conception of the self-determining will, which finds expression in the idea of social freedom. In other words, the means by which the rational social order secures the conditions of personal and moral freedom must themselves realize a kind of freedom; more than being merely a means to freedom's realization, they must also be an instance of it.

Bringing together the various requirements that social freedom is supposed to meet yields a statement of its essential features: in addition to securing the necessary conditions of personal and moral freedom, social freedom will incorporate self-determination in two senses. The first of these concerns the wills of individual social members. Such individuals will be self-determining in the sense that, because their self-conceptions are linked to the social roles they occupy, their participation in the institutions of Ethical Life will be not only voluntary but also activity through which they constitute – give real existence to – their very identities.

The second sense of self-determination – the least intuitively evident but most distinctively Hegelian aspect of the *Philosophy of Right*'s treatment of freedom – is based on the following thought: if self-determination is to be fully realized in securing the conditions of the first two forms of practical freedom, it is not enough that the individuals who make up the social order have self-determined wills; it must also be the case that the social order as a whole, regarded as a living, self-reproducing system, embodies the characteristics that define a fully self-determining will, one more thoroughly self-sufficient than any individual will on its own could be. On this conception, the actions of socially free individuals count as 'their own' in two respects: their social participation flows from and gives expression to their own consciously embraced identities; and, in acting in accordance with those identities, they actually produce the totality of social conditions that make their own (personal and moral) freedom possible, as well as the 'self-determination' (or self-sufficiency) of their social order.

Finally, let us return to the idea that philosophical comprehension gives a rational *form* to an already existing content that, prior to such comprehension, is merely implicitly rational. As suggested, this involves coming to see an apparently patternless collection of existing institutions and practices as systematically ordered in accordance with the concept of practical freedom and its Idea (the requirements of its realization). In other words, philosophy makes explicit the initially hidden systematic character of our practices of Right by regarding them through the single lens of – as multiple but related instantiations of – the concept of practical freedom. Its business is to give form to what otherwise appears formless, but its form-giving is not an *imposing* of form on to an external content. We can make sense of this claim by referring again to the account of Abstract Right given above. For that account reveals the rationality of property rights by showing our existing practices to be essentially – though not in every detail – ways in which the social world realizes practical freedom of a specific sort. Regarding existing schemes of individual rights in this way is an act of *interpretation*; that is, it takes those schemes to be aiming at something – or to have a point – and then makes that point explicit by articulating the conception of freedom that best makes sense of, and unifies, the various types of rights recognized in modern societies. This point makes it possible to see how philosophical comprehension systematizes (and legitimizes) existing practices of Right without imposing a form on them from without. What can appear to be merely different types of individual rights – to property in the narrow sense, to one's body and life, to the liberty to act in various ways unimpeded by others – are shown by philosophy to have their point in their relations to a single conception of freedom. As we progress from one domain of Right to another, we apprehend systematic relations of a similar sort among social practices – most notably, family life, economic life and the life of citizens – that appear to be even more diverse than the types of individual rights at issue in the first of those domains.

The systematicity that rational comprehension reveals to exist among the domains of Right is of two main types: one concerns systematic connections among the *conceptions* of freedom that underlie each domain respectively; the other consists in systematic connections among the ways in which institutions *realize* those conceptions. The first form of systematicity is demonstrated by the *Philosophy of Right*'s conceptual argument, in its necessary progression from the freedom of personhood to that of moral subjectivity to that of social membership. The second is revealed by showing how the institutions and practices of Right made necessary by specific conceptions of freedom are, in roughly the form in which we already know them, constituted so as also to contribute to realizing freedom in the forms underlying not only their own but also the other domains of Right. Part of what it is for philosophy to give a rational form to what is, then, is to show how specific instances of Right, though grounded primarily in one conception of freedom, also cooperate with other instances in realizing the forms of freedom distinctive to their domains. One version of this second type of systematicity can be found in the ways in which the institutions of Ethical Life realize not only social freedom but also the freedoms of personhood and moral subjectivity. (Participation in the family is a way of realizing social freedom, but in its fully rational form it also promotes the personhood and moral subjectivity of family members.) Another version of the second type of systematicity is located in the ways in which the aims individuals pursue in one institution of Ethical Life converge with the aims they pursue in the other institutions. (In their productive activity in civil society, men not only pursue their own particular ends but also fulfil their duties as fathers insofar as their labour satisfies the needs of their respective families.) It is by demonstrating how institutions of Right systematically realize the Concept of freedom in these senses (and in others discussed in this essay) that Hegel takes himself to have shown that 'the state' – the modern social order that incorporates Abstract Right, Morality and the institutions of Ethical Life – is '*an inherently rational entity*' (PR *Preface*, 21[26]).

CHAPTER 2

Property, Use and Value in Hegel's Philosophy of Right

Stephen Houlgate

Hegel is aware that it is only in the modern world, with the emergence of civil society, that 'the *freedom of property* has been recognized here and there as a principle' (PR § 62R).[1] Nonetheless, he contends, property is made necessary by the very idea of freedom itself. The purpose of this essay is to explain why this is the case by tracing the logic that leads in Hegel's *Philosophy of Right* from freedom, through right, to property and its use. I conclude by briefly comparing Hegel and Marx on the topic of 'value'.

Free Will and Right

The first task is to explain why freedom, or the free will, must give itself the form of *right* (*Recht*). What Hegel calls 'intelligence' is the knowing of what *is* (PM § 465). Will, in contrast, seeks to realize, and realizes, its subjective aims in the external world. It is, therefore, the activity of giving objective 'existence' (*Existenz*) to the content of its aims (PR § 8; PM § 469).[2] Insofar as will actively objectifies itself in this way, it is 'self-determining' and *free*. Initially, however, its aims are determined by nature, rather than by itself: they are its immediately given needs, drives and inclinations. Accordingly, Hegel maintains, will is at first not fully free, but free only implicitly or 'in itself' (*an sich*) (PR §§ 10–11; PM §§ 471–475).

Will is, however, explicitly free, or free 'for itself', insofar as it distinguishes itself in thought from its given drives and inclinations and understands itself to be the power to *choose* which aims it will realize: the

[1] See also PR § 182A, and VRP 3: 565, 641. Translations from VRP are mine.

[2] In Hegel's logic there is a difference between *Existenz* and *Dasein*. This difference, however, plays no role in the discussion of abstract right in the *Philosophy of Right*, so in this essay both terms are translated as 'existence'.

power of *Willkür* or 'arbitrariness' (PR §§ 12–15; PM §§ 476–478). Yet, as such, will is still only implicitly free, since the aims among which it can choose remain determined by nature. Arbitrariness is thus contradictory, even though it is what most people take true freedom to be: for, although it is the explicit and unfettered freedom to choose, it can choose only what is given to it and so is completely *dependent* on the latter (PR § 15A; VRP 3: 134).

Will avoids this contradiction and is truly free, Hegel contends, when its principal content is not just a given need or drive but its *freedom* itself (PR § 21; PM § 480). The truly free will is thus '*the free will which wills the free will*' (PR § 27). This will, however, is still subjective and so still seeks to give, and gives, *objectivity* to its content (PR §§ 25–26). It is thus 'the absolute drive … to make its freedom into its object' *in the world*, both as the 'rational system' of freedom and as an 'immediate actuality' (PR § 27). In the words of Hegel's *Encyclopaedia*, the truly free will aims to give 'existence' (*Dasein*) to its freedom (PM § 469). That *existence* of freedom in turn is what Hegel understands by 'right' (*Recht*): '*right* is any existence [*Dasein*] in general which is the *existence* of the *free will*' (PR § 29; PM § 486). Right, for Hegel, thus does not belong to what is merely alive and sentient but without consciousness of freedom; right is *freedom* as something objective and existing.[3]

We do not yet know all that right will prove to be, or exactly what is meant by 'freedom'; we know, however, that the truly free will cannot just be the will that exercises choice (since the latter is caught in contradiction), but must be the will that wills its freedom as right. Moreover, this will both *aims* to give its freedom the form of right and *actually gives* its freedom 'existence' as right. As such, the truly free will is '*actually free will*' (*wirklich freier Wille*), whereas the choosing will is merely the '*capacity*' (*Vermögen*) for freedom (PM §§ 480, 482; PR § 22). This is not to deny, by the way, that the will may not always be able to realize its freedom as right (for example, under conditions of poverty) (see PR § 244; VRP 4: 609); but, if this happens, the will will not be truly free.

There is, however, another modal category, besides 'actuality', that is inseparable from the concept of right, namely 'necessity'. Right is the 'existence' that the truly free will *actually* gives to its freedom, but also that it *must* give to its freedom if it is to be truly free. In Hegel's (largely) *a priori* philosophy of spirit, each form of freedom is shown to be logically

[3] Animals, therefore, have no rights (which is not to say that we should not protect, feed and conserve them); see PR §§ 47A, 56A; VRP 3: 225; VRP 4: 173, 183, 195.

necessary. For philosophy, therefore, it is necessary that freedom take the form of choice (before proving to be the willing of right). Freedom of choice itself, however, consists in the absence of necessity, that is, in not *having* to affirm any particular inclination or object but *being able* to affirm whichever one pleases: the freely choosing 'I' is the pure '*possibility* [*Möglichkeit*] of determining myself to this or to something else' (PR § 14).

In contrast, the truly free will *must* have itself and its freedom as its content – as what it aims to realize, and actually realizes, in the world – since this is the only way it can avoid the complete dependence that accompanies choice (PR § 23). Moreover, such necessity is there not merely for philosophy but also for the free will itself, and it forms part of the latter's concept of right.

The choosing will is free 'for itself' since it is explicitly aware of its capacity to choose, yet it is also still only free 'implicitly' (*an sich*). This means not only that it is not truly *free* (but dependent on what is given to it), but also that it is not truly *for itself* and so is not aware of its contradictory character (though it can be made aware of it). This is why the choosing will takes itself, mistakenly, to be completely free (PR § 15R). The truly free will, on the other hand, has its own *freedom*, rather than something given, as its 'content and purpose' and so is truly '*for itself as free will*' (PM §§ 480–481). This means that, in contrast to the choosing will, the truly free will is, and must be, *aware* of the character of its freedom; and that in turn means that it understands its freedom to entail *having* to will itself and give itself objective existence. For the truly free will, therefore, its right is not only the 'existence' of its freedom, but also the existence that it *must* give to its freedom if it is to be free. For the free will, in other words, its right is its own freedom, conceived as that which it must will and affirm – that which it must aim to realize and actually realize.

This moment of necessity is integral to Hegel's concept of right and explains why right commands respect. A right does not have the compelling force of a natural event or law and so cannot actually prevent us from disregarding it; nonetheless, it demands recognition from the will and thereby confronts the latter with normative, if not natural, necessity. As Hegel shows in his discussion of crime, it is always possible for a free will to violate the rights of another; yet, if such a will does not understand that the rights it violates must be respected, then it does not understand what a right is. A right is thus the objective existence of freedom that, as a norm, leaves the free will no choice but to affirm it, even if such a will can in fact choose not to affirm it. This moment of normative necessity in right is not made fully explicit in the *Philosophy of Right* itself. It is made explicit, however, in Hegel's lectures: 'People say that the will is free, because it can *choose*. Rational freedom, the will in and for itself, does not choose, but also has necessity ... Right is *necessary* [*Das Recht ist* notwendig]' (PR 1821/22, §§ 14, 29).[4]

Right and the Person

The free will that no longer merely exercises choice, but that wills, and knows it must will, its freedom as right, is the *person*. We will now consider the logical structure of the person and his freedom in more detail.

In speculative philosophy, as Hegel conceives it, the examination of a concept always begins with the latter in its undeveloped immediacy.[5] The truly free will, or person, in its immediacy is the will that relates immediately to *itself* and so, Hegel maintains, is the '*inherently individual* [*in sich einzelner*] will of a *subject*' (PR § 34). It is not just a will in general, but the will of a specific individual. Furthermore, such a will, like the choosing will, still has given drives and inclinations that supply it with particular aims, and it still confronts an 'external', immediately given world in which it must realize its freedom.

Yet the free will is also the 'self-conscious, but otherwise contentless and *simple* relation to itself in its individuality' (PR § 35; translation modified). As such it is an utterly indeterminate, non-specific, and in that sense *universal*, will. As Hegel explains in § 5 of the *Philosophy of Right*, the self-conscious subject first becomes an explicitly (though not yet truly) free will by distinguishing itself in thought from its particular 'needs, desires, and drives' and conceiving itself as a purely abstract, universal 'I'. This abstract will then chooses between those drives (and their objects) and so gives itself a particular content. When it becomes truly free, however, it has its abstract *universality* as its content. The 'freedom' to which the will gives, and must give, objective existence as right is thus precisely this abstract universality.

[4] Translations from PR 1821/22 are mine. See also VRP 4: 149; *Werke* 7: 81: 'it is *necessary* that I be a person *with rights* [*eine* rechtliche *Person*]' (translations of Hegel's marginal notes to PR are mine); and Stephen Houlgate, 'Recht und Zutrauen in Hegels Philosophie des Rechts', in Gunnar Hindrichs and Axel Honneth (eds.), *Freiheit. Stuttgarter Hegel-Kongress 2011* (Frankfurt am Main: Vittorio Klostermann, 2013), 615–616.

[5] See EL § 238: 'The moments of the speculative method are (α) the *beginning*, which is *being* or the *immediate*'.

Yet the free will in its immediacy is also always a specific, individual will. It thus is, and knows itself to be, both specific and universal at the same time: the will that in its 'finitude' is '*infinite, universal,* and *free*' (PR § 35). The free will, or the person, therefore, is, and understands itself to be, *this* 'I' that is equally a bare, indeterminate 'I' like any other – an 'I' that is utterly abstract and universal in its specificity (PR § 35R). Accordingly, the freedom that the will affirms as its right is the universality or 'personality' that is inseparable from being a specific individual.[6]

Now in the *Encyclopaedia* Hegel argues that the individual free will necessarily relates to other individual wills (PM § 483). A similar point is made in Hegel's 1817–18 lectures on the philosophy of right, when he draws on the logic of the 'one' (*Eins*) in the *Science of Logic* to claim that 'the immediate one of personality is a repulsion into infinitely many ones' (LNR § 31; translation slightly modified). We have also just seen, however, that the personality the free will must will as its right is abstract, non-specific and so *universal.* It does not, therefore, belong to just *one* person but belongs to *all* persons alike. Accordingly, in willing his own freedom as his right, the person must also will the freedom of all other persons as *their* right, because the freedom that any will affirms is the same in all of them: each person must affirm the right of the person in *every* person. The 'commandment of right' is thus not just 'respect my freedom as a person' but '*be a person and respect others as persons*', and the sphere of right is that of *mutual recognition* between persons (PR § 36).[7] Earlier in the *Encyclopaedia* Hegel showed that mutual recognition is a logical precondition of all reason and spirit (see PM § 436). At the start of the *Philosophy of Right,* however, mutual recognition is made necessary by the logical structure of the person (as the bearer of right): for in recognizing that he must will his own abstract and thus 'universal' freedom, the individual person recognizes that he must will the same freedom in all persons, and every person recognizes this in exactly the same way.[8]

Note that right precedes and makes necessary mutual recognition and is not itself constituted by the latter. It is, therefore, not true that 'right is

[6] See Klaus Vieweg, *Das Denken der Freiheit. Hegels Grundlinien der Philosophie des Rechts* (Munich: Wilhelm Fink, 2012), 97–102.

[7] See also PM § 490; LNR § 31.

[8] In PR § 49R Hegel suggests that at this point there are not yet 'several' (*mehrere*) persons. Yet what he means, I think, is that we are not yet in the sphere of *contract,* in which there is a 'plurality' (*Mehrheit*) of wills (VRP 4: 179) and freedom has its *existence* in 'the relation of will to will' (PR § 71). He is not denying altogether that, prior to contract, a person relates to other persons. (On my reading, by the way, Hegel's claim in PM § 490 that my personality has its 'existence' in being recognized by others also anticipates contract, even though contract is not introduced until PM § 492.)

grounded in mutual recognition'.[9] Hegel will argue later in the *Philosophy of Right* that rights must be generally recognized and codified in law if they are to attain 'the power of actuality', and that this occurs in civil society; yet laws confer universal 'validity' on what is already 'right *in itself*' (PR §§ 210–211). Recognition through law does not, therefore, first establish the sphere of right; right is made necessary by the concept of the person and commands that there be, rather than presupposes, mutual recognition between persons.

The concept of the person also gives a distinctive character to the right that arises from it. Like the choosing will, the person sets his wholly abstract, 'universal' identity apart from his particular desires. Accordingly, such 'particularity' – unlike individuality – is 'not yet contained in the abstract personality as such' (as it will be contained in the moral and ethical subjects) (PR § 37). This in turn means that there is no right, inherent in being a *person*, to satisfy this or that particular desire. It is already clear that I do not have a right to something just because I *desire* it, since right is grounded in freedom, not desire. We now see that my freedom as a person does not itself confer rights on particular desires. If a particular desire were built into being a person, then I would have to will it and it would have a right to be satisfied. No desires are built into being a person, however, since personality is utterly abstract. Accordingly, persons have the right to be free *as* abstract persons, and that is all.

Yet precisely because a person is conscious of himself as an abstract I, just like the choosing will, the freedom of the person – like freedom of choice – consists in being able to (though not having to) affirm any of one's desires, that is, in the *possibility* of such affirmation. Unlike the choosing will, however, the person is conscious of his freedom as his right, as that which *must* be willed by the free will. The person thus understands his freedom to consist in the *necessary* possibility of willing any particular desire (and its object). Accordingly, the right of the person, which just *is* this necessary possibility, is, in Hegel's words, 'a *permission* or *warrant*' (PR § 38). I am thus permitted as a person to affirm whatever desire I choose; but I do not have to affirm any particular one, and, as we have just seen, none of my particular desires itself has the right to be satisfied. If a person satisfies a desire, therefore, it is because he, as a free person, is entitled to do so, not because any 'right' of the desire requires him to.

[9] Robert R. Williams, *Hegel's Ethics of Recognition* (Berkeley, CA: University of California Press, 1997), 138. There is a similar misunderstanding in Dudley Knowles, *Hegel and the Philosophy of Right* (London: Routledge, 2002), 102.

Yet right, as we know, is the objective existence or 'actuality' of freedom. The necessary possibility of affirming a desire (and its object) – in which the person's freedom consists – must, therefore, be actualized if the person is truly to enjoy his right. This is why Hegel will later insist that every person must own *some* property, even if they do not all have to own the same amount (PR § 49A; VRP 3: 216–218). Nonetheless, the right that the person enjoys in *actually* affirming a desire (and owning something) consists in the necessary, rightful *possibility* of so doing: it is the actual embodiment of the person's 'warrant' or entitlement. The person is entitled, therefore, to withdraw his will from that desire (and its object) and invest it in another, if he so wills.

The fact that personality is abstract and empty means, further, that no particular, positive commandments follow from it. Accordingly, all a person's right requires is that it be respected and not be violated. 'Hence', Hegel writes, 'there are only *prohibitions of right*, and the positive form of commandments of right is, in its ultimate content, based on prohibition' (PR § 38). The 'positive' commandment 'respect others as persons' thus in fact just directs us *not* to violate their rights.

Personality's abstract character also means that no particular conditions must be met for the person to have rights beyond understanding oneself to be a person and 'realizing' one's freedom in the world. In other words, there is nothing one needs to do, or can do, to *merit* rights: one cannot earn rights, for example, through good actions, or deserve them through being needy (PR § 37). Right belongs *immediately* to a person, as soon as he asserts or 'realizes' his freedom in the world in a way that enables, and requires, others to recognize it.

Note that the immediate – or what Hegel calls 'abstract' – right of the person is not a *natural* right that one has simply by virtue of being human (though it is what others call 'natural right' [*Naturrecht*]).[10] Abstract right belongs only to those who are explicitly conscious of their *freedom* and who give that freedom 'existence' both in their own eyes and in those of others. Yet it is a right that *anyone* conscious of his freedom, whatever his social or legal status, can give himself.[11] This applies as much to slaves as to other people.

[10] See PR 1819/20, 67. Translations from PR 1819/20 are mine.

[11] Under Roman law, Hegel notes, rights came with a particular social and legal 'status' (*Stand*) (PR § 40R). For us, however, right is independent of status, since freedom itself is 'not a status at all' (*gar kein Status*) (PR 1819/20, 69–70).

Slaves, in Hegel's view, do not need to earn their freedom; as he states in 1817–18, 'even if I am born a slave … I am free the moment I so will it, the moment I come to the consciousness of my freedom' (LNR § 29). The slave then turns that freedom into his right the moment he gives it objective existence by, for example, running away. In his 1824–25 lectures, Hegel maintains that 'the slave has the absolute right always to run away' (VRP 4: 239). It accords more with Hegel's concept of right, however, to say that the slave establishes his right precisely *by* running away. His consciousness of his freedom, if it is properly developed, will bring with it the necessity of asserting that freedom as right; yet it is only in actually being asserted – for example, in flight – that it becomes a right that others must respect. This explains Hegel's otherwise harsh suggestion (in 1819–20) that no 'injustice' (*Unrecht*) is done to one who, in the eyes of his captors, lets himself be enslaved (PR 1819/20, 73). For Hegel, all human beings are born to be free, so there is a clear moral demand not to enslave anyone; but I can demand respect for my *right* only if my freedom 'shows itself in existence' *as* right (PR 1819/20, 74). If I fail to realize my freedom in this way, therefore, I cannot claim that my *right* is being violated (though as soon as I do realize my freedom, my right is established and commands respect). In Hegel's view, each person must aim to promote, and must actually promote, the rights of all persons; but, equally, an individual must show others that he *is* a person, if his rights are to be promoted and respected by them.[12]

Property

As we have seen, the person conceives of himself as such by abstracting himself from all that is merely given to him. Indeed, the person *excludes* such givens from himself (PR § 34). The latter are thus reduced to merely external 'things' (*Sachen*) without any personality, and so without any freedom or right, of their own (PR § 42). Such things, however, are actually of two different kinds.

The first is the '*natural* existence' that is inseparably attached to, but also distinct from, the person: namely, his body together with all his particular needs and desires. The second comprises those things that are

[12] Since rights are not natural but dependent on the consciousness of freedom, all children, as *implicitly* free, must be raised to such consciousness through *education* (PR §§ 174–175). In a rational state, therefore, all will be aware of their freedom and right and there will be no slavery (*Werke* 7: 124–125).

distinct from both the person and his body: namely, inanimate objects and living things in the external world (PR §§ 34, 43, 47).[13] These two kinds of 'thing' thus constitute what Hegel calls the 'external sphere' in which the person must give his freedom objective 'existence' (PR § 41). Moral freedom will be embodied in the actions of the subject itself, and ethical freedom will be embodied in human institutions governed by habit and law. Personal freedom, however, must be embodied in 'things' that are immediately distinct from the person and so are 'unfree'. As Hegel puts it, therefore, 'personal right is essentially *right over things* [*Sachenrecht*]' (PR § 40R; translation modified).

When the person embodies his freedom in a thing, he places his will in it and *appropriates* it, and in this way the thing becomes the person's *property*. The person, for Hegel, thus has the 'absolute *right of appropriation*' over things (that have not been appropriated by another person), or the right to property (PR § 44). More precisely, the person has his right *in* property: for his freedom becomes something objective and external only in a thing owned. This is not to deny that the person conceives of his right of ownership before he appropriates something; but what he is conceiving of, and aiming to realize, is his right *as* ownership itself. My right to own is thus – and must become – coextensive with my actually owning something.

An important consequence of this conception of property is that property is not – or not principally – a *means* towards furthering the person's freedom. Property is, rather, the 'first *existence* [*Dasein*] of freedom' itself and as such is 'an essential end for itself' (PR § 45R). *Pace* Alan Patten, therefore, we do not own property so that we can develop and maintain 'the capacities and self-understandings that make up free personality'.[14] Persons own property because it is only *in* such ownership that they are actual bearers of right, both for themselves and for others (see PR § 51).

Since the external sphere comprises not only external objects but also my body, I must appropriate the latter and place my will in it (for example, by training it to do what I will), if it is to embody my right (PR §§ 47–48; VRP 4: 195). When I do this, my body commands respect from others and so 'may not be misused as a beast of burden' or enslaved (PR § 48R). (Slaves can thus assert their freedom and right, not only in running away, but also in the way they hold their bodies.) As free, I can, if I choose, 'withdraw into myself from my existence' and deny that harm

[13] On living things as 'external' to the person, see PR § 44A; VRP 3: 209.

[14] Alan Patten, *Hegel's Idea of Freedom* (Oxford: Oxford University Press, 1999), 140.

done to my body affects my person as such. For *others*, however, my body – once I have appropriated it – is the objective 'existence' *of* my personal freedom. Others may not, therefore, inflict harm on my body, because in doing so they violate my *right* as a person: in Hegel's words, 'violence done to *my body* by others is violence done to *me*' (PR § 48R).[15]

For Hegel, therefore, the right to bodily inviolability is an integral component of my right to property (PR § 57). There is, however, a significant difference between my ownership of my body and that of other things. All things are external to the freedom of the person, and so no thing, *qua* thing, is such that my freedom requires that I own it. My freedom as right consists, therefore, in the rightful possibility, but not the necessity, of owning any particular thing, and anything I own can thus be disowned or 'alienated' (PR § 65). My body, however, is not merely a *thing*. It is, indeed, a thing in the world distinct from my abstract personality, yet it is also 'the real possibility of all [my] further-determined existence' (PR § 47; translation modified) and so the natural condition *of* my personality. My right as a person cannot, therefore, include the right to alienate my body (and my life), since in doing the latter I would forfeit all right as such (PR § 70; see also PR 1821/22, § 70). Accordingly, as a person I am not just permitted to own my body, but I must do so and must continue to do so.[16]

Ownership of my body and of other things coincide, however, in requiring that I actually 'take possession' of the thing concerned; for only in this way do I give objective existence to my freedom and so turn the latter into a right able 'to be recognized by others' (PR § 51). Yet Hegel points out that possession itself does not constitute ownership of *property*. I possess something when I have it in my 'external power' (in ways we will consider in a moment) (PR § 45). A possession counts as my property, however, only when it embodies my right as a person: property is *rightful* possession (PR § 45; VRP 4: 186). Only free beings, as bearers of right, can own property, therefore, whereas any being with a need or desire for a thing can seize possession of it.

[15] Children, who are not yet persons, are protected by the family (and if necessary by the state) (PR § 174; LNR § 85). Adults who, for whatever reason, are not able to train their bodies to do their will can appropriate their bodies (as they can other things) through the use of signs; see PR § 58.

[16] In Hegel's view, therefore, there is no right to suicide (PR § 70; VRP 3: 260–261). On the 'inalienability' of a person's body (and mind), see Peter G. Stillman, 'Property, Contract, and Ethical Life in Hegel's *Philosophy of Right*', in Drucilla Cornell, Michel Rosenfeld and David Gray Carlson (eds.), *Hegel and Legal Theory* (London: Routledge, 1991), 210–212.

Hegel points out that families and communities, such as religious ones, can own property (PR §§ 169–171, 270R).[17] In the sphere of abstract right, however, property is owned by *persons*, and this in turn explains two further features of it. The first is that such property is by its nature *private*. A subject is a person, insofar as he is conscious of his abstract identity and freedom as an 'I'; but such a person is also conscious of being an immediate individual (among other such individuals) (PR §§ 34, 36). Thus, if property is to embody the person's freedom and right, it must embody his universal right as an *individual*. That in turn means that it must be the private and exclusive property of the individual concerned (PR § 46; LNR § 26). Private property, for Hegel, is thus not simply the product of a social order based on the division of labour (though it emerges in history in such a society), but is made necessary logically by the very concept of a person (which is in turn made necessary by the nature of freedom). This is not to say that the right of private property cannot be trumped by other concerns. Hegel insists, however, that exceptions to the rule of private property 'cannot be grounded in contingency, private arbitrariness, or private utility, but only in the rational organism of the state', which is itself the highest embodiment of freedom and so the highest right (PR § 46R).[18]

The second feature of property to be noted here is that, in the sphere of abstract right, every person has an equal right to own (some) property but there is no need for possessions to be equal (PR § 49). The right to property is grounded in the 'personality' that is the same in all individual persons, so everyone has the same right to own (some) property. What we take into possession, however, is determined by our particular needs and desires, and the latter, as particular to us, will differ in some respect from those of others. What different persons take into possession will itself, therefore, be different and unequal. In his later account of civil society, Hegel shows that great differences in wealth between people can deprive the least well-off of their well-being (and so deny them their moral right to satisfaction). Civil society thus needs to be organized into corporations to prevent such great differences emerging (PR §§ 243–244, 253R).[19] Hegel also argues, however, that there is nothing at the level of abstract right to prevent the excessively unequal distribution of possessions (provided that every person owns something). This is a clear indication, therefore, that,

[17] See also *Werke* 7: 109, 421; VRP 3: 212.

[18] Moral concerns can also limit a person's right to property; see PR § 127R; LNR § 8.

[19] On the role of the corporations in preventing the emergence of poverty in civil society, see Stephen Houlgate, *An Introduction to Hegel: Freedom, Truth and History*, 2nd edn (Oxford: Blackwell, 2005), 204–206.

although personal right is the necessary beginning of freedom, it does not exhaust all that freedom can and must be.

Property and Its Use

Property, for Hegel, is rightful possession, and the fact that a *person* owns property requires the possession it involves to take different forms. A person is an *individual* who is conscious of being an abstract, *universal* (and thus free) 'I', so the 'modes of taking possession' must 'contain the progression from the determination of individuality to that of universality' (PR § 54A; VRP 4: 204).

Since the person in his immediacy is an individual with *this* body, here and now, rightful possession must first involve 'physical seizure' of a thing, seizure that is limited in space and time (PR §§ 54–55; see PR §§ 43, 47). In his marginal notes to the *Philosophy of Right*, however, Hegel points out that the person has property 'as a *thinking* human being' and what such a person '*wills* as thinking is the *whole*, the *universal*' (*Werke* 7: 120). The first step towards possessing something universal, rather than limited, is taken by '*giving form*' to a thing (for example, by tilling the soil): for in this way my will's presence in the thing has an '*independently existing* externality' that continues *beyond* this place and this moment in time (PR § 56). The second step then involves taking possession of the whole thing (the 'universal') in my mind and making this clear to others through a *sign* (PR § 58; VRP 4: 212). This, Hegel contends, is the 'most complete' mode of taking possession since it has the widest range, though it can also be 'ambiguous' and 'indeterminate' (as when a cross is placed on a coast to indicate 'that the whole land is mine') (PR § 58A; VRP 3: 227; *Werke* 7: 126).

Property, however, involves not just the possession, but also the *use* (*Gebrauch*) of the thing. Such use, like the different modes of possession, is made necessary by the fact that property is owned by a person or free will. In taking possession of a thing, Hegel writes, 'the will has a *positive* relationship to it' (PR § 59): it sees in the thing the 'existence' of its own freedom. At the same time, by making the thing 'mine' the will deprives it of its independence and in that sense *negates* it. This negation of the thing is made explicit in the use of the latter, which, as Hegel puts it, involves 'the alteration, destruction, or consumption of the thing' (PR § 59). The use of a thing is thus the 'completion of my ownership of it' (*Werke* 7: 128; PR 1821/22, § 59).

Now the person, as well as being an individual conscious of himself as an abstract, universal 'I', is also a particular subject with particular needs and desires (PR § 37). The latter determine what we take into possession, but our personality as such is indifferent to them. Consequently, a person, *qua person*, at first regards things solely as potential property, not as objects of need. A person's relation to things changes, however, when he takes them to be objects of use: for, *qua person*, he then regards them both as property *and* as objects of need. This change is grounded in the doctrine of the 'concept' in the *Science of Logic* and is not completely intelligible without reference to the latter. Put simply, the concept as something universal and as something individual is essentially self-related (even though the individual is one among 'many *other* ones'), whereas the concept as particular is essentially differentiated from, and so explicitly related to, another particular (SL, 601, 606–607, 621). Accordingly, as a bare owner, conscious of my individuality and universality as a person, I just relate to my own personhood in my property; as a user of property, however, I negate, and so differentiate myself from, the thing and in so doing take both the thing and myself explicitly to be *particulars* in relation to one another. This does not alter the fact that my right to own and use things is based purely on my being a person, *not* on my having particular needs. Nonetheless, as a rightful user (rather than mere owner) of things, I regard the latter explicitly as particulars related to my particular needs (rather than just as things that are owned) (PR § 59). As we shall see in the next section, this means that property has to have 'value' for its owner.

For Hegel, then, use is the logical extension of ownership, since it renders explicit the fact that my free will negates a thing by appropriating it. Since my freedom is given objective existence in use itself, the latter is a further embodiment of my right as a person. A person, therefore, has the *right* to use his property, and property ownership without the right of use would be incomplete (which is not to deny that moral and ethical considerations might limit how I use my property). Furthermore, since property in the sphere of abstract right is private, I have the right to full and exclusive use of it (though I can give another temporary use of it without forfeiting my ownership) (PR §§ 61–62). Conversely, if I have the right to full use of the thing, then I am its owner and 'nothing remains of the thing which could be the property of someone else' (PR § 61). A feudal relation, in which a serf has full use of the land but the lord retains ownership of it, is thus incompatible with the idea of property (see PR § 62R).

Value

In § 63 of the *Philosophy of Right* Hegel notes that an object of use is an individual thing 'determined in quality and quantity'. This object also satisfies a particular or 'specific' need (as we have just noted) and so has a 'specific utility'. Such specific utility is '*comparable*' (*vergleichbar*) with that of other things in relation to the same need: this scarf may be more useful than that one in keeping me warm. Furthermore, different needs are themselves comparable in that one may be more urgent than another. This means in turn that a thing's utility in relation to one need must be comparable with the utility of things that meet *different* needs. Yet, since there is in this case no one need that all things satisfy, such things cannot be more or less useful in meeting one *specific* need. So how can their utility be compared? This is possible, in Hegel's view, only insofar as the things are more or less useful in meeting 'need at all' (*Bedürfnis überhaupt*) (PR § 63; translation modified). Things with a different specific utility must, therefore, have a comparative utility in relation to needs that, in the comparison, are not specified but just count as needs *tout court*. This is not to deny that my raincoat may keep me dry (and so meet its specific need) better than my scarf keeps me warm (and so meets its specific need). The two objects can be compared directly, however, only insofar as there is a common measure – namely, need as such – and my coat is just understood to meet *a* need of mine more successfully than the scarf does. The objects can be compared directly, in other words, only in relation to needs that are left unspecified.

Note that a thing's comparative utility, in the sense just explained, is not utterly separate from its specific utility, but is the latter *compared with* the specific utility of a thing meeting a different need (as in the example of the coat and scarf above). A thing's utility can become directly comparative, however, only when we disregard its connection to a specific need – and so disregard its own specificity – and conceive of it as an unspecified utility serving an unspecified need (in comparison with another such utility). My scarf keeps me warm, not dry, and my raincoat keeps me dry, not warm. The *comparative* utility of each, however, is not relative to the specific need that it serves, but is relative to need as such: the coat is simply better than the scarf at meeting a need of mine at all.

Since a thing's comparative utility is unspecified in this way, Hegel argues, it is something 'universal' (PR § 63; VRP 3: 239). Such 'universal utility', it should be noted, does not consist in wide-ranging *specific* utility, in being useful in many specific ways. A thing's comparative utility is 'universal' because it *abstracts from* the thing's specific utility and consists in its ability, compared with that of other things, to meet needs that are not further specified – in the simple 'possibility of satisfying a need' (*Werke* 7: 136). The name that Hegel gives to this comparative utility is 'value' (*Wert*). An object of property, therefore, must have *value*, and to understand it to do so is to disregard its specific utility and to consider it just to be comparatively useful at all (PR 1819/20, 76; VRP 3: 236–240). The value of a thing, in other words, is its comparative (or relative) unspecified usefulness.

Now, as we have noted, an individual thing owes its specific utility to its 'quality and quantity'. Yet when the comparative utility, or value, of a thing is considered, abstraction is made from the thing's 'specific quality' (PR § 63), so that value must take the form of a 'quantitative determination' – quantity being, in Hegel's view, the mode of being that is 'indifferent' to quality (PR § 63A; VRP 3: 238–239). The value, or relative unspecified utility, of a thing can thus only be 'more' or 'less' than – or equal to – that of another.[20]

Hegel insists, however, that the specific quality of a thing is not completely absent from its quantitative value but is preserved in it, since the *magnitude* of that value is itself a function of its specific quality and utility. A thing's value is its being 'more' or 'less' useful than another; yet it is not indeterminate but has a definite character, expressed as a quantum or ratio: a thing is three or four times more valuable than another, and so on. That quantum, Hegel insists, is ultimately determined by the specific quality and utility of the thing concerned. Various factors, in Hegel's view, contribute to determining a thing's value, including the rarity of the thing and the '*time* and talent' required to produce it (*Werke* 7: 136–137; see also VRP 4: 228–229). Above all, however, the magnitude of a thing's relative unspecified ability to meet a need is determined by its specific utility: my coat is more valuable than my scarf at all because it meets my (unspecified) need better than my scarf does, but the coat is *four* (rather than three) times more valuable than the scarf because of its specific ability to keep me dry and to do so well (and perhaps because of my greater need or desire to stay dry). Accordingly, 'the qualitative supplies the quantum for the quantity, and is, as such, both preserved and sublated [*aufgehoben*]' in it (PR § 63A; translation modified; VRP 3: 239).[21] The quality, or specific

[20] Hegel also thinks that things of the same utility are comparable only as '*quantitatively* determined' (PR § 63).

[21] See Jean-Philippe Deranty, 'Hegel's Social Theory of Value', *The Philosophical Forum* 36(3) (2005), 315. Christopher Arthur, in contrast, insists that Hegel 'makes no attempt to derive a *measure* of

utility, of a thing is 'preserved' in the thing's value, since it determines the latter; but it is also 'sublated' or hidden in that value, since the mere fact that a coat is worth four times as much as a scarf does not tell us what the coat is good for.

Note that, for Hegel, value is made necessary – before contract and exchange – by the fact that property must be used and, in being used, is explicitly related to need.[22] More precisely, the person, who thinks of himself as something universal (as well as individual), seeks the *universal* in the specific thing he uses; he thus takes the thing to relate not only to specific needs, but also to 'the universal of my needs' or my needs as such, and so deems it to have a relative unspecified utility or value (VRP 4: 226). The person becomes conscious of the value of things, therefore, through 'bringing out the universal' in objects of use (*Werke* 7: 136).

It is thus, ultimately, my being a *person* – not just need (and certainly not exchange) – that makes it necessary for my property to have value. Moreover, the fact that a person's property is by its nature private and exclusive means that I must be the exclusive owner of that value. When a thing is understood not just to be a thing, but also to have value, it is understood to be a 'good' or 'ware' (*Ware*); and when value becomes something objective in its own right, it becomes money. Ownership of money – alongside the ownership and use of things – is thus integral to being a person; indeed, Hegel states, money is 'the most intelligent [*verständig*] possession, which is worthy of the thought of the human being' (VRP 4: 228–229).[23]

Contract

As a person, I must own some property, but I am not required to own any particular thing; I own this, rather than that, only because I choose to. I can, therefore, always choose to own something else instead: I can always withdraw my will from this thing and 'alienate' it by abandoning it or handing it over to another person (PR § 65). Alienating a thing also completes the process of negation that becomes explicit in use. By owning

value from utility'; see Christopher J. Arthur, 'Hegel on Political Economy', in David Lamb (ed.), *Hegel and Modern Philosophy* (London: Croom Helm, 1987), 113.

[22] In 1817–18 Hegel does not yet see (or, at least, highlight) the logical connection between use and value, and maintains that things acquire a value in being exchanged. He also contends that 'value depends on the labor needed to produce the thing' (as well as the latter's 'rarity') (LNR § 37). From 1819–20, however, Hegel understands value to be a thing's (relative) unspecified utility; see PR 1819/20, 76.

[23] On Hegel's concept of value, see also Vieweg, *Das Denken der Freiheit*, 129–130.

something, I reduce it to an embodiment of my will and so implicitly negate it. I negate the thing explicitly through use, in which I change or consume it. I then negate it even more profoundly by declaring that it is *no longer* the embodiment of my will and thereby freeing my will from it (VRP 4: 228). As noted above, however, I can alienate only external objects distinct from my body; I cannot alienate my body, except for a limited period (see PR §§ 67, 70).

Note that, in alienating things, I implicitly acknowledge that no *thing* can adequately embody my free will for me and that my will must rather become objective *as will*. In contract (*Vertrag*) my alienating of a thing coincides *explicitly* with my will's becoming objective in and for another will (PR §§ 71–73).

My will becomes objective *for* another will by being *recognized* by the latter (which I recognize in turn) (PR § 71R). My property is, of course, already recognized by others before the emergence of contract, but in that case my will has its objective 'existence' in the thing owned. In contract, in contrast, my will has its objective existence precisely in being recognized as a property owner by another will. In contract, however, my will is objective not just for, but also *in* and *as*, another will, since the other will wills what *I* will. Our wills thus form an identity. Yet we also remain distinct wills, so the 'identity' we form is in fact just a 'common will' 'posited' and sustained by the two of us (PR §§ 71, 73, 75). My freedom has its objective existence, therefore, in a common will that is also 'a relation of will to will' (PR § 71).

Contract, as Hegel conceives it, takes two fundamental forms (each of which has variants). The first is 'formal' contract, in which one party hands over property to another as a gift (though both still recognize one another as persons and property owners) (PR § 76). The second is 'real' contract or exchange. In this case, each party hands over property to the other (and so *ceases* being an owner), but also receives property from the other (and so *becomes* an owner). Furthermore, each party to the exchange *remains* the owner of the property with which he begins. This occurs because the goods exchanged are of the same value, and so each party retains that value (PR §§ 74, 77). Value, which is made necessary by the use of property, thus makes possible contracts of exchange.

Now such exchanges occur because a person needs or desires something that is owned by someone else (just as we appropriate something in the first place because we need or desire it). Hegel insists, however, that contracts are also made necessary by reason, since it is only in contract that a person's will becomes objective in the form of will, rather than a mere thing. It is thus not just need (or the division of labour within civil society) but rather the *logic of freedom, right and personhood* that makes contract necessary, just as it also makes necessary property, use and value.

Marx and Hegel on Value

To conclude this essay I will now briefly consider a difference between Hegel and Marx on the topic of value. This difference is subtle, but, I believe, significant.

Hegel derives the idea of value directly from property and its use. Marx, in contrast, maintains that value emerges only in the exchange of goods or 'commodities' (*Waren*).[24] Every commodity, for Marx, has – or is – a 'use-value', which is a specific utility or capacity to satisfy needs and which resides in the 'physical properties' or *quality* of the commodity (Cap. 125–126, 133).[25] This use-value, however, is distinguished by Marx from the commodity's 'value' (*Wert*), which is expressed in the latter's 'exchange-value' (Cap. 128, 152). This exchange-value is the 'quantitative relation' in which a commodity stands to another one (1:3, 1:4, and so on). Indeed, it just *is* a certain quantity of another commodity: so the exchange-value of one quarter of wheat *is* '*x* boot-polish, *y* silk or *z* gold, etc.' (Cap. 126–127). Note that a commodity will have several different exchange-values, but each expresses the *same value* of the commodity.

Marx insists that every commodity must have both a use-value *and* an exchange-value (or value) (Cap. 131, 138, 310). Yet he also argues that there is an 'opposition' between the two 'latent' in the commodity (Cap. 181). This is due to the fact that a thing's 'value is independent of the particular use-value by which it is borne' (Cap. 295). This sharp difference reflects a further logical difference between quality and quantity: 'as use-values, commodities differ above all in quality, while as exchange-values they can only differ in quantity, and therefore do not contain an atom of use-value' (Cap. 128; see also Cap. 176). Since this difference is so sharp, the value of a commodity, for Marx, is not determined by the latter's specific utility or quality (as it is for Hegel). The magnitude of that value is determined, rather, solely by the 'socially necessary labour-time' required to produce the commodity, that is, the labour-time required under normal conditions

[24] Karl Marx, *Capital. Volume 1*, trans. B. Fowkes (London: Penguin Books, 1976) (hereafter Cap.), 138–139, 166, 179.

[25] See PR § 63.

and 'with the average degree of skill and intensity of labour prevalent in a society' (Cap. 129, 186, 293).

My aim here, however, is not to examine Marx's theory of value in detail, but to note the important implication that Marx's distinction between value and use-value has for his understanding of wage-labour. In wage-labour both the capitalist employer and the worker consider the latter's labour-power to be a *commodity* to be bought and sold (for a limited period) (Cap. 270–273, 342–343). As such, labour-power exhibits the dual nature of commodities in general. On the one hand, labour-power is concrete, comprises the specific 'mental and physical capabilities', or *qualities*, of a human being, and (when set to work) produces 'use-values' (Cap. 270, 283). On the other hand, labour-power is a *quantity* of '*congealed labour-time*' – namely, the time required to produce and sustain it – and so has a *value* (expressed in its exchange-values) (Cap. 130, 277). This value, which abstracts altogether from the specific quality of labour-power, is what enables the latter to be an exchangeable *commodity*, just like any other. *As* such a commodity, therefore, labour-power is not the specific power of *this* or *that* individual, but simply labour-power in the abstract – power that can be used by the purchaser, just like any other commodity, 'such as a horse he had hired for the day' (Cap. 292).

To repeat: labour-power must be the power of a specific individual and produce use-values. As a commodity, however, that labour-power is also exchangeable for any other. It counts, therefore, not as the power of a specific individual, but simply as abstract labour-power, available in certain quantities. Furthermore, the capitalist purchases labour-power to produce not just use-values, but also new value, and indeed surplus value (Cap. 293, 301). To produce these, labour-power must again be abstract, for it must realize itself in a certain *quantity* of labour and labour-time (Cap. 296, 302–303).

The surplus value produced in the labour process – the value that exceeds that of the labour-power itself – belongs to the capitalist, rather than the worker, because he has purchased the latter's labour-power for the day. Yet the capitalist could, of course, share some of that surplus value with the worker. He does not do so, however, for three reasons. First, he is driven by 'selfishness' and 'private interest' (Cap. 280). Second, he sees it as his right to appropriate the surplus products of the labour-power whose use he has purchased (Cap. 303, 342). Third, insofar as labour-power is a commodity, and so an embodiment of value, it is labour-power in the abstract; the capitalist thus does not see it as the labour of this or that specific individual, and so has no reason to share surplus value with any such individual. This third point, I think, is especially important: the capitalist is not just selfish and concerned with his rights, but is prevented from seeing the specific quality – and concrete human character – of labour-power by conceiving of such labour-power as an exchangeable commodity with a certain quantum of value. This in turn reflects the fact that the quantitative value of a thing is independent of, and bears no trace of, the quality and specific utility of that thing. Note, too, that it is not just the capitalist (as Marx understands him) who sees nothing of the quality and specific utility of a thing in its value; Marx himself thinks that value abstracts from, and blinds us to, the distinctive quality of things and human labour-power. That is why he insists that value and exchange-value must be abolished and with them the private production and exchange of commodities.[26] The problem with capitalism, for Marx, is not just that it extracts surplus value and leads to poverty, but that it is built on value and exchange-value that, by their very nature, 'do not contain an atom of use-value' and so completely hide the latter from view (Cap. 128).

In this respect, Hegel's conception of value provides a significant alternative to Marx's conception. Hegelian value does not coincide exactly with Marxian use-value or exchange-value. It is not the former because it does not consist in specific utility, and it is not the latter because it precedes, and so is independent of, exchange. It does, however, resemble Marxian *value*, insofar as it is a 'quantitative determination' of things that 'abstracts' from their 'specific quality' (PR §§ 63, 63A; VRP 3: 239). Yet, in Hegel's view, value is not (or not principally) 'congealed labour-time', but the relative unspecified *utility* of a thing: its being more or less useful to us. Such utility is 'unspecified' because it is simply the capacity of a thing to satisfy a need at all. Hegel insists, however, that the unspecified utility or value of a thing 'arises out of the thing's particularity' (and specific utility), and that 'the qualitative [thus] supplies the quantum' for the value (PR § 63A; VRP 3: 239). A trace of such particularity and quality must, therefore, be contained in a thing's value. This does not mean that the specific quality and utility of a thing will be directly visible in its value; but the latter will *itself* indicate that the thing has a specific

[26] Karl Marx, *Selected Writings*, ed. D. McLellan, 2nd edn (Oxford: Oxford University Press, 2000), 257: 'the Communistic abolition of buying and selling'. See also Patrick Murray, 'Value, Money and Capital in Hegel and Marx', in Andrew Chitty and Martin McIvor (eds.), *Karl Marx and Contemporary Philosophy* (Basingstoke: Palgrave Macmillan, 2009), 179: 'The point of *Capital* is not to redistribute surplus value . . .; it is to abolish value'.

utility and will suggest something of its strength (which is not the case for Marx).[27]

For Hegel, value arises, prior to exchange, out of the use of property, but it makes the exchange of goods possible and so in such exchange can be considered to be 'exchange-value'. In Hegel's view, however, *contra* Marx, value and exchange-value must contain a trace of the specific quality and utility of the thing, and so the former do not by their nature blind us to the latter. This does not mean that employers cannot disregard the humanity of their employees and selfishly appropriate the 'surplus' goods they produce. It means, however, that value and exchange-value do not themselves abstract completely from the quality of things and human beings, and so are not inherently dehumanizing. That in turn means that the system of economic exchange, which is inseparable from value, does not need to be abolished, as Marx contends, but rather needs to be made *ethical*.[28]

Marx borrows much from Hegel, including an often subtle grasp of the workings of dialectic in history. In his account of capitalism, however, Marx proves himself to be a thinker of the 'understanding', rather than dialectical reason: for, despite recognizing that a commodity must have both (exchange-) value and utility, he insists on the sharp distinction between the two (and, in this respect at least, also between quantity and quality).[29] In contrast, Hegel shows that a trace of a thing's specific utility is contained *in* its value, and in so doing he proves himself to be a thinker not of understanding, but of reason.

[27] To repeat: a commodity, for Marx, must have both a use-value and a value (or exchange-value); but the latter, which is simply congealed labour-time, does not contain 'an atom' of the former and so does not *itself* indicate that the commodity has a use-value.

[28] See Houlgate, *An Introduction to Hegel*, 206.

[29] In a different context, Marx also recognizes 'the law discovered by Hegel, in his *Logic*, that at a certain point merely quantitative differences pass over by a dialectical inversion into qualitative distinctions' (Cap. 423).

CHAPTER 3

Hegel on Morality

Allen W. Wood

It is a commonplace that Hegel is a proponent of what he calls 'ethical life' (*Sittlichkeit*) and a critic of what he calls 'morality' (*Moralität*). Associated with this commonplace is the belief that the latter term is nothing but Hegel's disparaging nickname for the moral philosophies of Kant and Fichte. Common interpretations contrast *Sittlichkeit* – whose ordinary German sense implies the morality of custom and tradition – with *Moralität* as an individualistic and rationalistic stance, which might be critical of commonly accepted social practice. Hegel is supposed to be a proponent of the former and a foe of the latter. This consorts well with another commonplace: that Hegel is a social and political conservative, a foe of critical reason and also an enemy of individuality. Like many commonplace thoughts, both in philosophy and outside it, this one contains a grain of truth, but it oversimplifies and distorts that truth, and for this reason, when people allow such a commonplace to shape their thinking about the topic, it can badly mislead them.

The Development of Hegel's Conceptions of Morality and Ethical Life

The kernel of truth in the commonplace about Hegel on ethical life and morality is that, during his Jena period, Hegel adopted a critical attitude towards the philosophy of Fichte, who had just departed the university under a cloud, driven out by accusations of 'atheism'. It is also true that philosophers in Hegel's day, and for a long time afterwards, tended to identify Kant's moral philosophy with that of Fichte, and to take Fichte's *System of Ethics* (1798) as the definitive statement of Kant's views on ethics as well as Fichte's.[1] Hegel's expression of these criticisms, which is clearest

[1] The truth of this (perhaps surprising) claim is well documented by Michelle Kosch, 'Fichtean Kantianism in Nineteenth-Century Ethics', *Journal of the History of Philosophy* 53(1) (2015): 111–132.

in his early essay *The Scientific Ways of Treating Natural Right* (1802), does make use of the terms *Moralität*, as the name for a standpoint Hegel wants to transcend, and *Sittlichkeit*, as a higher standpoint (*Werke* 2: 459–468; NL, 75–82). Ethical life is the standpoint he identifies with the spirit of ancient Greece, celebrated in some of Hegel's unpublished earlier writings, in which there was supposed to be an immediate fusion of individuality and universality – individuals feel an immediate identity with their social order and its customary ways. Morality seems to be a modern falling away from this, in the direction of social atomism and a loss of cultural cohesion.

Things become more complex several years later, however, in the *Phenomenology of Spirit*. Hegel there uses the same contrast, but in a rather different way. In Chapter 6 (Spirit), 'ethical life' refers to the first or immediate stage of 'spirit', a shape of consciousness that transcends 'reason'.[2] In the chapter on Spirit, e*thical life* is only the first or immediate stage, corresponding to the shape of consciousness Hegel locates in ancient Greek society. *Morality* represents the outcome of the historical process, resulting from the breakdown of the beautiful immediacy of Ethical Life, and passing through the Condition of Right (Rome), Spirit in Self-estrangement (Christianity), the dialectic of Faith and Pure Insight, then Enlightenment, culminating in Absolute Freedom and Terror (the French Revolution) and ending with Morality. Morality is Spirit 'certain of itself'. In a fairly straightforward sense, then, within the structure of the system, modern Morality is presented in the *Phenomenology* as the highest stage of spirit, higher than the stage of ancient ethical life.

Of course, like all shapes of consciousness presented in the *Phenomenology*, Morality too suffers its own dialectic, and breaks down, leading to paradoxes of conscience, the need for forgiveness, and passing over into the higher stage of Religion. Moreover, even in the *Phenomenology*, Hegel retained his nostalgia for Greek *Sittlichkeit*. He therefore describes *Moralität* critically, pointing to the incoherences he finds in the moral psychology he attributes to Kant and Fichte, and to their view of the relationship of individual moral action to the order of

[2] The advance from 'Reason' to 'Spirit', however, represents a revision of Hegel's original plan for the work, and raises a number of vexed questions about the overall structure and subject matter of the *Phenomenology*. A recent presentation of these issues – one which takes the true end of the project of the *Phenomenology* to be Chapter 5, is to be found in Eckart Förster, *The Twenty-Five Years of Philosophy*, trans. Brady Bowman (Cambridge, MA: Harvard University Press, 2012), Chapter 14, 351–372. A more positive outcome to Hegel's decision to alter the structure of the *Phenomenology* is presented in considerable detail by Michael Forster, *Hegel's Idea of a Phenomenology of Spirit* (Chicago, IL: University of Chicago Press, 1998), Chapters 13–18.

the world (PhG, 365–383). These criticisms began even earlier, in the chapter on Reason, to which Ethical Life seemed to offer the solution (PhG, 228–235, 252–262). Hegel's discussion of morality at the end of the chapter on Spirit feels like a continuation of these criticisms. So, despite the structural superiority of morality over ethical life, it is understandable that those who get their impression of Hegel's views from the *Phenomenology* would naturally think that here, as in the 1802 essay on natural right, he has a favourable attitude towards ethical life and a negative attitude towards morality.

But there remains a tension, even a contradiction, in the way Hegel treats the two in the *Phenomenology*. Modern spirit, which has gone through the experience of self-estrangement, the struggle of Enlightenment with superstition and the trauma of the revolution, should have emerged as something higher and deeper than the innocent immediacy of ethical life with which the historical process began. But, in the *Phenomenology*, Hegel seems still unable to conceptualize the way in which modern morality is higher than ancient ethical life. That is why, despite the structural superiority of morality implied by the structure of the system of stages of consciousness, Hegel still gives the impression that ancient ethical life is to be preferred to modern morality. In the chapter on Reason, Kant seems to be the problem, Antigone the solution (PhG, 261–262). Yet the stage of spirit represented by Antigone has now vanished forever, and for good reasons. We are left with Kant (or Kant filtered through Fichte) and with the Romantic turmoil of conscience that ensues from critical reflection on the moral view of ourselves and the world (PhG, 383–409). Religion comes to the rescue, but only by transporting us to a higher stage. The paradoxes of morality motivate religious consciousness, but they have not been resolved on the practical level.

It was over a decade later that Hegel again took up these questions, first in the Heidelberg *Encyclopaedia*, then in his lectures on right and – now definitively – in the *Philosophy of Right*. The superiority of ethical life to morality is now given a structural form. Ethical life is the concrete shape, the truth, of the abstract spheres of right: abstract right and morality (PR §§ 33, 141). But ethical life itself has undergone a decisive transformation in Hegel's thought during the intervening years. It is no longer a nickname for ancient Greece. What it now names is the distinctive rationality of *modern* society. In *modern* ethical life, the fusion of individual and universal (of the self and the social order) no longer takes only the form of beautiful, innocent immediacy, as it did in ancient Greece, but now can be grasped as a series of increasingly reflective stages, passing through immediacy to faith and conviction, then the one-sided insight of the understanding, and it finally reaches fulfilment in conceptual thought, the rational system which the *Philosophy of Right* itself proposes to offer (PR § 147R). It is only here that ethical life is truly to be found.

Ethical life, as modern ethical life, is also rationally structured differently from ancient ethical life. In ancient ethical life, the only institutions were the family and the state, represented in Sophocles' play by Antigone and Creon: and their immediate juxtaposition led to the tragic clash, which was the downfall of the beautiful harmony of universality and individuality (PhG, 266–289). Between 1806 and 1816, Hegel began to appreciate – and began to give a name to – a distinctively modern institution, which determines the shape of both the modern family and the modern state, and explains the way in which modern ethical life is superior to every pre-modern social order. His name for this institution is 'civil society' (*bürgerliche Gesellschaft*). This term might be even more accurately translated as 'bourgeois society', since its basis is economic, rather than political, so it is *bürgerlich* in the sense of the French word *bourgeois* (urban middle-class participant in a modern market economy), rather than the French word *citoyen* (member of a political state) (PR § 190R). Civil society determines the modern character of the *family*, which is the bourgeois nuclear family, not the pre-modern feudal 'clan' or 'kinship group' (*Stamm*) (PR § 172). It also determines the character of the modern *state*. In the modern state, citizens have a distinct sphere – the 'private' social sphere of their estate (*Stand*), grounded on their trade or profession (*Gewerbe*) within the market economy – in which to develop their individuality and what Hegel calls their 'subjective freedom'. From the standpoint of civil society, one's estate is one's private life, but through it one is also social, since estate membership is one's organic connection to the life of society. It is the *Stände* that constitute the representative body within the legislature in the *political* state (PR §§ 308–314). It is the principle Hegel calls 'subjectivity' – manifesting itself most purely in the moral sphere (*Moralität*) – that determines every aspect of modern society, constituting its decisive superiority over the ancient Greek world, and over every pre-modern social and political form. Social harmony and individuality are now seen to be reconciled not immediately, as in the beautiful, innocent harmony of ancient Greece, but reflectively and rationally. Hegel's criticism of Plato (essentially the same as Karl Popper's) is that Plato's philosophy, along with ancient ethical life itself, did not recognize the standpoint of subjectivity but instead tried to suppress it (PR §§ 185R, 185A, 206R, 262A). In modern ethical life, personal particularity and individuality, in the form of subjective freedom, at last reach fulfilment; they do not subvert the modern state, but, on the contrary, constitute its strength, just as the modern social order gives individuality its true significance: 'The principle of modern states has enormous strength and depth because it allows the principle of subjectivity to attain fulfilment in the *self-sufficient extreme* of personal particularity, while at the same time *bringing it back to substantial unity* and so preserving this unity in the principle of subjectivity itself' (PR § 260).

Moral Subjectivity in Hegel's Mature Thought

If we are to understand Hegel's mature concept of morality (*Moralität*) in the *Philosophy of Right*, we must leave behind the thought that his only stance towards morality is a negative one. For in the section on Morality (PR §§ 105–140), Hegel is attempting to develop an alternative conception of the moral subject, which incorporates elements of Kantian–Fichtean moral philosophy, but locates them within Hegel's systematic development of the concept of right, giving modern subjectivity its due as an element in the ethical life of the modern world.

Morality emerges from the dialectic of abstract right, and specifically from the breakdown of this sphere in the determination of 'wrong' or 'injustice' (*Unrecht*). The concept of wrong is that of an abstract free will, the 'person', in which its own individual volition stands in opposition to the universal volition of (abstract) right. The possibility of this opposition leads to a new conception of the free will. The person actualizes free will only in relation to external objects or things. But once the will of the person is divided, as in wrong, between the universal will that wills the right and the individual will that opposes it, this internal opposition within the free will gives rise to a new concept of it: that of the moral subject (PR § 104).

The free will is the will that is 'with itself in an other' (PR § 23). The only 'other' for the person (the free will as abstract right) is the external world. But once the will itself has been sundered into universal and particular, freedom can take a new form: that of the *moral subject*, where the possibility of being with oneself can be actualized within the will itself, through its own actualization of the universal in its individuality. This actualization has several different aspects.

(1) The moral subject recognizes as valid for it only what belongs to it as its own (PR § 107). The moral subject is self-governing, not governed

by external coercion, as happens both in wrong and in its cancellation through punishment (PR §§ 100–102).

(2) In this self-governing, the relation of the universal to the particular takes the form of 'obligation or requirement' (PR § 108). The moral subject stands under a norm or duty, a law that is self-imposed, its own universality to which its particular volitions ought to conform.

(3) The subject, like the person, stands in relation to an external, objective sphere in which it acts. So the conformity of individuality to universality is to be manifested in relation to this objectivity; and the objectivity of its action places the moral subject in relation to the will of other moral subjects (PR §§ 110–114).

Hegel's exposition of morality is then divided into three sections. They do not follow these three moments separately, but deal with three different ways in which all three are combined in the action of the moral subject. The first section deals with the way the moral subject recognizes external occurrences subject to obligation as its own: responsibility or imputability (PR §§ 115–118). The second deals with the way the moral subject fulfils its own individuality through action: the role in moral action of the subject's self-satisfaction or welfare (*Wohl*) (PR §§ 119–128). The third covers the moral conception of the *good* (*Gut*) to be actualized by the moral subject, and the way this good is determined by the subject's *conscience.*

Hegel's Theory of Moral Responsibility

Many theories of moral responsibility are concerned not directly with actions – events in the external world – but with inner mental events, such as volitions, which are taken to be the causes of actions. These theories ask about the kind of causal relations that volitions have to actions, and also about the way the volitions themselves are caused in the psychology of agents. We are held responsible for what we do if our doing is related in the right way to willing, and we are responsible for willing if our volitions are caused psychologically in a way that manifests who we are as agents.

Hegel's approach is quite different from this. He does presuppose, based on his account of the free will in PR §§ 4–21, that the human will is free (like Fichte, he regards an unfree will as a contradiction in terms, PR § 4), and he holds that this freedom consists in the capacity both to abstract entirely from our particularity and also to identify with the particularity of who we are and what we will (PR §§ 5–6). But he thinks of volition as essentially related to external happenings, rather than being merely an inner event (PR §§ 7–9). He supposes that it is up to us to take up different attitudes towards ourselves, our natural drives and desires, and also to *choose* to identify with some rather than others, and between different expressions of our free will (PR §§ 10–15). But none of this as yet, as Hegel sees it, settles questions about 'imputability' – about what we are morally responsible for: which events in the world are 'ours' in the sense pertaining to moral subjectivity, and how we should think about these events as ours, regarding moral credit or blame.

Hegel has three basic concepts in terms of which we are to think about the relation of moral subjectivity to happenings in the world. The first of these is 'being responsible' (*Schuld sein an*), a purely causal notion of responsibility for objects or events, where something about us – such as our bodily motions – brings about an object or state of affairs. A deed (*Tat*) is an alteration in the objective world for which the will is 'responsible' in this sense (PR § 115). We can be responsible in this causal sense in cases where we do not impute what happens at all to ourselves as moral subjects.

The other two concepts of 'responsibility' for deeds on which imputation depends have to do with the way the effects of outer behaviour are cognized or thought about by the moral subject. There are two such concepts, which Hegel designates by the German words *Vorsatz* ('purpose') and *Absicht* ('intention'). Neither corresponds precisely to the meaning of the English word 'intention', but that word might in the right contexts translate either word as it is used in ordinary German. The ordinary uses of these words, however, matter somewhat less because Hegel provides his own rather technical accounts of them.

'It is … the right of the will to recognize as its *action*, and to accept *responsibility* for, only those aspects of its *deed* which it knew to be presupposed within its end, and which were present in its *purpose*' (PR § 117). The purpose of a deed, in this sense, is whatever I knew would happen as a result of the deed. It is the *intention* of the deed in the sense in which we say that something I do might be done either intentionally or unintentionally. Even those aspects of my deed I regret or wish I could have avoided belong to my purpose, because, since I know they will occur, I necessarily do them intentionally rather than unintentionally. My will is not held responsible for what is done *unintentionally* in this sense – what I did not know would happen – but only for what belongs to my purpose. Hegel therefore calls this 'the right of knowledge' (PR § 117). Hegel's example of someone who is not responsible for an aspect of his deed, because it did not belong to his purpose, is Oedipus, who did not know he was killing his father, and is therefore not responsible for committing parricide (PR §§ 117R, 118R). Hegel takes it to be an important difference between the ancient and the modern world – connected with the emergence of the idea of moral subjectivity in modernity – that, for the ancients, Oedipus was held responsible for the entire compass of his deed, even what did not belong to his purpose (see PhG, 281–284).

The intention (*Absicht*) of a deed, however, is that universal concept in terms of which I think of the deed when I will it (PR § 119). It is the *intention* in the sense of what you were trying to do, *what you intended* to do, in your deed. The subjective will has the right that it should be held responsible for its deed, and that part of its deed that constitutes its purpose, by considering the deed in terms of the universal conception or description under which it willed the deed. If the fireman ruins your books by spraying water on them when he puts out the fire in your house, the ruining of your books might belong to his purpose, but it would not belong to his intention, because the concept under which he was doing it was 'putting out the fire' not 'ruining the books'. When we are held responsible for a deed, we have the right that it should be judged in the light not only of its purpose, but also of its intention. This Hegel calls 'the right of intention' (PR § 120).

But there is an important qualification to be appended both to the right of knowledge and to the right of intention. Hegel says we are to include both in the purpose and in the intention of a deed whatever belongs to the 'nature' of the action. According to Hegel, the 'nature' of anything includes what we would grasp about it from rational reflection on it and its connection with other things (EL § 23). In the case of a deed, these include connections with its consequences (PR § 118). Consequently, the nature of an action includes all the consequences that would be known by rational reflection: 'In general it is important to think about the consequences of an action because in this way one does not stop with the immediate standpoint but goes beyond it. Through a many-sided consideration of the action, one will be led to the nature of the action' (*Werke* 4: 230). Both the purpose of an action – what makes it intentional rather than unintentional – and also its intention – the concept or description under which the agent is regarded as intending it – include anything that rational reflection would have brought to light, even if a careless, thoughtless or negligent agent did not in fact think of them. I am held responsible not merely for my failure to be reflective, but also for whatever I did that I would have realized I was doing if I had been as reflective as I should have been. Consequently, corresponding to the 'right of intention' is also 'the right of the objectivity of the action to assert itself as known and willed by the subject as a thinking agent' (PR § 120).

One result of including the 'nature' of the action as part of its purpose and its intention is that, if a certain development can be known to be a possible consequence of the action, then the agent cannot disclaim responsibility for it on the ground that it occurred by 'bad luck'. In acting, a thinking agent accepts responsibility for all the consequences that belong to the nature of the action, even if they occurred as a result of misfortune. An arsonist, for example, must accept responsibility for the destruction of an entire neighbourhood, even if his aim was only to destroy a certain dwelling, or a certain stick of furniture, because the possibility that a fire might spread out of control belongs to the nature of that kind of action (PR § 119, 119R, 119A): 'By acting, I expose myself to misfortune, which accordingly has a right over me and is an existence of my volition' (PR § 119A). Because we are originally responsible for external deeds, not inner volitions, there is nothing 'the same' in the deed of an arsonist who, through good fortune, destroyed little or nothing and an arsonist whose deed brought about a terrible conflagration.

The provision that the purpose and intention include everything belonging to the nature of the action applies especially to aspects of the action that have significance from the standpoint of abstract right, morality or ethics. A deed is to be judged as right or wrong depending on the agent's 'cognizance' (*Kenntnis*) – that is, what a thoughtful rational agent would have known about it, even if a thoughtless or misguided agent did not know or believe it. Neither a 'good intention' nor beneficial consequences can justify or excuse a deed which is wrong (PR § 126).

Moreover, the wrongness of wrong action must be considered to be part of the agent's intention as well as the agent's purpose (PR § 132). An action of whose wrongness the agent had cognizance – because it is contrary to abstract right, moral duty or ethical duty – need not be thought of as intending wrong for its own sake (unless that is the description under which the agent intended the action), but our conception of the agent's intention must take account of the fact that the agent had cognizance of its wrongness. We might express this by saying that 'The agent knew, or should have known, that it was wrong, and intended to do it anyway'.

Hegel's theory exculpates only those who are not fully functioning rational subjects. It implies that 'the *responsibility* of children, imbeciles, lunatics, etc. for their actions is either totally *absent* or diminished' (PR § 120R). Hegel's theory thus allows both for mental or agential incapacity, and for degrees of it, in determining the responsibility of subjects for their deeds. His theory also allows for *liability* – harm or wrong done by things, animals or non-responsible persons (such as children) which are in my possession or under my care (PR § 116). By possessing or caring for them, I take responsibility for the effects they bring about, just as I take responsibility for the results of any good or bad fortune my actions carry with them as part of their nature.

Subjective Satisfaction and Welfare

The moral subject as a rational agent must care about the external outcomes which are its deeds, and take an interest in them as regards their content (PR § 122). Hegel distinguishes two sides of this interest, the formal and the material. Formally, the subject finds satisfaction in the successful exercise of its agency, especially as regards its positive effect on other people. It belongs to my welfare, and my happiness, that I have done certain things, that my projects have succeeded, that I have promoted whatever causes and achieved whatever ends I set myself. Materially, I also care about, and consider part of my own welfare and happiness, the particular 'needs, inclinations, passions, opinions' that belong to the intention of my action (PR § 123). These are for Hegel a positive aspect of my moral subjectivity. If doing good for others also benefits me, or if I receive honour and fame on account of my good deeds, this is nothing to be ashamed of. The self-satisfaction I take in what I have done is not something for which I need to apologize, or from which I ought to abstract myself in my moral action. On the contrary, it constitutes something essential to the expression of my subjective freedom, which is the fundamental value constituting moral action.

Here Hegel does part company decisively from both Kant and Fichte. Kant thinks that I should feel self-contentment when I have done my duty, but this is no part of my happiness (KpV, 119). For Kant, it is no ground for reproach that I am beneficent because I have an inclination to make others happy, or promote the common good out of a love of the honour that it brings me; indeed, these inclinations are amiable and deserving of praise and encouragement; but they do not give my actions that inner, true or authentic worth that is central to morality. That belongs only to actions done from duty (G, 397–399). And even if I do perform good deeds also from these inclinations, I ought to cultivate a moral character that gives priority to doing my duty solely for the sake of the moral law and it alone (G, 390; KpV, 81). Self-satisfaction cannot be a motive for moral action, since it is felt only when we are conscious of obeying the moral law and of the inherent value of conformity to it for its own sake (KpV, 38). Fichte is even stricter than Kant on this point. He thinks that self-satisfaction for its own sake is the direct opposite of morality (SW 4: 260; SE, 249). Morality involves tearing yourself away from the drive to enjoyment for its own sake (SW 4: 141–142; SE, 134–135). Like Kant, he thinks the pleasure of self-approval has nothing to do with happiness or self-interest (SW 4: 147; SE, 140). But Fichte goes further: 'The ethical drive must … be involved in all acting' (SW 4: 156; SE, 148). Moral action must not seek one's own good or one's own glory: it must be entirely selfless: 'It is precisely by means of this disappearance and annihilation of one's entire individuality that everyone becomes a pure presentation of the moral law' (SW 4: 256; SE, 245).

For Hegel, in contrast, what matters chiefly is what one accomplishes in the world: 'What the subject *is*, *is the series of its actions*. If these are a series of worthless productions, then the subjectivity of volition is likewise worthless; and conversely, if the individual's deeds are of a substantial nature, then so also is his inner will' (PR § 124). Hegel even identifies the 'motive' (*Beweggrund*) of a moral action with 'the particular aspect of the intention' (PR § 121A). In other words, what motivates any moral action is precisely the self-satisfaction the subject takes in the action, the way it contributes both formally and materially to the subject's self-interest. The subject has a right to find self-satisfaction in its action (PR § 121). And since 'the *subjective* satisfaction of the individual himself (including its recognition in the shape of honour and fame) is also to be found in the implementation of ends *which are valid in and for themselves*', it is 'an empty assertion of the understanding' to separate the two, and 'to take the view that … objective and subjective ends are mutually exclusive' (PR § 124).

The distinctions of the understanding, Hegel thinks, lead to the envious pettiness of moralists who condemn those that do genuine good because they find personal satisfaction, including the satisfaction of honour and fame, in their accomplishments. It was a well-known saying: 'No man is a hero to his own valet'. But Hegel adds 'Not because the former is not a hero, but because the latter is only a valet' (PR § 124R). This seems to me a dispute on which the truth cannot lie only on one side. Hegel is surely right that the satisfaction an agent takes in the success of a good action is part of the value of moral subjectivity itself. It is an indispensable aspect of the very autonomy that philosophers like Kant and Fichte place at the foundation of morality.

Kant thinks we are permitted to pursue our own happiness, and there is nothing morally wrong or shameful about it. But we must not treat this as the same as duty, or confuse the good of our person with the good of our condition, or think we have done good just because we have done what serves our self-interest, or brings us honour (KpV, 110–113; TP, 278–289; MS, 385–387). What worries Kant is that as soon as we allow our own happiness, and especially our self-conceit, to have pride of place among our motives, we are in danger of no longer doing what is right and good for their own sake, and subject to the self-deception that leads corrupt agents to do whatever benefits them – especially what might bring them honour and fame – whether or not it is substantively right.

Fichte seems to agree with Hegel that the ethical drive involves self-satisfaction (SW 4: 152, 156; SE, 144–145, 148), and even that our happiness consists in doing our duty: 'Not *what makes us happy is good*, but rather, *only what is good makes us happy*' (SW 6: 299; EPW, 151). Hence those who seek the good because it makes them happy are, in Fichte's view, likely not to do what is truly good, and if they do it because they suppose it will make them happy, then it is not going to make them truly happy either. Happiness is not to be got by pursuing it directly. People will be happy when they unselfishly serve the moral law, seeking their own freedom, the freedom of others and the ends on which all can agree – especially when others do likewise.

Hegel seems to be right, but Kant also seems to be right, and Fichte as well seems to be right. Perhaps there is a way of reconciling the truth in Hegel's view with the contrasting truths found at this point in Kant and in Fichte. But I will leave it to another Fichte or another Hegel to synthesize or mediate these opposites and determine where exactly that truth lies. The point I wish to emphasize is that Hegel here shows a distinctive conception of moral subjectivity. Even as he criticizes Kant and Fichte, he does so not by rejecting morality, but by developing a positive conception of morality that contrasts with theirs.

The Moral Good

> The *good* is the *Idea*, the unity of the *concept* of the will and the *particular* will, in which abstract right, welfare, the subjectivity of knowing and the contingency of external existence [*Dasein*], as *self-sufficient for themselves*, are superseded; but they are at the same time *essentially contained* and *preserved* within it – [The good is] *realized freedom, the absolute and ultimate end of the world.* (PR § 129)

The good, as presented here, is the good proper to morality – that is, the good *will.* It is also the good regarded as the end of moral striving, the end of the *world.* Both aspects of the good have their precursors in Kant, but in Hegel both are transformed.

For Kant, the good will is the will that acts in accordance with good principles, or the moral law. The other Kantian idea involved in Hegel's presentation of the moral good is that of the highest good, the end of the world. For Kant, this is morality or virtue (goodness of will), combined with the well-being or happiness of which that will has made itself worthy (KrV, A804–819/B832–847; G, 392; KpV, 110–113; KU, 447–459; R, 4–6).

In Hegel's presentation, both are significantly modified. The good will is not a will that acts according to some principle, but the will whose intention and insight accord with the good (PR § 131). The good with which they accord involves a conditional relation between two elements, and the second or conditioned element in both cases is well-being or happiness; but the conditioning cannot be the same as those in the Kantian highest good, because in Hegel what makes for a good will is determined by the will's relation (of insight and intention) to the good, so the good will cannot (on pain of vicious circularity) be determined, as in Kant, by reference to the relation between goodness of will and well-being. Instead, the conditioning element in the good is abstract right. The good is that external existence which includes well-being or happiness, but well-being that has been achieved without violation of abstract right. The good will is the will whose intention and insight are directed to the good in this sense. Both abstract right and welfare are necessary to the good: 'welfare is not good without *right.* Similarly, right is not the good without welfare (*fiat iustitia* should not have *pereat mundus* as its consequence)' (PR § 130). Further, the welfare that is in question here is no longer only the welfare of the individual moral subject, but must be conceived as the universal welfare of all, the common weal or welfare of the state (PR § 126R).

The moral will, or subjectivity, must be judged by the way in which it knows and intends the good. This Hegel calls its 'right of insight into the good' (PR § 132R). Both its insight and its intention must accord with the good. That is, the will must produce the good, and do so under the abstract concept 'good' (welfare conditioned by right); and it must have insight into what is objectively both right and good. It is therefore to be judged by its cognizance (*Kenntnis*) of the good, as well as its intention (PR § 132). A will that intends the good in the abstract, while being mistaken about what it consists in – thinking its volition is good even though it produces no welfare, or even though the welfare it produces involves the violation of right – is not a good will. We will see presently, in relation to conscience, that this feature of the good will for Hegel puts him at odds with the theorists of morality who are his most immediate predecessors – Kant, Fichte and Fries.

From the moral standpoint, what is willed by the good will is understood under the concept of *duty* (*Pflicht*). Hegel agrees here with Kant, and also with the proposition that duty must be done for the sake of duty (PR § 133). But he parts company with Kant over the question 'What is duty?' and over how this question is to be answered (PR § 134). Kant thinks that it can be answered by applying to particular circumstances the supreme principle of morality. Fichte parts company with Kant at this point, arguing that the principle of morality itself is purely formal, and that its content must be supplied by a separate deduction (SW 4: 54–65; SE, 56–67). Moreover, an adequate doctrine of duties cannot be developed without developing the concept of a rational society, and the roles or estates people might occupy in it (SW 4: 343–365; SE, 324–344). Hegel follows Fichte on both these points, but unlike Fichte he interprets them to mean that the moral standpoint as a whole, and Kantian ethics in particular, is incapable of developing an adequate objective theory of duties (PR §§ 135, 148, 148R).

Conscience

Fichte and Hegel are agreed on one further point as well. Both think that, from the subjective standpoint, that of the ordinary moral agent (Hegel would say: from the standpoint of the moral subject as such), questions about what to do must be answered by *conscience*. Hegel's treatment of conscience in the *Phenomenology* differs somewhat from his later treatment in the *Philosophy of Right*. In the earlier work, he recognizes no objective standard of moral rightness. Conscience functions through the subjective reflection of individual moral agents, and also through their relation to other moral consciousnesses. Conscience functions as long as others accept an agent's assurance that the agent has reflected honestly and that the action accords with the agent's conscientious conviction (PhG, 383–401). It breaks down when the possibility is recognized that the agent may not be sincere, or that others may not accept the agent's assurances to that effect (PhG, 401–403). This leads to an opposition between the acting consciousness and a pure or judging consciousness, the 'beautiful soul': the agent may be judged hypocritical and evil; but the judge remains unable to act without incurring the same accusations, and is therefore just as hypocritical and evil in its own way (PhG, 403–407). The resolution comes when both confess and are reconciled in forgiveness, passing on to the higher realm of Religion (PhG, 407–409). The contradictions in conscience remain, from the practical standpoint, unresolved.

In the *Philosophy of Right*, Hegel draws a crucial distinction: between merely *formal* conscience, which is subjectively certain of its convictions and its action according to them, and *true* (or truthful, *wahrhaftig*) conscience, whose convictions accord with objective standards of rightness and goodness determined by ethical life. True conscience has 'fixed principles'; it wills 'what is good in and for itself' (PR § 137). It alone commands recognition even from the moral standpoint. But equally, the right of moral subjectivity is that whatever the subject does must conform to its subjective insight and its formal conscience (PR §§ 136–138).

There remains, however, the possibility of opposition between what moral subjectivity, in its conscientious reflection, should determine for itself to be good, and what is good objectively according to correct standards of right, morality and ethical life. From the limited and abstract standpoint of morality, to the extent that it has not yet been taken up into that of ethical life, there persists the possibility of a conflict between the right of subjectivity, which is essential to the moral sphere, and what is objectively right in and for itself. This possibility represents moral *evil.*

Evil

Every phase of the *Philosophy of Right* constitutes a determinate stage in the actualization of freedom. But each is a limited actuality – there is always something beyond it, which it cannot comprehend. For this reason, each stage ends with its own downfall or opposite, requiring a transition to something higher. Abstract right ends with wrong or injustice (*Unrecht*), passing over into Morality (PR §§ 82–104). The phases of ethical life end the same way: the family dissolves with the death of the father and the maturation of the children (PR §§ 173–181). Civil society reaches its culmination in the honour of one's estate as member of a corporation, whose ends are particular, not universal. Universality is achieved only in the state (PR § 256). Even the state reaches its limit in its external relations with other states and its limited place in world history (PR §§ 341–360). It is not unique to morality, therefore, that its exposition ends with its opposite, its downfall – with evil. It did the same, as we have seen, in the *Phenomenology*, though Hegel tells us that conscience and evil were explained differently there (PR §140R), as I have tried to show above.

Hegel has a general concept of moral evil. Morality and evil have for their common root the 'self-certainty' of the moral subject. The good will is the conformity of the moral will to what is objectively right and to universal welfare. The evil will, in contrast, is the withdrawal of the subjective will into itself, its *Insichsein* (PR § 139R). Evil occurs, on Hegel's account, when the self-certainty of the subject is affirmed in its particularity in opposition to what is universally and objectively right and good. But evil also exists in degrees or stages. In PR § 140R, Hegel presents six stages of the corruption of moral conscience. They consist in a descent from the least aggravated or serious form of evil towards more aggravated forms. As the descent progresses, the conflict between conscience and the evil or wrong action diminishes. This might, in one way, seem a good thing, since you might think, naively, that conflict is bad and harmony is good. Hegel's point, however, seems to be that, when it comes to evil, the harmony of conscience with an (evil) action is a bad thing, not a good thing. Hegel's stages of evil have it in common with Kierkegaard's *The Sickness unto Death* that they represent a dialectical development which, unlike most dialectical movements in the works of Fichte, Schelling and Hegel himself, does not progress from lower to higher, but instead descends from lower to lowest. Perhaps Kierkegaard saw himself as presenting an ironical satire on German idealist dialectical theories, which represent the rational development of a subject matter (or of human history) as progressive and good. Kierkegaard's view is that the progressive development of human despair into sin leads downwards, not upwards, as the sinful human being asserts his own prideful reason against the authority of his Creator. But Hegel's treatment of the stages of evil shows that a rationalist can just as well do the same thing, when the subject matter requires it.[3]

Hegel's Six Stages of Evil

Stage (a). Acting with a bad conscience. Here the action, and, to that extent, also the moral agent, is wrong, corrupt and evil. But the agent's conscience is not corrupted. It tells the agent that what she

[3] See Allen Wood, 'Evil in Classical German Philosophy: Evil, Selfhood and Despair', in Andrew Chignell and Scott MacDonald (eds.), *Evil* (Oxford: Oxford University Press, Forthcoming). This article discusses Kant, Fichte and Kierkegaard, but, for reasons of space, I was unable to include Hegel. I hope the present section of this essay helps to compensate for that omission.

is doing is wrong. This stage is the starting point of the slide of the conscience itself into evil.

Stage (b). Hypocrisy. The moral agent is doing wrong, and knows it, but pretends that it is not wrong, or attempts to deceive some subject into thinking it is not wrong, or at least not believed by this agent to be wrong. There are two sub-stages.

(i) **Objective hypocrisy**. The agent herself clearly knows the action is wrong, but pretends to others that it is not wrong (or at least pretends to others that the agent herself does not think it is wrong, even if these others do think it is wrong).

(ii) **Subjective hypocrisy**. The agent knows the action is wrong, but deceives *herself* into thinking it is not wrong.

Stage (c). Probabilism.[4] The moral agent is confronted with a situation where she cannot be certain which of two alternatives is right and which is wrong. There are reasons on both sides. We assume for the sake of argument that the agent chooses the action that is objectively wrong. But let us suppose that it seems to the agent, ingenuously, that the action she chooses is more probably right than the alternative. The corrupt attitude of probabilism is involved when the agent convinces herself that, since it is more probable that the action she chooses is right, that suffices to make it right, in the sense that she cannot be blamed for doing it (even if objectively it is wrong). Here the agent permits the judgment that, given her present information, her action is probably right to supplant the whole question of whether it really is objectively right. This is a level of corruption one step deeper than subjective hypocrisy, since it in effect involves a hypocritical *principle* – that of substituting the mere probability that an action is right for the objective fact concerning its rightness or wrongness.

Stage (d). Willing the abstract good. Here the agent performs a wrong or evil action, but claims that her intention (in the sense discussed in PR §§ 120–122) is good, that is, that the universal under which she brings the action in willing it is 'the good'. Since the action itself is (*ex hypothesi*) wrong or evil, this good must be

[4] Probabilism is an ethical doctrine associated with the Jesuits, which was criticized by Blaise Pascal in his *Provincial Letters*. (Pascal was a Jansenist; Jansenists were the theological and political enemies of Jesuits in seventeenth-century French Catholicism.) Hegel makes several references to Pascal in the *Philosophy of Right*, all of them favourable.

the good in the abstract – in other words, it must be some positive feature or property of the action which the agent can cite as its 'subjective essence' in willing it. In probabilism, there was still the remnant of uncorrupted conscience that might distinguish between an action's being 'probably right' and being 'really and truly right'. At this further stage, the fact that the agent wills the good in the abstract is taken to be sufficient for conscience to consider the action right or good – ignoring or suppressing the possibility that the action in particular is wrong.

Stage (d′). The end justifies the means. Hegel categorizes 'the end justifies the means' as a sub-stage under this form of evil conscience. The positive aspect under which the agent brings the evil action is here: 'it promotes a good end'. This deceptively ignores or suppresses the possibility that an end that is good in the abstract might be an evil thing to promote if the means are evil.

Stage (e). The ethics of conviction.[5] At the previous stage, the agent persuaded herself that an action could count as objectively right if only it were willed with an abstractly good intention. But this still allows for a distinction to be made between an action that is willed with an abstractly good intention and an action which is nevertheless wrong considered in its particularity (even if the point of the previous stage was to conceal or suppress this distinction). At this new stage, the agent lets the action count as good or right in particular whenever the agent's conviction concerning this particular action is that it is right. It is no longer allowed that the action was objectively wrong, as long as it is willed with the conviction that it is right.

Stage (f). Irony.[6] Here the agent's subjectivity takes itself to be sufficient to justify an action, irrespective of all moral standards whatever. Irony is self-detachment from all objectivity – by implication, subjectivity as such or in itself is regarded as authoritative for the agent.

[5] Hegel associates the 'ethics of conviction' with J. F. Fries. This characterization of the ethics of conviction is not an accurate portrayal of Fries' position. For a further discussion of this topic, see my book *Hegel's Ethical Thought* (Cambridge: Cambridge University Press, 1990), 178–194.

[6] Hegel associates this ultimate stage of evil with Friedrich Schlegel's theory of irony. Again, the association is unfair, and misses the point of Schlegel's position in discussing the place of irony in art, communication and life.

Concluding Remark

The aim of this essay is to show that, for the mature Hegel of the *Philosophy of Right*, 'morality' does not designate merely an error found in Kant and other moral philosophers. Hegel's positive conception of morality represents the value of subjective freedom characteristic of modern ethical life. In this essay I have attempted to expound Hegel's conception of moral subjectivity, responsibility, the good, conscience and moral evil. Hegel has an affirmative account of moral subjectivity that contrasts interestingly with those of Kant and Fichte, and constitutes an important part of his mature ethical thought.

CHAPTER 4

Hegelian Conscience as Reflective Equilibrium and the Organic Justification of Sittlichkeit

Dean Moyar

In this essay I analyze two of the major conceptions of justification in the *Philosophy of Right* and unpack the relation between them. I argue that we should link Hegel's conception of conscience to the account of reflective equilibrium introduced by John Rawls because Hegel's view of conscience contains the holism, as well as the back and forth between universal principles and individual judgments, that are central to the reflective equilibrium account. In the transition from 'Morality' to '*Sittlichkeit*', Hegel switches the locus of justification from the moral individual to the whole ensemble of social institutions of modern life. This system of institutions is justified because of its organic, living structure characterized by the productive interplay of universal and particular ends. In contrasting these two models, my goal is to figure out just what Hegel thinks is wrong with the reflective model and what is gained in the move to organic justification. The main difference hinges on Hegel's orientation by *action* rather than by *judgement*, where the action-based organicism proves superior because it includes a public feedback process that supports a dynamic, self-correcting model of political justification.

Preliminaries

The recent proliferation of readings of the *Philosophy of Right* has not resolved a central interpretive issue. The issue is how to explain the relation between Hegel's theory of individual freedom, on the one hand, and his theory of the organic rationality of *Sittlichkeit*, on the other. Hegel does take pains to discuss the individual at every level of the account, yet he addresses some of his strongest polemic at political theories based on the individual will, and it is clear that the distinctiveness of his theory stems from his thesis about the social whole. There has been renewed attention to Hegel's concept of the free will as laid out in the *Elements of the Philosophy of Right* §§ 5–7, but that account of the structure of the will is compatible with emphasizing the primacy of the whole over the individual members of that whole. The persisting questions are the following: how strongly holist is Hegel's organicism; and is it compatible with core liberal democratic commitments?[1] While not offering a full answer to these difficult questions, I will argue that the organic model has much to contribute to contemporary discussions on social and political justification.

To frame the discussion of the text that follows, I lay out here what I see as the main elements of any adequate account of Hegel's conception of the justification of the political. This is meant to be a preliminary characterization that is relatively uncontroversial, drawing on familiar aspects of his account. The main issue of the essay is how the first and second elements are related, with the other five elements playing important roles in adjudicating the main issue.

(1) Norms and institutions are justified if they conform to Hegelian rationality, for that rationality is the form in which anything at all can be justified. While the exact terms of this rationality are contested, the general picture is fairly clear. Norms and institutions are rational as a systematic whole in which universals, particulars and individuals stand in a dynamic interrelationship. In Hegel's terminology, it has the three-moment structure of the Concept and the systematic, 'actualized' character of the Idea.

(2) Norms and institutions should be such that they are affirmed by the individuals embedded within them. Thus Hegel's main description of freedom is 'being with oneself in otherness', a criterion of identification or non-alienation. This affirmation includes a component of reflective endorsement, though it is more important to Hegel that individuals identify with norms by acting in ways that realize the norms, finding the result of their actions to be an expression of their freedom.

(3) The norms and institutions must provide social *stability*. This is a hallmark of nearly all political justification, but is most prominent in Hobbes's *Leviathan* owing to his predominant aim of preventing civil strife.

(4) The norms and institutions must be characterized by *mutual recognition*. The theme of recognition runs very deep in Hegel's philosophy, and it shows up in places in the *Philosophy of Right*, yet it takes

[1] For a good overview of current thinking on this issue, see Alison Stone, 'Gender, the Family, and the Organic State in Hegel's Political Thought', in Thom Brooks (ed.), *Hegel's Philosophy of Right: Essays on Ethics, Politics and Law* (Oxford: Blackwell, 2012), 143–164.

some work to figure out just how to understand its overall function in the text.

(5) For Hegel any justifiable conception of political institutions will have to include legal rights and equality before the law. This domain of 'Abstract Right' is also a domain of mutual recognition, though one in which the particular differences of individuals are inessential. One of the most pressing questions for Hegel's conception of *Sittlichkeit* has always been the extent to which the rights of the individual are *aufgehoben* within the institutions, that is, how to understand the subordination of individual rights to the organic system.

(6) The norms and institutions must operate to realize the overall conception of value that Hegel calls the Good.[2] By itself this is not saying very much, since there are many ways for norms and institutions to be oriented towards achieving the Good, though it does cut against the grain of the line of liberal thinking that takes political institutions to shun all ideals. An important corollary of this component is that there is a consequentialist element in Hegel's account that has to figure into any account of justification.[3]

(7) Whatever we end up saying about the previous six aspects, Hegel makes it clear in many remarks that the justification of norms and institutions is not going to be the justification of a timeless ideal, but rather one that is actual in the here and now. One can call this element historicist or pragmatist, but more important than any label is its demand to be responsive to changes on the ground.

The most obvious issue with this list is simply how long it is. Full Hegelian justification can seem terribly unwieldy and thus useless for any guidance in resolving practical disputes. Yet the truth of politics might just be that complex, and Hegel's frequent charges of superficiality against his contemporaries do show that he expected comprehension of the domain he called Objective Spirit would be difficult.[4] Complexity and difficulty do not preclude justification in specific cases, since in the real world pretty much all cases involve holistic considerations. As a pioneer of holism, Hegel does provide resources for thinking through how a system of rational considerations can justify. His theory of rationality as

[2] When I capitalize the Good I am referring to Hegel's conception in PR § 129.

[3] I discuss this in Dean Moyar, 'Consequentialism and Deontology in the Philosophy of Right', in Thom Brooks (ed.), *Hegel's Philosophy of Right: Essays on Ethics, Politics and Law* (Oxford: Blackwell, 2012), 9–42.

[4] See, for example, PR § 272A.

the interrelation of the particular, universal and individual enables him to think of multi-layered justification as a dynamic, contextually sensitive process. In this respect his theory looks quite similar to the most prominent holistic model of justification in political philosophy, namely reflective equilibrium.

Reflective Equilibrium and Hegelian Conscience

The deep affinities between Hegel's *Philosophy of Right* and Rawls' *A Theory of Justice* are now well known. While on the surface more Kantian than Hegelian, major elements of Rawls' project – the basic structure as subject, the social bases of self-respect, the reconciliatory function of political theory – derive from Hegel. I introduce Rawls here not in order to rehearse the argument for their similarity, but rather to focus on one key, and rather neglected, point of comparison. The idea of *reflective equilibrium* was pivotal in Rawls' resuscitation of political theory, as it gave him a way to think of political justification that both appealed to common sense and avoided the theoretical pitfalls of excessive formalism and foundationalism. I will give a sketch of this conception of justification and then argue that we can see Hegel's conception of conscience in the *Philosophy of Right* as a precursor of Rawls' approach. Understanding this affinity will help set up the subsequent move to Hegelian *Sittlichkeit* and the different conception of justification operative there.

Justification might seem like an unlikely point of contact since one might think that for Rawls justification simply is the procedure of the original position, a *contractualist* position that has little in common with Hegel's more holistic, non-formal understanding of justification. Yet for Rawls the formalism or proceduralism of the original position is only one element of an essentially holistic view. His initial presentation of reflective equilibrium is contained within the section 'The Original Position and Justification', which makes it seem that the contractualist ideas are primary and the equilibrium considerations secondary. But the central justificatory strategy is to consider *all of the factors* that enter into the proper description of the rational choice of the two principles of justice. It would not be hard to spell out correlates in Rawls for all but the first of the elements of justification that I listed in Hegel, though for several of these correlates there will be crucial differences. The point I want to stress is that the holistic justification to an individual in reflective equilibrium is compatible with taking these six elements seriously (even the organic conception could be given a Rawlsian interpretation, though I will not explore that possibility here). As Rawls says in a Hegelian vein at the very end of *A Theory of Justice*, 'Thus what we are doing is to combine into one conception the totality of conditions that we are ready upon due reflection to recognize as reasonable in our conduct with regard to one another'.[5]

Rawls writes of the method of reflective equilibrium as justifying and adjusting principles based on how well they lead to results that match our 'considered convictions':

> We can note whether applying these principles would lead us to make the same judgments about the basic structure of society which we now make intuitively and in which we have the greatest confidence; or whether, in cases where our present judgments are in doubt and given with hesitation, these principles offer a resolution which we can affirm on reflection.[6]

The principles are tested by seeing whether they produce judgements (at all levels of generality) that are concurrent with those we already make. The equilibrium is between our particular judgements and abstract principles, and it is achieved by adjusting both those elements and the procedure that is supposed to model them. He writes that, 'By going back and forth, sometimes altering the conditions of the contractual circumstances, at others withdrawing our judgments and conforming them to principle, I assume that eventually we shall find a description of the initial situation that both expresses reasonable conditions and yields principles which match our considered judgments duly pruned and adjusted'.[7] The 'reasonable conditions' include, most prominently, the veil of ignorance. The veil is supposed to represent our moral intuitions that the terms of justice should not be based on unfair bargaining positions and that no one deserves credit for the circumstances into which they are born.

Notice that for Rawls there are two kinds of justification that take place in reflective equilibrium. *First*, there is the justification of *specific judgements* through the principles of justice. This justification is tentative, for it is answerable to our considered convictions or intuitions. If those intuitions contradict the proposed justification through the principle, then the principle has to be adjusted to deliver better results. *Second*, the *whole theory of justice* is justified through reflective equilibrium. The principles, together with various circumstances or facts, should allow us to produce results for a broad range of issues in political philosophy, and the overall theory is justified insofar as those results and the principles together

[5] John Rawls, *A Theory of Justice*, Revised Edition (Cambridge, MA: Belknap Press, 1999), 514.
[6] Rawls, *A Theory of Justice*, 17.
[7] Rawls, *A Theory of Justice*, 18.

amount to a coherent whole. While one can assess cases and principles one by one using the first type of justification, in the end that type will depend on the second, overall kind of justification in reflective equilibrium.

What Rawls calls a problem for rational choice is what Hegel would call a problem of the free will, so it is not at all far-fetched to think of Rawls' holistic consideration of what the rational agent would choose under the right conditions as a relative of Hegel's grounding of right in the free rational will. Virtually nothing in Rawls' account hinges on the element of contractualism that Hegel most criticizes – dependence on the contingent, arbitrary will. Rawls is aiming to secure a *system* of justice that does not depend on any given individual's contingent choice to opt in or opt out. Rawls' principles of justice are principles *designed to govern the basic structure*, where that structure consists primarily of just those institutions (specified differently, of course) that Hegel conceives of as *Sittlichkeit.* However, Hegel does not present the transition to *Sittlichkeit* as what the fully rational will would choose upon reflection. Rather, he unites – with explicit reference to his speculative logic – the universal principles of the Good with the particularity of individual conscience in a social system that is justified because of its organic, living character.

To understand conscience as reflective equilibrium, we need to take one step back in the account to the point at which Hegel introduces the Good. Hegel presents this Good as an all-inclusive conception of the formal rights previously introduced in the *Philosophy of Right.* Hegel calls the Good 'the Idea' and '*the ultimate purpose of the world*' (PR § 129; translation modified), a claim that despite appearances is compatible with the Good being what Rawls would call a 'thin theory of the good'.[8] It includes only those general rights that anyone would need in order to pursue more substantive conceptions of the good. Hegel initially presents the relation of the Good to the will in terms of the abstract universality of Kantian duty, then follows with his famous objection that the categorical imperative is formal and empty. The *realization of the Good* demands that the *particularity* of the will come into play, and thus that the individual conscience take on the role of specifying which realizations of the Good are justified.

There is an apparent peculiarity in Hegel's treatment of conscience that brings out why it makes sense to align it with reflective equilibrium. Hegel introduces conscience as '*particularity* in general' and 'the determining

[8] See Rawls, *A Theory of Justice*, 347ff. See Frederick Neuhouser, *Foundations of Hegel's Social Theory: Actualizing Freedom* (Cambridge, MA: Harvard University Press, 2000), 266ff., for an argument that Hegel's Good is considerably thinner than usually supposed.

and decisive factor' (PR § 136), and he tends to stress that it is the perspective of the actual individual judging in specific situations what is right. Yet Hegel also thinks of conscience as the act of rising above one's specificity: it is 'that deepest inner solitude within oneself in which all externals and all limitation have disappeared – it is a total withdrawal into the self. As conscience, the human being is no longer bound by the ends of particularity, so that conscience represents an exalted point of view ...' (PR § 136A). How, if conscience is the subjective certainty of the particular individual in a particular situation, can it also be the perspective from which the 'ends of particularity' have disappeared?

These two seemingly opposed aspects are in fact just the two poles of reflective equilibrium – we must take some fixed points of reference in our particular judgements, but we aim at justification in reflecting on those judgements and attempting to fit them with other judgements and principles into a rational whole in which the universal perspective predominates. Conscience is the perspective of the individual arriving at a holistic justification, where that justification takes into account both the particular judgements and the universal principles. Hegel thinks of conscience primarily as a mode of ethical judgement in specific cases – what set of considerations *justifies* this specific action? But he clearly thinks of conscience as a candidate for Rawls' second sense of justification through reflective equilibrium – how do the totality of principles (formal rights) and specific judgments hang together? Hegel's critique of conscience is in part a critique of the latter function for reflective equilibrium – conscience cannot be the *medium* of overall justification, but must see itself as embedded within an actual system of ethical institutions. The organic character of that system is a reflection of the fact that it has developed in conjunction with the authority of individuals to judge for themselves on specific cases, but ultimately the system *justifies itself* through its dynamic, self-correcting realization of the Good.

From Independent Centre of Justification to Dependent Agent in a Justified System

If reflective equilibrium represents the holism of justification for an individual reasoner, the organic model of justification of *Sittlichkeit* is a holism of justification at the system-wide level in which individual reasoners are one element of the whole. Hegel is very worried about the potentially disruptive nature of individual holistic justification. Rawls, in contrast, does not mention the sense in which reflection can *undermine* attachment to important principles or judgements. He does not worry about this because he is considering an idealized individual behind the veil of ignorance who is evaluating principles for a basic structure in which all individuals will be fully compliant. In Hegel's worries about 'formal conscience', we see that the holism of justification itself is disruptive when we take the issue of individuality – and non-compliance – seriously. For Hegel, the holism of reflective equilibrium in judgement is not the proper medium of ultimate justification because its way of connecting universal principles and particular judgements remains too unstable. Because the process is internal to the reflecting subject, there simply is too much room for interpretation when one goes to connect one's general principles to particular judgements. There are always numerous ways in which one can imagine the principles playing out in specific cases. For the ethical individual the process of principle–judgement equilibrium is indispensable and, while it is not infallible, it is generally the right model for moral deliberation. But in the case of the justification of a social and political system, of its laws and institutions, such an internal process is inadequate.

Without something like an actual experiment to test the principles, the connections between universal principles and particular cases are liable to be mostly conjecture, or at least liable to be seen that way by the other agents who are supposed to be subject to the justified system. Hegel stresses the internality of conscience when he writes of conscience that 'This subjectivity, as abstract self-determination and pure certainty of itself alone, *evaporates* into itself all *determinate* aspects of right, duty, and existence [*Dasein*], inasmuch as it is the power of *judgement* which determines solely from within itself what is good in relation to a given content …' (PR § 138). Hegel uses change-of-state metaphors (in other places he writes of 'dissolving') to express the way in which principles have to be provisionally suspended in order to arrive at an overall judgement, an overall justification for action. Hegel is worried about what we can call *particularized conscience*, a shape of subjectivity that tends towards preference for one's own good over the universally good (a preference that Hegel calls evil), but also towards the self-righteous judgement of others for failing to conform to one's own abstract conception of the good.

Yet Hegel finds in the particularized conscience itself an element that makes reflective conscience push through its own individualistic boundaries to *Sittlichkeit*. The key to understanding Hegel's transition is that he thinks of conscience both as a kind of *judgement* and as a kind of *action* that implicates the agent in externality and in the particularity of specific interests. In this sense conscience tracks an ambiguity in *practical reason*, which we also think of both as an individual's deliberative activity and as the action that follows from that activity. Hegel holds that the concept of the free will includes the agent's *particularity*, and that particularity gives the Good *actuality* as opposed to mere abstract universality. Hegel already invokes actuality in § 138, where after the above passage about 'evaporating' he writes that this subjectivity is 'at the same time the power to which the Good, which is at first only represented and an *obligation*, owes its *actuality*' (PR § 138; translation modified). Unlike the Rawlsian agent behind the veil, the agent of Hegelian conscience does not bracket his own interest, for the agent of conscience does not aim simply to arrive at principles, but rather to *act*. For Hegel it is not a sign of corruption that we act on interests, so we need not set our justification at an unrealistic level that we must simply strive (in vain) to attain. This view of *actual* moral action also gives us a way to think of a perspective of justification that includes the moral agent without taking that agent's internal perspective as ultimate. An action takes place in a context and includes both prior intention and actual outcome. The *holism of action* thus includes an external perspective and a dynamic connection between the internal and external.[9]

The question before us concerns the rationality of the shift from the individual reflective perspective to the perspective of *Sittlichkeit*. A contractualist might ask the following question: in what sense is it rational for the agent to consent to a social system in which his judgment of what is right does not have the ultimate authority and in which he is subject to the demands of political holism (including, as Hegel often reminds us, the possible sacrifice of one's life for the whole)? Hegel does not frame the issue as one of consent because he has shifted the issue from one of judgement to one of *action*. His question is rather the following: in what way should we conceive of the ethical world such that the actions that accord with my particularity are also the ones that serve the universal good? Both the particular side and the universal side are elastic concepts here, but the overall point is clear. The solution to the individual's inadequacy as a locus of justification is not to look for an objective truth of the matter apart from all my interests, but rather to locate institutional contexts of action in which interest and moral value are in harmony.[10]

[9] The shift from judgement to action is also a shift from judgement to the *inference* (*Schluß*) as the form of fully rational relations. I explore this theme in Dean Moyar, *Hegel's Conscience* (Oxford: Oxford University Press, 2011), Chapter 5.

[10] Part of the obscurity surrounding the move to *Sittlichkeit* has to do with the reference to his speculative logic in § 141. The logical underpinnings are clearer when Hegel makes the same move away from reflective justification in intersubjective terms in the *Phenomenology of Spirit* in the famous scene of confession and forgiveness at the end of 'Spirit'.

In the move to organic justification in *Sittlichkeit*, Hegel reconceives the universal–particular dynamics that Rawls aims to capture with universal principles and particular judgments. Hegel thinks of the universal as a purpose or end rather than a principle (the Good is the 'final purpose of the world'), and the particulars are the purposes or ends in which the universal is realized. Because those realizations are public events, the match (or mismatch) between the universal and particular is open to public assessment rather than confined to internal equilibrium. This is not to say that the particular ends must conform to universal ends in some simplistic manner. It is essential to Hegel's organic story that the particular ends can disrupt existing universals, which must modify themselves in response. But it is also essential that these particular ends are dependent for their value on the universal ends and on the institutional powers that embody those ends. Since individual human beings are mainly concerned with particular ends, Hegel thinks of individuals themselves as dependent on the whole. We can see this dependence as a replacement for Rawls' veil in the sense that it serves the function of displacing the ultimacy of the individual's interests. Yet it also preserves those interests and therefore allows for an *actual* and *dynamic* equilibrium. Instead of conscience determining what counts as a realization of the Good, the standards for the valuation of actions are set by the institutions of *Sittlichkeit*. The organic justification of the whole is in the end a way for the actual results of laws and policies to be evaluated in public and then the laws and policies altered in the light of that evaluation. Like an organism interacting with its environment, the system generates new results that are initially external but then are fed back to the system so that legislators, judges and civil servants can correct and render more determinate the existing laws and policies.

Organic Justification and Civil Society

Hegel's typical claim about the organic is that we misunderstand *Sittlichkeit* or the state if we do not think of them in organic terms, where this sounds like an argument that *Sittlichkeit* or the state does not *need* to be justified because its very existence justifies itself. In the lecture notes introducing the state we find the claim that we should focus on 'the Idea [of the state], this actual God', and then,

> Any state, even if we pronounce it bad in the light of our own principles, and even if we discover this or that defect in it, invariably [*immer*] has the essential moments of its existence within itself (provided it is one of the more advanced

> states of our time). But since it is easier to discover deficiencies than to comprehend the affirmative, one may easily fall into the mistake of overlooking the inner organism of the state in favour of individual aspects. (PR § 258A)

Insofar as it exists, the state 'invariably' possesses 'the essential moments' and we are misguided if we think that it requires justification or deserves criticism. Principles of justification do not really apply because the modern state always is what it ought to be.

Our trouble digesting Hegel's view is that, while he takes it as a virtue that there is no standpoint outside the social organism from which to judge it, we tend to think that genuine justification has to be able to bring external standards to bear. Hegel's model is 'inner purposiveness' as opposed to the 'external purposiveness' that would justify something through its use for a purpose separate from its internal relations. When we ask whether this car is a good car, we assume that it has all the working subsystems of a functional whole, but we are asking whether it serves *our* purpose of transportation in comfort and safety. Hegel's thesis depends on a fundamental difference between functional commodities and organisms: the organism's purpose is not anything external to itself, but rather is its own survival and flourishing. I can ask myself whether I am justified in buying a car, since I can get along without one. But if I seriously ask myself why go on living, typically something has already gone very wrong in my life. Hegel's organic account of the state is suspicious because he seems to be saying that, if we ask why the state has a right to exist, to go on living as a state, then either the state has already ceased to exist or we have totally misunderstood the nature of the state, which 'is an absolute and unmoved end in itself [*Selbstzweck*]' (PR § 258).

Before I begin my sympathetic (and selective) reconstruction of Hegel's organic account of *Sittlichkeit* and the state, I should note that my focus will be somewhat different from most recent engagements with the organicism issue. Because organicism is closely tied to the idea of functional differentiation, it seems to lead Hegel in an inegalitarian direction. Given that a predominant liberal concern is with equality, much of the focus has been on determining whether Hegel's organicism really commits him to some of the inegalitarian conclusions he actually draws, or whether we can see his view as compatible with the idea that each individual should have opportunities to participate at all levels of *Sittlichkeit*.[11] While this is an important issue, I think that it tends to

[11] See Stone, 'Gender, the Family, and the Organic State in Hegel's Political Thought', both for an overview of the general debate on this issue and for a specific account of its impact on Hegel's view of the family.

obscure another important dimension of Hegel's organicism, namely the way in which the differentiated members of the whole realize ethical value and provide feedback to the laws and institutional agencies governing the subsystems and the state as a whole. I take it that this aspect of his account remains fruitful even though many of his specific proposals about societal differentiation (such as his views of the separate roles of men and women) are not justifiable. At the very least, his organic model can serve as a corrective to the highly individualized and formal models of justification that predominate in liberal democracies. The organic model allows us to see how social forms become more rational, better justified, in *actuality* rather than in the political imaginary that is often the medium of political philosophy.

Hegel clearly thinks of the organic character of the state as providing *stability*, but what we need is a conception of stability *for the right reasons*. The social organism must be oriented by something more than self-preservation, for that would be compatible with an authoritarian politics and with a stability based on fear of revolution rather than on mutual recognition. Hegel has already offered in his account of the Good a basis for justification of the social system, a standard that the system has to meet to count as flourishing. He confirms this when he opens '*Sittlichkeit*' with the following: 'Ethical life [*Sittlichkeit*] is the *Idea of freedom* as the living Good which has its knowledge and volition in self-consciousness, and its actuality through self-conscious action' (PR § 142). Recall that Hegel's Good is an inclusive concept of freedom that incorporates all the elements of the *Philosophy of Right* up to that point. The Good is the result of the conflict between rights that Hegel resolves in 'the right of necessity', in which he endorses the right of life or welfare *over* the abstract right of property claims. This is significant because it provides a motivation for restrictions of individual liberty based on the demands of that liberty itself, and thus a grounding for the substantive moral dimension of justice that comes from within the right. While individual conscience could not stabilize the realization of the Good, *Sittlichkeit* as 'the living Good' is able to set the competing considerations in a dynamic equilibrium in which realizing individual freedoms does not come at the cost of realizing the common good. For Hegel, 'rationality consists in general in the unity and interpenetration of universality and individuality [*Einzelheit*]' (PR § 258R). Only the organic model in which universality and individuality are mediated by particularity is capable of achieving such rationality. This organic rationality delivers a model of stability for the right reasons because it sees the strength and stability of the whole as deriving from the freely chosen purposes of the individuals and as nesting those purposes within more universal institutional purposes.[12]

Hegel thinks of organic life as the model for *Sittlichkeit* as a whole, offering an inclusive conception that I call *societal organicism* to contrast it with his *political organicism* that deals specifically with political activity in the state. In the rest of this section, I discuss the way in which civil society, which on the face of it is the realm of mere particularity, is essential for Hegel's societal organicism. The development of particularity in civil society both allows the individual to see why the state is justified *for her* and contributes to the justification of the state as a stable self-determining system. Hegel writes that 'The principle of modern states has enormous strength and depth because it allows the principle of subjectivity to attain fulfilment in the *self-sufficient extreme* of personal particularity, while at the same time *bringing it back to substantial unity* and so preserving this unity in the principle of subjectivity itself' (PR § 260). For a society to be organized and living it must have both elements – the members striving for their personal particularity and the universal bringing the particular back into line with the whole.

Civil society represents the oppositional or external element within *Sittlichkeit*, a self-disrupting element that leads to the expansion and refinement of mediating institutions subordinate to the state. This point is hard to appreciate because Hegel's claims about externality tend to focus on individuals in their activity against each other. But, as the domain of externality in general, he is thinking of the self-interested actions of individuals as a way in which society is external to itself. I think this is what Hegel is getting at when he claims that civil society represents the moment of 'irritability' in the organism (see PR § 263A). Irritability is the drive of the organism to outward movement and the ability to react appropriately to external stimuli. By building this externality into their internal structure, modern states have found a way to provoke their own self-regulation and self-correction. Hegel often writes that the city-states of ancient Greece were fragile and vulnerable because they relied on '*original* natural intuition' (PR § 185R). They really were not stable because they had no room for the particular subjectivity that came on the scene in the form

[12] This argument does find an echo in Part Three of *A Theory of Justice* in Rawls' argument for the congruence of the right and the good. In my view it is unfortunate that Rawls largely abandoned this view in the move to *Political Liberalism*.

of the sophists.[13] Modern states are stable because they have developed institutional structures to allow particularity free reign and to channel its externality back into the power and value of the common good.[14]

For all its merits, civil society on its own is not an organism and cannot organize itself. The market may claim to be able to regulate itself, but Hegel is very clear that this is a dangerous illusion. To make civil society work in the organic system the state needs to regulate the commercial activities. This type of regulation gives more definition to the kinds of policies that are actually justified through the organic dynamics. Hegel writes that

> The differing interests of producers and consumers may come into collision with each other, and even if, *on the whole*, their correct relationship re-establishes itself automatically, its adjustment also needs to be consciously regulated by an agency which stands above both sides. (PR § 236)

Hegel has some faith in the self-correcting character of the market, but he is suspicious of attempts to claim too much autonomy for the market. He writes that 'This interest invokes freedom of trade and commerce against regulation from above; but the more blindly it immerses itself in its selfish ends, the more it requires such regulation to bring it back to the universal' (PR § 236R).

Now one might argue that such concern with the public good is available to any form of justification of public institutions. Hegel's argument would be that in the social contract model one can *try* to justify such intervention, but given the starting point in individual freedom such arguments will be hard to make.[15] The individual liberties of property owners will tend to win out over the claims of the universal. Hegel's

[13] Hegel contrasts this all-important dimension of the modern state with the ancient one, in which particularity 'had not been released and set at liberty and brought back to universality ... Thus, the universal must be activated, but subjectivity on the other hand must be developed as a living whole' (PR § 260A).

[14] I have argued in *Hegel's Conscience* that Hegel thought that modern societies with strong civil societies are held together in large part because of the development of conscience in Protestant Christianity. In terms of this essay's argument, the claim is that organic justification of *Sittlichkeit* does depend on the reflective equilibrium of individual conscience, so, while Hegel argues that Rawls' reflective equilibrium is appropriate only for individual deliberation, there remain for Hegel important connections between the individual and institutional levels.

[15] Among social contract theorists, Rousseau and Fichte stand out for trying to build into their theories an argument against the ultimacy of private property rights. Their theories are best described as a kind of holistic contractualism, and I doubt that in the end they are stable. I have argued that they are unstable in Dean Moyar, 'Fichte's Organic Unification: Recognition and the Self-overcoming of Social Contract Theory', in Gabriel Gottlieb (ed.), *Fichte's Foundations of Natural Right: A Critical Guide* (Cambridge: Cambridge University Press, 2016).

organic model gives him the resources (admittedly not extensively enough employed) to justify state action to contain business interests and mitigate inequality. There are formal property rights that must be respected, but they are subordinate to the interest of the whole. Contrast the organic justification of state action to Rawls' use of the Difference Principle to promote equality. There is an enormous obstacle to implementing this principle, namely the 'lexical priority' of the first principle that guarantees individual liberties. Secondly, as a general principle applicable to the basic structure, the Difference Principle must travel a long road before it can justify specific state intervention even if the first problem can be overcome. It is unobjectionable as a moral principle, but it remains very unclear how to think of its actuality. The justification of Hegel's *Sittlichkeit* also depends on protections for individual welfare against the exploitative interest of the commercial interest, but Hegel's account is very closely linked to the authorization of power to check that exploitation.[16]

A key part of the story of the reintegration of the particular in the universal is that within civil society itself there are what Hegel calls 'corporations'. These are a crucial normative element in the societal and political organicism, a crucial part of what makes society a living whole. If we can say that without these the organicism would not go through, we have an argument that our society itself will not be justifiable without something akin to corporations. In Hegel's vocabulary, individuals must have 'actuality both as private and as substantial persons' (PR § 264) in civil society. Without the 'corporate' element of civil society, the organic justification would not go through – 'the state must hang in the air' (PR § 265A). Deciding what would qualify as a corporation in Hegel's sense is no simple task, but I do think that this demand to find a more universal sense within civil society itself is something we can draw on as we justify or critique our existing institutions. The most important 'corporations' are trade unions and professional organizations, institutions that provide some measure of financial stability and a sense of belonging and self-respect. We can argue that our *Sittlichkeit* is not justified if it is lacking in such stabilizing institutions for workers. The justification would not go through because the workers' identification with their particular occupational role will not be

[16] The biggest objection to this picture for Hegel himself was the existence of the *rabble*, the poor, shapeless, *unorganized* class that is a necessary by-product of modern civil society. If an organic system produces such an inorganic element, that would seem to jeopardize its justificatory status, or at least severely weaken it.

sufficiently recognized and because they will not have an adequate basis for *political* efficacy.

Organic Politics and Representative Interests

Discussions of the Hegelian state tend to focus on the problematic theory of monarchy at the apex of the doctrine of *political organicism*, yet the economic issues of civil society are also central for the political doctrine and will be my focus here. He thinks of the state powers as an interlocking, mutually reinforcing set of powers rather than as a system of checks and balances. He writes of such a system of mutual limitation that, 'In this view, the reaction of each power to the others is one of hostility and fear, as if to an evil, and their determination is such that they oppose one another and produce, by means of this counterpoise, a general equilibrium rather than a living unity' (PR § 272R). The view of an equilibrium of forces would be one that is preoccupied with possible abuses of authority. The idea of a living unity, in contrast, is one in which each part of the state (monarch, executive and legislative) is intertwined with the others and informs the work of the others. The subject matter of governmental action is largely the economic interests discussed within 'civil society', providing the direction and control for the productive elements of society.

Hegel's theory of the executive brings civil society and the state into very close contact. In fact, he writes that the executive 'includes the powers of the *judiciary* and the *police*' (PR § 287). It is also here that he clarifies the role of the corporations: 'The *particular* common interests which fall within civil society … are administered by the corporations (see PR § 251) which represent the communities and the various professions [*Gewerbe*] and estates, with their authorities, supervisors, administrators, etc.' (PR § 288). These officers must in turn be led by 'executive *civil servants* and the higher consultative bodies' (PR § 289), for 'we here encounter the conflict between private interests and particular concerns of the community, and between both of these together and the higher viewpoints and ordinances of the state' (PR § 289R). What justifies the actions of these executives if they are acting on the organic model? Hegel writes that 'The *organization* of official bodies accordingly faces the formal but difficult task of ensuring that civil life shall be governed in a *concrete* manner from below, where it is concrete, but that the business in question shall be divided into its *abstract* branches and dealt with by distinct bodies' (PR § 290). Against the caricature of the organic model in which too much authority is invested in the head, Hegel's organic argument here is against centralization. The executive officers must take pains to see that the effects of policies – the considered judgements of those 'below' who are directly affected by them – are used to improve the policies.

Voting and representative politics are of course naturally thought of as feedback mechanisms. It is thus not hard to see how they are supposed to function as an essential part of the organic system of interrelated functions. Hegel writes of the beneficial relation of the estates to the executive officials as having largely to do with the effects of the *publicity* of the assembly on the government's deliberations and decisions. He writes that the benefit 'lies in the effect which the expectation of criticism, indeed of public criticism, at the hands of the many has in compelling the officials to apply their best insights, even before they start, to their functions and to the plans they intend to submit, and to put these into effect only in accordance with the purest of motives' (PR § 301R). The publicity brings the dynamics of society's 'living unity' into the open, showing what interests are served by which policy and what results or considered judgements are being taken into account.

In writing about the legislative power Hegel is clearly concerned about stability, seeing the estates as one way not only to make sure that people do not get lost in a mere aggregate, but also to make sure that the people does not become a destabilizing 'massive power in opposition to the organic state' (PR § 302). Hegel thinks that the way to prevent this is by having political representation and participation follow the same economic organization as that of civil society. He writes as follows:

> But the state is essentially an organization whose members constitute *circles in their own right*, and no moment within it should appear as an unorganized crowd. ... The idea that those communities which are already present in the circles referred to above can be split up again into a collection of individuals as soon as they enter the sphere of politics – i.e. the sphere of the *highest concrete universality* – involves separating civil and political life from each other and leaves political life hanging, so to speak, in the air; for its basis is then merely the abstract individuality of arbitrary will and opinion, and is thus grounded only on contingency rather than on a foundation which is *stable* and *legitimate* in and for itself. (PR § 303R)

Reprising his claim about the dependence of the state on the elements of society in which individuals have their particular interests satisfied, Hegel argues that political representation in the estates must reflect the distinction of interests in civil society. Provided that one can imagine the interests of workers actually being represented by their elected officials, paradigmatically in the form of heads of labour organizations, Hegel's proposal here sounds rather sensible. The foundation of the political body would be the economic life, which forms the stabilizing element in society as a whole.

Our attachment to voting rights as rights of individuals *as individuals*, and especially our sense of voting rights as a symbolic feature of modern politics, make Hegel's main arguments very hard to swallow. Yet it is here more than anywhere that we should take to heart the critique of illusory individual rights that Marx made so famous. Does our ability to show up at the ballot box every few years guarantee that our interests, and the interests of the polity as a whole, are served? Hegel is clearly not inclined to accept the idea that a democratic procedure somehow automatically justifies the decisions of a representative body. He writes that '[t]he idea that *all* individuals ought to participate in deliberations and decisions on the universal concerns of the state … seeks to implant in the organism of the state a *democratic* element *devoid of rational form*, although it is only by virtue of its rational form that the state is an organism' (PR § 308R).

We are likely to be uncomfortable with Hegel's argument against democratic participation, but we must also acknowledge the truth of his claim about what happens when political representation and participation are conceived atomistically. He writes that,

> If the deputies are regarded as *representatives*, this term cannot be applied to them in an organic and rational sense unless they are *representatives* not of *individuals* as a crowd, but of one of the essential *spheres* of society, i.e. of its major interests … As for mass elections, it may also be noted that, in large states in particular, the electorate inevitably becomes *indifferent* in view of the fact that a single vote has little effect when numbers are so large; and however highly they are urged to value the right to vote, those who enjoy this right will simply fail to make use of it. (PR § 311R)

Voting trends in the United States certainly confirm Hegel's claims here. We are inclined to blame 'voter apathy', and to bemoan the fact that people 'vote against their interests', but the problem is just that there is no straightforward way for most people to see that their vote counts and their interests are served in elections. This is not to say that Hegel's proposals are at all feasible for a society as differentiated as the United States, but it points to a real problem, a real disconnection between our democratic rhetoric and the way in which democracy fails to serve the interests of the people who most need political power to work for them.

Hegel's reflections here can be compared with Rawls' reflections on the issue of the fair value of the political liberties. Rawls acknowledges that the formal right to participate is inadequate on its own and must be supplemented by measures that preserve the fair value of equal political liberties for all.[17] Hegel's concern in the passages above is clearly that individuals be able to appreciate the value of their vote. The contrast between the two thinkers on this issue is sharper than usual. While Rawls thinks that the answer is public funding for parties and disconnecting politics from economics, Hegel thinks that representation should be tied directly to economic interests. Once the issue has been expressed in terms of value, the rationale for Hegel's view is easy to appreciate: if the main public value in your life is the value placed on your work, you will find your political representation valuable to the extent that it supports the interests of your employment. The objection to this view is that such a politics will simply replicate the entrenched inequalities of civil society. But why should it? And why should we think that disconnecting the two would serve to counteract economic inequality? In any case, Hegel's view is supposed to be dynamic and progressive in the sense that the economic interests are channelled into the public good in ways that combine the concreteness 'from below' with the publicity and transparency of executive and legislative acts. If one's concern is with the power relations entrenched in civil society, one should demand a state that takes as its business the transformation of civil society's power into the universal ends of the country as a whole. The challenge is to make sure that it is not only the private interests of profit-seeking owners, but rather the interests of ordinary workers that are represented in the estates. Hegel would justify the efforts of workers to 'organize', as we say, for it is the only way to make sure you see the value of your representation.

The Embedded Philosopher

I conclude with the question of how to think about the final picture of Hegelian justification in relation to reflective equilibrium. This question arises because it does seem that a philosopher in some sense *always* relies on his or her considered judgements and universal principles. Hegel's organic model of justification in the account of *Sittlichkeit* certainly involves lots of claims about how that model fits with considered judgements that derive from thinking of society and the state organically. It would seem that the organic justification must ultimately depend on the arrangement or presentation of the organic system by the philosopher, and thus it would always take the form of reflective equilibrium. There are

[17] See Rawls, *A Theory of Justice*, 194–200.

two parts to answering this challenge. The first would be to say that the organic model must rely to some extent on the historical record, on what has actually happened as the result of principles and laws. The success or failure of a certain constellation is not supposed to be up to the construction of the philosopher, but rather up to the actual events that have resulted from enacting the laws.

The second part of the reply is that Hegel can admit the role of the philosopher's reflection and still argue for the priority of the organic by virtue of the philosopher's embeddedness within *Sittlichkeit*. Though in Hegel's system philosophy has a higher place than the state, he still holds that within the domain of action the philosopher is also a dependent member of the whole. His insistence that the philosopher is in some sense accountable to the state is part of his critique of philosophy's tendency to erect abstract ideals. This demand for accountability leads him to some disconcerting claims, such as when he writes that it is 'a stroke of *good fortune* … that this philosophizing … has come into closer contact with actuality' (PR *Preface*, 19[23–24]). When we notice this readiness to sell out the scholar (especially Fries) to the state, we are likely to recoil in horror at what looks like an invitation to violate the conditions of free inquiry and speech. It seems to reinforce the fear that the organic model is really a covert way for the powers of the whole to be justified in suppressing the activity of the members when those members step out of line.

The question of the philosopher's relation to the organic state is surprisingly similar to the question of the moral individual's relation to the state. The issue is claiming a privilege that one can justify only through action, where action implicates one in contexts of value that tend to nullify the privilege. Insofar as the philosopher's reflective equilibrium remains withdrawn from action, the philosopher's doctrine is beyond reproach by non-philosophers.[18] But as the philosopher's voice moves from the professional conference to the classroom to the public square, the terms of justification are – and must be, according to Hegel – increasingly out of the philosopher's control. His point is that it would be better for the philosopher, as it is for the moral agent, to have continuous feedback from the world. Only then does the *rationality* of the philosopher's system stand a chance of being able to capture, and to inform, the *actuality* of the ethical world.

[18] In the 'Absolute Knowing' of the *Phenomenology of Spirit*, Hegel goes so far as to claim that the philosopher is close to the 'beautiful soul' that he aligns with the judge in the scene of reconciliation that I mentioned in note 10.

CHAPTER 5

Living the Contradictions: Wives, Husbands and Children in Hegel's Elements of the Philosophy of Right

Kimberly Hutchings

Introduction

This essay focuses on Hegel's discussion of the family as an essential component of modern ethical life in *Elements of the Philosophy of Right*.[1] Hegel's arguments about the nature of marriage, the sexual division of labour within the family, the relation between parents and children and the necessary role of the family in relation to state and civil society have inspired a range of sympathetic and critical responses. Many such responses point to ways in which aspects of his arguments appear to put the ethical life of the family at odds with Hegel's broader narrative of the realization of freedom in the development of the modern state. It will be argued here that Hegel's presentation of the ways in which the family relates to both civil society and the state undercuts the possibility of reading this relation in a linear or hierarchical fashion in which either the family is subsumed by civil society, or the state satisfactorily resolves contradictions and tensions between the other two spheres. In this respect, Hegel not only shows us how the modern market state sustains and is sustained by certain kinds of personal relations and self-identities, but also reveals fault lines that threaten its stability. These are fault lines that challenge the temporal and spatial distinctions through which, on Hegel's own account, the specificity of the *modern* family is secured. They suggest that there is more at stake in Hegel's argument than a functional account of how the family serves the higher purposes of the state.

The argument of the essay proceeds as follows. First, I offer a reading of Hegel on the family, which highlights his emphasis on the *novelty* of the

[1] In this chapter I rely mainly on the *Elements of the Philosophy of Right*. I also make supplementary use of the earlier versions of the *Philosophy of Right* recorded in Wannenmann's lecture notes from 1817–18 and 1818–19. There is considerable overlap between the two texts, though the earlier lectures are differently organized, for example incorporating the discussion of inheritance in the section on family resources rather than in the section on the dissolution of the family.

nature of the family within modern ethical life. Second, I demonstrate how Hegel's account of this new kind of family is haunted and destabilized by a series of tensions in his analysis relating to the distinctions and transitions he traces between kinship and family (marriage); family and civil society (property); family and state (education). In all of these contexts wives, husbands and children challenge the smooth process of spirit's actualization of itself as free, individually and collectively. In conclusion, I suggest that Hegel's account of the family makes the fragility and contradictions of modern ethical life explicit. It is not something achieved, but rather something that is continually created and recreated through the lived experience of a complex range of identities, beliefs, practices and legitimating strategies, many of which are at odds with the idea of modern life that they are supposed to uphold.

Hegel's discussion of the family in the *Philosophy of Right* is quite short,[2] and, in comparison with the huge bodies of literature on the other sections, it is a relatively under-studied aspect of Hegel's argument. Nevertheless, all commentaries on the *Philosophy of Right* necessarily engage with the passages on the family, and there is a considerable body of work that relates his discussion of the family to his broader philosophy and draws on it to substantiate more general claims about the meaning of family relations in the modern state.[3] Within long-standing and more recent arguments about the significance of Hegel's account of the family we find the recurrence of familiar issues about how to approach Hegel's texts, as well as substantive disagreements about his meaning.[4]

[2] PR §§ 158–180, 199–218; LNR §§ 73–88.

[3] For example, David V. Ciavatta, *Spirit, the Family, and the Unconscious in Hegel's Philosophy* (Albany, NY: SUNY Press, 2009); 'The Family and the Bonds of Recognition', *Emotion, Space and Society* 13(1) (2014): 71–79; Robert Gillespie, 'Progeny and Property', *Women and Politics* 15(2) (1995): 37–51; Edward C. Halper, 'Hegel's Family Values', *The Review of Metaphysics* 54(4) (2001): 815–858; Axel Honneth, *Suffering from Indeterminacy: An Attempt at a Reactualization of Hegel's Philosophy of Right*, trans. J. Ben-Levi (Amsterdam: Van Gorcum, 2007); Kimberly Hutchings, *Hegel and Feminist Philosophy* (Cambridge: Polity Press, 2003); Douglas E. Jarvis, 'The Family as the Foundation of Political Rule in Western Philosophy: A Comparative Analysis of Aristotle's Politics and Hegel's Philosophy of Right', *Journal of Family History* 36(4) (2011): 440–463; Toula Nicolacopolous and George Vassilacopolous, *Hegel and the Logical Structure of Love: An Essay on Sexualities, Family and Law* (Aldershot: Ashgate, 1999); and Laura Werner, *The Restless Love of Thinking: The Concept of Liebe in G. W. F. Hegel's Philosophy* (Helsinki: Helsinki University Press, 2007).

[4] In summary, interpretive issues range from questions about whether Hegel should be read as prescribing a particular ideal for the family, especially when it comes to the role of women, see, for example, Peter Steinberger, *Logic and Politics: Hegel's Philosophy of Right* (New Haven, CT: Yale University Press, 1988); Harry Brod, *Hegel's Philosophy of Politics: Idealism, Identity, & Modernity* (Boulder, CO: Westview Press, 1992); and Carole Pateman, 'Hegel, Marriage and the Standpoint of Contract', in Patricia Jagentowicz Mills (ed.), *Feminist Interpretations of G. W. F. Hegel* (University Park, PA: Pennsylvania University Press, 1996), 209–233; to whether we should deduce the meaning of the *Philosophy of Right* from other parts of his philosophy, such as his treatment of Antigone in the

In terms of the reading that follows, it is the relation between Hegel's account of the family and the argumentative structure of the *Philosophy of Right* as a whole that is central to my interpretation. In my view, the overall argument of the *Philosophy of Right* should be read as a response to the question of how social and political arrangements that explicitly (self-consciously) embody freedom (the self-determination of spirit) can be articulated and sustained. It is a highly complex response in which a wide variety of identities, beliefs and practices, as well as institutional forms, are identified as necessary. Prominent amongst these is the internalization of a particular temporal and spatial understanding of contemporary ethical life in contrast to previous, or contemporaneously backward, forms of social and political organization. And it is in this respect that the discussion of the family becomes particularly interesting.

The Modern Family

The family in the *Philosophy of Right* is a novel kind of family. Hegel repeatedly distinguishes it from other types of familial structure in the past and in the present. Most frequently, Hegel compares the modern family with ancient models of kinship, in particular Roman ones.[5] But he also compares it with the family in other cultural contexts, in which either marriages are wholly a matter of the strategic advantage of birth families or polygamy holds sway.[6] And he stresses its transformed religious status within modern Protestantism.[7] Each of these distinctions draws attention to characteristics of the modern family. In contrast to ancient kinship structures, the modern family does not give priority to the broader kinship. Adult men and women do not remain attached to their birth families, they found new families. The ties to this new family are far more ethically significant than ties to parents or siblings. In contrast to the Greek world in which Antigone valued her relation with her brother

Phenomenology of Spirit, see, for example, Ciavatta, *Spirit, the Family, and the Unconscious in Hegel's Philosophy*; and Jagentowicz Mills, 'Hegel's *Antigone*', in Jagentowicz Mills, *Feminist Interpretations*, 59–88; to whether his philosophical categories (see, for example, Halper, 'Hegel's Family Values'; and Nicolacopolous and Vassilacopolous, *Hegel and the Logical Structure of Love*) or his historical context (see, for example, Werner, *The Restless Love of Thinking*; and Seyla Benhabib, 'On Hegel, Women, and Irony' in Jagentowicz Mills, *Feminist Interpretations*, 25–43) governs his meaning. For a more extended discussion of interpretive issues in the *Philosophy of Right* see Kimberly Hutchings, 'Hard Work: Hegel and the Meaning of the State in his Philosophy of Right', in Thom Brooks (ed.), *Hegel's Philosophy of Right* (Oxford: Blackwell, 2012), 126–129.

[5] PR §§ 172A, 173R, 180R; LNR §§ 84–85.

[6] PR §§ 162A, 167; LNR § 80.

[7] PR § 163R; see also HPW, 192–193.

above that with her future husband, the modern family gives supreme value to the relation between husband and wife. In contrast to worlds in which the participants in marriage have no say, the modern family is the coming together of two free consenting individuals for the sake of their relationship with each other, rather than for the sake of increasing their wealth or dynastic considerations. It involves a symmetrical relation between husband and wife in which the rights of each are equally protected, something that Hegel argues is impossible with polygamous marriages. And in contrast to Catholic doctrine, in which celibacy is valued and sexual relations denigrated and permitted only for the procreation of children, the modern family is the location of sacred love.

The modern family is ethical life in itself and as part of the bigger story of ethical life that connects it to civil society and the state. In contrast to modes of thinking characteristic of abstract right and morality and the realm of civil society, it is a context in which individuals do not understand themselves as autonomous and self-subsistent:

> The family, as the *immediate substantiality* of spirit, has as its determination the spirit's *feeling* [*Empfindung*] of its own unity, which is *love*. Thus, the disposition [appropriate to the family] is to have self-consciousness of one's individuality *within this unity* as essentiality which has being in and for itself, so that one is present in it not as an independent person [*eine Person für sich*] but as a *member*. (PR § 158)

Love is key to the ethical nature of the family, in which the interconnection and mutual dependence of self-consciousnesses are experienced naturally and directly. As he elaborates on the meaning of the modern family, however, it is clear that Hegel does not see it as straightforwardly natural. Relations between husband and wife, between heads of families and other family members and between parents and children spiritualize what initially appear to be natural connections of sexual desire and blood.

In his discussion of marriage, Hegel criticizes the identification of marriage with sexual relations, contract or romantic love,[8] none of which captures what marriage is in its essence. Concubinage is solely concerned with the satisfaction of sexual drives, but in marriage these drives are subordinate to 'love, trust, and the sharing of the whole of individual existence' (PR § 163). Here, Hegel insists on the *religious* character of marriage and the family, it is spiritual commitment to each other, and has to have a stability and longevity that he argues is incompatible with the predominance

[8] PR § 161A.

of passion, which inevitably is 'extinguished in its very satisfaction' (PR § 163). Hegel criticizes Kant's argument that marriage involves a contract for the mutual use of each other. Rather than being a contract between two people, the marriage ceremony is the public constitution of an ethical bond, it transcends a relation of exchange or mutual subordination to the other's needs. And in this respect legal and religious formalities play an important part in making marriage what it is. Just as Hegel objects to Kant's contractual argument, so he objects to Schlegel's romantic celebration of love as not needing external legal or religious validation in a marriage ceremony. For Hegel, Schlegel's *Lucinde* reduces love to sensuous inclination and inner feeling; it takes away the distinctively ethical character of love.[9]

The inadequacy of the identification of marriage with sexual relations, contract or romantic love has to do with the incompatibility between an institution that is premised on the abandonment of the particular will of its participants and feelings and behaviours that are inherently particular in the modern sense of being the products of a contingent will. To reduce marriage to sexual gratification, mutual gain or romantic love is to misunderstand the lack of individual freedom in marriage. This is a lack of freedom which is a constituent part of a broader reality of ethical life within which, paradoxically, free individuality is produced and reproduced. This becomes clearer as Hegel outlines the sexual division of labour in the modern family, and then moves on to discuss family property and the bringing up of children.

As we have seen, Hegel is insistent on the distinction between marriage and the satisfaction of natural sexual drives. The ethicality of marriage concerns its transcendence of individual particularity, and it accomplishes this through the distinctive and complementary ways in which men and women embody different aspects of spirit. Natural sexual difference is produced as a new kind of complementary spiritual difference by the relation of marriage itself:[10]

> The *one* [sex] is therefore spirituality which divides itself up into personal self-sufficiency with being *for itself* and the knowledge and volition of *free universality*, i.e. into the self- consciousness of conceptual thought and the volition of the objective and ultimate end. And the *other* is spirituality which maintains itself in unity as knowledge and volition of the substantial in the form of concrete *individuality* [*Einzelheit*] and *feeling* [*Empfindung*].

[9] PR § 164A.
[10] LNR § 76, 76R.

> In its external relations, the former is powerful and active, the latter passive and subjective. (PR § 166)

Hegel goes on to explain that the husband finds his substantial life in work and struggle in the wider world. In effect, he lives a dual private and public existence, with the private very much subordinate to, and supportive of, the demands of the public. The wife, in contrast, has her vocation within the family, her work is there, and she is unfit for the demands of public existence. Rather than by thinking, pursuing and acquiring knowledge, women are educated through feeling. In contrast to men, women are unable to appreciate the universal; for them everything is understood in terms of immediate, contingent relations, which makes them dependent on inclination and opinion rather than truth, and renders them untrustworthy of any kind of public office.[11]

Hegel argues that property takes on an ethical form within the family.[12] This is in contrast to the individual contingent possession characteristic of abstract right, but also to earlier forms of property relations, in which husbands and wives remained bound to kinship relations beyond the immediate family in ancient and feudal law.[13] Once again, the novelty of the modern family is stressed. It is a collective person, whose property is owned collectively and for a '*communal purpose*' (PR § 170). The husband, as the head of the family, represents its legal personality and is responsible for acquiring, administering and distributing its property. Legal restrictions on family property (for example in marriage settlements) are justified insofar as they guarantee the access of both husband and wife to resources. The key point, however, is that property is now essentially connected to marriage rather than to 'the wider circle of their blood relations' (PR § 172A).

Property continues to be a significant theme as Hegel moves on to discuss the place of children within the modern family, and what he calls its 'dissolution'. Married love, we are told, remains subjective and inward, it is only with parenthood that the unity of husband and wife becomes objectively present through their joint love for their children as the reproduction of themselves. This is not, however, a lasting unity. In this section, Hegel again emphasizes the specificity of the modern family. In contrast to ancient modes of family organization, oriented towards the survival of a kinship, where children remained in perpetual nonage, the child of the

[11] PR § 166, 166R, 166A.
[12] PR § 170.
[13] LNR § 83.

modern family is a free individual and must be made to be able to live as a free individual.[14] In this respect, Hegel rejects views of education that affirm the value of being childlike by emphasizing the importance of play and failing to point to the inadequacy of a child's view of themselves and the world. It is the duty of parents to provide emotional stability for their children in a context of 'love, trust, and obedience', but only as the basis on which the child can develop beyond indulgence of their arbitrary will.[15]

> The end to which punishments are directed is not justice as such; it is rather of a subjective and moral nature, seeking to have a deterrent effect on a freedom which is still entrammelled in nature and to raise the universal into the children's consciousness and will. (PR § 174)

The punishment and discipline of children is part of the necessary pattern of the modern family in which the family unit dissolves as the children grow up into free individuals and found their own families.[16] However, this dissolution brings with it complications in relation to family property. The permanent dissolution of the family comes with the death of the parents, but since their children may already have set up families of their own the question of inheritance becomes open to arbitrariness and caprice, in ways that it was not under previous modes of family relation. Hegel is extremely critical of the ways in which inheritance worked in Roman law, but is equally critical of modern individuals making wills and identifying their heirs on the basis of affection or ties of friendship. Family property should be passed on to family members equally, not in ways that favour some members over others, for example through the setting up of trusts that favour sons over daughters or the eldest son over other children. At the same time, however, this can be insisted upon only in relation to the nuclear family, the boundaries of which become unclear once offspring have formed their own families. And Hegel suggests that it may in any case need to be limited by considerations of preserving property, in some instances, specifically for the first (agricultural and landowning) estate by a right of primogeniture.[17]

At the end of the section on the family, we have been told that the modern family is a distinct mode of family organization, which fits with the specificities of modern ethical life in terms of personal and property relations. It is a sphere of ethical life in which freedom is experienced

[14] PR §§ 175, 175R, 180; LNR § 85.
[15] PR § 175, 175R; LNR § 86.
[16] PR § 177.
[17] PR §§ 178, 178R, 179, 179R, 180, 180R, 180A.

through mutual identification with a whole that transcends any particular member. But it is also the context in which modern, property-owning individuals can be produced and sustained. It is temporally and spatially distinguished from the various modes of adult dependence characteristic of other forms of social relation, from Ancient Rome and Israel to feudal or Catholic Europe to contemporary India. Temporally it instantiates the progress of spirit; it is a new departure peculiar to the developing modern state and civil society. Spatially, it is geographically located in the protestant Germanic realm of northern Europe, but it also occupies a distinct 'home' space. Except in the case of the backward-looking classes linked to agricultural production, the modern family no longer dwells in the same location as productive labour. The modern family is somewhere that the head of the family has, literally and metaphorically, to 'leave' in order to engage in the activities peculiar to civil society. It is marked by a clear sexual division of labour, in which men and women bring complementary strengths to marriage and the bringing up of children. It is sharply distinguishable from other families and from the public realm of civil society and the state. At the same time it is necessarily sustained and supported by the state through the regulation of all of its three aspects. The modern family is both the culmination of a historical progression in the work of spirit, in which it has become possible for spirit to understand itself in terms of self-determination, *and* operates in terms of a cyclical temporality of formation and dissolution. It recognizes the ethical significance of its own repeated breaking apart as the only way to reconcile family relations with modern ethical life as explicitly instantiating the idea of spirit as self-determination.

Contradictions

The success and plausibility of Hegel's account is secured through a series of distinctions, which underwrite the stability not only of the family but also of the bigger edifice of modern ethical life encompassing civil society and the state. A distinction between modern family and older forms of kinship secures the notion of modern marriage. A distinction between modern family and civil society secures the notion of family property, which cannot be the same as ordinary private property. And a distinction between family and state secures the possibility of educating children for the purposes of freedom, a process which is incapable of completion within the confines of the family itself. If we look more closely at these three points of distinction, potential sources of disruption for Hegel's overarching argument for modern ethical life as the self-conscious work of freedom come to the surface.

Liberal, feminist and Marxist critics have long noted that there is something odd in Hegel's account of modern marriage. From the liberal point of view, it is unclear why Hegel denies a woman's capacity to act as an individual person, in particular given his emphasis on husband and wife as free, consenting individuals.[18] For many feminist commentators, Hegel's treatment of women implies their exclusion, or radical limitation, from or in the work of spirit and stands at odds with his identification of modernity with spirit's identification of itself as free.[19] Marxists have argued that Hegel underestimates the thoroughness with which market relations structure the private sphere of reproduction and subordinate it to the realm of production and exchange, and read his account of marriage as inaccurate and romanticized.[20] The puzzle here is what appears to be a kind of anachronism, specifically identified with the role of women, within what is claimed to be a radically novel version of the family form. The difficulty is to understand, in Hegel's own terms, how women's connection with essentially unchanged earlier or culturally distinct modes of family life can be reconciled with his insistence on the distinction between the modern family and kinship.

The distinction between family and kinship is claimed to be that women's exclusive identification with the familial sphere is now rational and freely willed:[21] 'The *natural* determinacy of the two sexes acquires an *intellectual* and *ethical* significance by virtue of its rationality' (PR § 165). However, although he is clear that the family is not natural but ethical, natural sexual difference still figures in Hegel's account of how men and women come to play different even if equal roles within marriage. Men experience and spiritualize the sexual difference as their ongoing connection to, but ultimately transcendence of, nature and contingency, whereas women experience and spiritualize it rather as identification with nature and contingency. Antigone exemplifies family piety in her determination to bury her brother, and her unwillingness (or incapacity) to acknowledge any law but the divine law as determinate.[22] The

[18] Richard D. Winfield, *The Just Family* (Albany, NY: SUNY Press, 1998).

[19] Patricia Jagentowicz Mills, *Woman, Nature, and Psyche* (New Haven, CT: Yale University Press, 1987); and Hutchings, *Hegel and Feminist Philosophy*.

[20] Siegfried Blasche, 'Natural Ethical Life and Civil Society: Hegel's Construction of the Family', in Robert B. Pippin and Otfried Höffe (eds.) *Hegel on Ethics and Politics*, trans. N. Walker (Cambridge: Cambridge University Press, 2004), 183–207.

[21] LNR § 77.

[22] PhG: 274–275; PR § 166R.

modern wife exemplifies familial piety in her care for husband, children and household and in an unwillingness (or incapacity) to acknowledge any law but that of subjective feeling as determinate. Hegel still refers to Antigone in the *Philosophy of Right* as instantiating familial piety in its highest form through her ethical connection to her brother, even though in modern terms her concern should rather have been with her betrothed. He also reiterates the view, previously stated in the discussion of the dissolution of Greek ethical life in the *Phenomenology of Spirit*, that women are unfit for a public role and if given political power will subvert the ends of the state.[23] It seems that modern wives are still in some sense connected to divine law in a way that in its fixity reflects an identification with natural rather than spiritual determination and which, should they escape the confines of the intimate sphere, makes them likely to subvert rather than support modern ethical life. Wives and mothers are not only anachronistic, they are dangerous.

It is possible to interpret this danger in different ways. For feminist philosophers such as Irigaray, Hegel's account of the threat women pose to the state is an acknowledgement of the possibility of a radically other, non-patriarchal way of being and thinking, which is quite literally unspeakable in the terms of Hegel's masculinist philosophy.[24] Less radically, Ciavatta sees the ongoing relevance of Antigone to Hegel's argument in *Philosophy of Right* as signalling a deep tension between the kinds of relation characteristic of the family and those characteristic of the public sphere. In the case of the family, the particular interests of concrete others are internalized affectively by each member as part of themselves. Rather than relating as separate individuals, family members relate to each other as already connected and in terms of specific identities (mother, son, daughter etc.). Women, therefore, are construed as dangerous to the public sphere because they represent a mode of mutual recognition that is fundamentally incompatible with recognition in relations of individual property owners and citizens.[25] Though different, both of the above interpretations of the meaning of women's threat to the public sphere present it in trans-historical terms that work across the millennia that separate Antigone's ethical life from the form of ethical life being described in the *Philosophy of Right*. In this respect, they concur on the view that women's position in

[23] PhG: 288; PR § 166A.

[24] Luce Irigaray, *Speculum of the Other Woman*, trans. G. C. Gill (Ithaca, NY: Cornell University Press, 1985).

[25] Ciavatta, *Spirit, the Family, and the Unconscious in Hegel's Philosophy*, 60.

the Hegelian family undercuts the idea that the actualization of spirit as self-determination is a historically unified and singular narrative.

In terms of the immanent logic of Hegel's argument, the danger posed by women is to the requirement that all aspects of the family can be understood as part of modern ethical life with all that this implies in terms of the development and maintenance of the modern market state through subjective identification with its ethical relations, from relations of buying and selling to citizens sacrificing their lives in war. Women are crucial to the family as an institution and to the support that institution gives to ethical life in the public realm, but they are presented either as only ambiguously inhabiting the institution that has been defined as their sphere, or as entirely outside of it. They inhabit the modern family only partially, in the sense that they blur the boundary between family and kinship; their consent and their understanding of what marriage and the family means are always limited. Unlike sons, daughters do not move from family to family via their individual existence in civil society. Instead, like Antigone, or like Roman women, they identify their fate, and are educated, to the extent that they are educated at all, with and in terms of roles into which they are born and which do not allow them to move beyond an identification with concrete universality. When Hegel identifies women with a principle which is self-consciously embraced but incapable of development, 'the law of emotive [*empfindend*] and subjective substantiality' (PR § 166R), it is not just that women's place within the family, and therefore within ethical life more broadly, is ambiguous, it is alien. Women are outside the historical stage of modern ethical life, which is characterized by the capacity of individual and collective subjects to identify themselves with spirit as self-determination. Women 'do not possess the ideal' (PR § 166) and are incapable of possessing it, and in this respect do not participate in it as individuals or citizens; they are untimely and resistant to government.

Hegel's positioning of women puts his distinction between kinship and the modern family, and therefore between *now* and *then*, into question. His account of family property creates problems for his distinctions between family and civil society and between family and state. Hegel is insistent that the family is a form of ethical life with a distinct mode of ethical relation, that of love or subjective feeling. In order for its separation from the principles instantiated within civil society to be possible, the family must be able to support itself in ways that do not disrupt and undermine this distinctiveness. This implies not only that families need resources, but also that these resources should not be arbitrarily distributed, but should be genuinely collectively owned by the family for the good of each member. Given Hegel's account of abstract right and the principle of individual ownership in the first part of the *Philosophy of Right*, and his view that the realm of production and exchange had shifted from its traditional location in the household or kinship to civil society, this means that family property cannot simply be an aggregate of individual earnings or capital, it has to be different in kind.[26]

As we saw above, the meaning Hegel assigns to family property necessitates a complex interaction between the realms of family, civil society and state. Family property is collectively owned but it is individually controlled by the head of the family, who is also a participant in the realm of civil society. Although the head of the family does not own the family property as an individual, it is possible for him to treat that property as if he were an individual, to dissipate or accumulate, and to distribute it according to his own will and desires, like any other member of civil society.[27] For this reason, the state may need to step in to regulate the maintenance and distribution of family property, not only whilst the head of the family is alive, but also when it comes to the distribution of property after his death. This account fits well with an understanding of the Hegelian state as mediating the contradictions thrown up by clashes between the realms of family and civil society. However, as we saw in the discussion above, in invoking the state's capacity to respond to the encroachment of civil society into the sphere of the family, Hegel's argument also testifies to the fragility of the boundary between family and civil society, and to the ongoing significance of the principle of kinship within the architecture of his modern state. In this case, it is men, husbands and fathers, whose liminal position destabilizes the temporal and spatial distinction through which the meaning of the modern family is secured. If women are ambiguously situated between the modern family and ancient kinship, then men are ambiguously situated between modern family and civil society on Hegel's account. Heads of families and future heads of families self-consciously identify themselves both with the surrender of individuality in their family membership and with the principle of particularity in their participation in civil society and the principle of free universality in their participation in the state. In Hegel's discussion they move literally and metaphorically between private and public spheres.

[26] See Ciavatta, *Spirit, the Family, and the Unconscious in Hegel's Philosophy*, for an interesting alternative reading of the meaning of family property in Hegel.

[27] PR § 170; LNR § 83.

> Man therefore has his actual substantial life in the state, in learning [*Wissenschaft*], etc., and otherwise in work and struggle with the external world and with himself, so that it is only through his division that he fights his way to self-sufficient unity with himself. In the family, he has a peaceful intuition of this unity, and an emotive [*empfindend*] and subjective ethical life. (PR § 166)

For a man, therefore, maintaining the distinctiveness of the ethical life of the family is particularly difficult and vulnerable to failure. His 'peaceful intuition' of his self-sufficient unity within the family is at odds with his struggle towards self-sufficient unity within civil society and the state. He knows that an 'emotive and subjective ethical life' is not enough. And in his accumulation and control of family property he is subject to the dual demand to act like a husband and father and to act like an individual owner of property. Unsurprisingly in these circumstances, Hegel identifies the danger of heads of families using family property for private purposes. If women may corrupt the ends of government, then men may corrupt the ends of the family. But whereas women's threat to government is presented as in some sense perennial, men's threat to the family is peculiar to the modern form of the family. This danger did not exist in a world in which production and exchange were organized at the level of household and kinship. For this reason, whereas the solution to the threat women pose to the state is to keep them out of it, the solution to the threat posed by men to the family is to bring the state into the family's domain.

Even though it is fundamentally at odds with the spirit of modern ethical life, in which the acquisition and transfer of property has been relocated into civil society, Hegel argues for the need for the state to step in to regulate family property to make sure it remains secured to the family as a whole. This is for the protection of wives' and children's rights.[28] He has more difficulty working out how to respond to the changes in principles governing inheritance in a world in which the family as a collective owner of property is, in the person of the head of the family, inherently internally conflicted and temporary. Although the modern family is said to dissolve with the death of the parents (particularly the husband[29]), Hegel discusses the difficulties that arise when parents die after children have formed new families in terms of the wrongs involved either in privileging distant over closer kin relations, or in allowing arbitrary will to enter into the disposition of family goods.[30] He is also concerned about cases

[28] PR § 172R.
[29] PR § 178.
[30] PR §§ 179, 179R, 180, 180R.

where following the principle of equal shares for the children of a nuclear family would potentially break up and damage the value of its assets. His response to these concerns includes state validation of the principle of primogeniture. Both in the Heidelberg lectures and in the 1821 *Philosophy of Right* Hegel identifies the value of this anachronistic principle in relation to the agricultural estate.[31] Men connected to the land as the source of their subsistence, like women, occupy a position somewhere in between traditional kinship relations and the modern family – and are therefore peculiarly identified with the familial sphere and its incapacity to *know*, as opposed to *feel*, the ideal.[32] For commentators such as Blasche, this indicates a fundamental flaw in Hegel's analysis, which is that he tries to *fix* the meaning of the family in ways that contradict his shifting historical present.[33] However, surely Hegel is in fact drawing our attention to the instability of the boundaries between family, civil society and state, and also of the temporal boundary between the *then* of kinship and the *now* of the modern family. The transitions between family, civil society and state challenge the claim of temporal novelty and spatial demarcations through which not just the meaning of the modern family but also that of modern ethical life as a whole is grasped in the *Philosophy of Right*.

Children, specifically male children, embody both the instantiation of the modern family as an ethical whole and its imminent dissolution. Sons, like husbands, are the agents of transition between family, civil society and state, and their education is the central purpose of the family's upbringing of children. Girls, who imbibe their spiritual destiny through a kind of osmosis, do not move on from their birth families in the same way as boys; like the women they will become, their ends are not in conflict with familial ethical life. Werner notes, for example, that, when Hegel discusses development through different stages of life in the third part of his *Encyclopaedia*, on the philosophy of spirit, it is the transition from boyhood through youth to manhood that is under examination.[34] It is the task of the family to provide an appropriate context for sons to learn how to transcend the family. Hegel suggests that in the very early years

[31] PR § 180R; LNR § 84.

[32] PR §§ 163, 164.

[33] 'Hegel fails to see that the *bourgeois* family is in the process of turning into the *petty bourgeois* form of family that pre-eminently lacks its own wealth and the security that that wealth once provided. This reveals once again that Hegel is in effect analysing only a specific historical and transitional form of family life, and therefore undermines his claim that the modern family is a definitively conceptualized self-contained institution constituting an *autonomous* intimate sphere of its own alongside society and the state.' Blasche, 'Natural Ethical Life', 193.

[34] Werner, *The Restless Love of Thinking*, 106; PM § 396R, 396A.

this is particularly a responsibility of mothers.[35] But he is also insistent that the loving relationship between parents and children, which is crucial to the child's emotional stability, is accompanied always by the recognition of the non-natural meaning of freedom: '… their upbringing also has the *negative* determination of raising the children out of the natural immediacy in which they originally exist to self-sufficiency and freedom of personality, thereby enabling them to leave the natural unit of the family' (PR § 175).

This leaving is one in which sons become husbands (heads of family) and daughters become wives in new families, but also one in which sons become individual persons and citizens. For sons this is a transition mediated by education. Hegel refers to the education of children (sons) at several points not only in his discussion of the family but also elsewhere, both in the *Philosophy of Right* and in the earlier lectures. In contrast to traditional family forms in which children are essentially the property of parents, who can do as they like with their children, Hegel is clear that education is ultimately a matter for, and a responsibility of, the state. In the Heidelberg lectures he notes both that parents are less effective educators than teachers from outside the family[36] and that in effect, in modern ethical life, 'Children become children of the state' (LNR § 158). But education in Hegel's account is not just about state provision of schools and training, but is also accomplished by the experience of the movement of spirit across various contexts of socialization and relations of recognition in civil society as well as the state. The education of spirit works through the internalization of a variety of identities, from the identity of the individual owner of property to that of the class and corporation to which particular individuals belong. It is through the experience of dependence on others as well as collaboration with them that individuals come to understand and identify themselves as self-determining beings. Above all the education of spirit leads to the internalization of the identity of the citizen in a way that incorporates but also supersedes family and other sub-state individual and corporate identities.[37] Citizenship is membership in the form of an explicit identification with the universal that conditions the possibility of all other aspects of spirit in its modern form. Within families, the identification of members with the family as a whole is love. Within states the identification of citizens with the state is patriotism. Patriotism, Hegel argues, is not a subjective feeling or opinion but is the

[35] PR § 175A.
[36] LNR § 85.
[37] PR § 187, 187R, 187A.

objective certainty that my individual interests and purposes are 'preserved and conserved' through the interests and purposes of the state.[38] Hegel rejects the idea that patriotism is predominantly about individual self-sacrifice or heroism. Nevertheless, it is patriotic certainty, internalized in habit and custom, that underpins the citizen's capacity to grasp the rationality of dying for the state – the radical undoing of the life-giving role of the family.[39] In this respect, the son's education through exposure to and engagement in the public realm links him to the forward movement of spirit, the clashes between nations and cultural forms with which Hegel completes his philosophy of right. This simultaneously distinguishes the son from women in general, from the agricultural or substantial 'class of innocence' (LNR § 103), from contemporaneous backward and barbarian people and from earlier historical stages of the development of spirit.

In order for the modern family to be sustained, the son must have defined himself in opposition to his identity as a birth family member. This entails, amongst other things, that he will not be sexually involved with other members of his birth family. It also entails that his wife is chosen. These two requirements could not be further from the example of Antigone as the exemplar of family piety, bound up in incestuous relations, due to marry her mother's/grandmother's nephew and experiencing her link to her family as necessary as opposed to contingent: 'What makes *our* tragedies so lifeless is the chance nature of the object that is loved. But with Antigone what happens is necessary: she is so firmly attached to this original bond of her family' (LNR § 87). The contingency of the founding of modern families is confirmed in their dissolution, which seems both a temporary moment of transition and a permanent swallowing up of family relations in the worlds of civil society and the state. It takes us back to the head of the household's ambiguous position in relation to family property. In order to maintain both private and public spheres men must be simultaneously family members, individual persons and citizens. And they constantly undermine the ethical specificity of the institution of which they are head and which they are required to sustain. In discussing the dissolution of old families and the founding of new ones, repeatedly in the *Philosophy of Right* we are presented with the modern family as located in the past, along with the agricultural class, women and barbarian cultures. But we are also constantly reminded of the specifically contemporary role that it plays in sustaining and being sustained by civil

[38] PR § 268, 268R, 268A.

[39] PR § 324.

society and the state. Hegel shifts between a temporal narrative, in which the proliferation of families becomes the basis of a people, and a spatial one in which the state encompasses and enables families' founding and maintenance.

Conclusion

In the *Philosophy of Right* Hegel's women are wives and daughters, whereas his men are husbands and sons, persons and citizens. Although very differently placed, in all cases the being and self-consciousness of family members is disruptive of Hegel's narrative, not only of the separateness of the ethical life of the family but also of the overarching story in which Hegel's state instantiates the explicit identification of spirit as self-determination. For Hegel it seems that women transcend time and may therefore not traverse the space that separates household from market or state. Men are able to traverse the space between family, market and state, but through moves that either leave them inexplicably dwelling in two worlds and multiple times, or suggest the subsuming of family into the space of civil society and state. The peculiar position of the family in Hegel's story has been interpreted in three different ways. The first underplays apparent anomalies and tensions and focuses on those aspects of Hegel's discussion that fit with his broader story, essentially subsuming family into the categories of civil society and the state, or arguing that Hegel ought to have done this even if he actually did not. On these interpretations, Hegel is speaking specifically of the family at the point of transition into capitalist market society, and Hegel's account remains firmly anchored in the terms of modern ethical life.[40] The second way is to embrace the idea of the temporal and spatial specificity of the family, underplaying those areas where it crosses or is crossed over by civil society and the state. On these interpretations, the dynamics of the family in itself and the ways in which those relations are in tension with the public sphere become the focus of scrutiny, and Hegel is held to be telling us perennial truths about human emotional, psychological and physical needs.[41] The third way is to read the family as the point through which Hegel's bigger story of the development of spirit can be criticized. On these interpretations the position of

[40] Blasche, 'Natural Ethical Life'; Steinberger, *Logic and Politics*; and Paul Franco, *Hegel's Philosophy of Freedom* (New Haven, CT: Yale University Press, 1999).

[41] Jessica Benjamin, *The Bonds of Love: Psychoanalysis, Feminism and the Problem of Domination* (London: Virago Press, 1988); Honneth, *Suffering from Indeterminacy*; and Ciavatta, *Spirit, the Family, and the Unconscious in Hegel's Philosophy*.

women or the clash between caring responsibilities and the pursuit of self-interest in the person of the head of the family demonstrates the political and ethical inadequacy of Hegel's idea of the meaning of spirit as self-determination and its instantiation in the modern market state.[42]

All of the above lines of interpretation can be supported on the basis of Hegel's text, and all of them tell us something valuable about the meaning of the family in Hegel's philosophy of right. However, none of them in isolation does sufficient justice to the complexity of Hegel's argument, which is neither a description of, nor a prescription for, modern family life, but rather an exposition of how it might be possible to reconcile the idea of spirit as self-determination with its concrete actualization in lived experience, identities, beliefs and institutions. Hegel tells us that the family is both inside and outside history, inside and outside civil society and inside and outside the state. We can understand this when we grasp Hegel's *Philsosophy of Right* as an investigation into how the modern state can be subjectively and objectively identified as the work of freedom. Essentially this can be possible only through a range of beliefs, identities and practices, some of which are sharply at odds with a linear temporal and spatial story, in which spirit is self-consciously actualized as self-determination in nineteenth-century Europe. In crude terms, Hegel shows us that, for the state to be understood in terms of freedom, not only does a great deal of unfreedom have to be in place, but also a constant effort has to be made to render that unfreedom intelligible in terms of freedom. Those efforts create meanings that are in perpetual tension with the overarching narrative they are intended to serve and therefore create an ongoing challenge to the workings of the modern state, whether through over- or under-identification with its self-understanding.[43]

As Hegel describes it, rather than being a secure structure, underpinned by solid, complementary building blocks of family and civil society, the modern state is fragile and vulnerable. The family is the sphere where this fragility and vulnerability is most obviously experienced. The state needs persons and citizens, but it can secure them only through a range of contradictory beliefs and practices in which the family is both separate from

[42] Jagentowicz Mills 'Hegel's *Antigone*'; Pateman, 'Hegel, Marriage and the Standpoint of Contract'; and Alison Stone, 'Matter and Form: Hegel, Organicism, and the Difference between Women and Men', in Kimberly Hutchings and Tuija Pulkkinen (eds.), *Hegel's Philosophy and Feminist Thought* (New York: Palgrave Macmillan, 2010), 211–232.

[43] Arguably, for Hegel problems arise primarily from an over-identification with spirit as self-determination at the level of the individual, since this leads women to meddle in the public sphere and men to neglect their duties as fathers and husbands.

and colonized by the public sphere. These contradictions have to be lived out in the self-conscious understanding and labour of family members. The family is a sphere in which women are equal and free, but also incapable of taking on a public role, where men need to be fathers and husbands but struggle to fulfil those roles in the face of the requirements of work and citizenship, where sons require the bonds of love and trust but also are obliged to shake off those bonds as soon as possible and to identify more absolutely with the state for which they may be willing to die than with the parents who gave them life. Regardless of what appears to be Hegel's normative stance on the nature of the modern family, his philosophical exposition of its presuppositions and implications undermines the representation of the family as a self-contained, safe ethical realm of private virtue which grounds and enables the proper operation of freedom in the public sphere. On his own account, the lived experience of wives, husbands and sons is always both necessary and dangerous to the work of freedom.

CHAPTER 6

'The Ethicality in Civil Society': Bifurcation, *Bildung* and Hegel's Supersession of the Aporias of Social Modernity

Andrew Buchwalter

One of the more complex features of Hegel's *Philosophy of Right* pertains to the normative status it assigns to civil society. While situated, along with the family and the state, in the work's section on Ethical Life (*Sittlichkeit*), civil society – which encompasses Hegel's account of modern market societies – is also presented as the very denial of ethicality. Characterized variously as the sphere of division, separation, fragmentation and bifurcation (*Entzweiung*), civil society for Hegel is gripped by a host of pathologies that undermine individual autonomy and societal well-being – features championed by advocates of market societies. Among other things, civil society promotes alienating work conditions, conspicuous consumption, the emergence of a societal underclass, colonialism and vast disparities in wealth between rich and poor. In this regard, Hegel's treatment of civil society anticipates the views of later social critics like Marx, Horkheimer, Adorno, Arendt, Foucault and Habermas, who in different ways question the rationality and normative possibilities of modern market societies.

On the other hand, Hegel does not claim that market societies are altogether bereft of possibilities for genuine autonomy or broader notions of community. He would not agree, for instance, with Habermas, for whom market economies denote a 'norm-free' self-regulating domain governed by the strategic calculations of individual utility-maximizers.[1] Instead, he maintains that considerations of morality and ethicality remain central to an account of modern civil society. He does so, moreover, in a manner arguably more robust than some of the champions of market societies. Not only does civil society realize the 'right of subjectivity' and the 'principle of subjective freedom', not only is it

[1] Jürgen Habermas, *The Theory of Communicative Action, Volume 2: Life World and System: A Critique of Functionalist Reason*, trans. by Thomas McCarthy (Boston, MA: Beacon Press, 1987), 185. See also Axel Honneth, 'Labour and Recognition: A Redefinition', in *The I in We: Studies in the Theory of Recognition*, trans. Joseph Ganahl (Cambridge: Polity, 2012), 57–58.

the domain for the realization of a notion of morality abstractly formulated earlier in the *Philosophy of Right*, but also it gives expression – especially in the concluding subsection on corporations – to an account of the relationship of individual and community illustrative of a modern account of ethical life. Indeed, the very designation civil society (*bürgerliche Gesellschaft*) references individuals not just in their capacity as self-interested utility-maximizers – the *bourgeois* common to the liberal tradition – but also as citizens (*citoyens*) who, in the tradition of civil republicanism, attend to their mutual well-being and the welfare of the community itself. In these respects, civil society, no less than family and state, comprises an account of ethical life.

In this essay I explore Hegel's distinctive account of the 'ethicality in civil society' (PM § 552R; translation modified). I do so, however, not by appealing, as some do, to notions of ethicality that may obtain despite or alongside the various bifurcations Hegel details in his discussion. I do not highlight modes of reciprocal recognition present in processes of commercial exchange, forms of solidarity implicit in the modern division of labour, or relations of ethicality antecedently undergirding social relations in market societies.[2] Whatever the merit of these approaches, they are insufficiently attentive to what arguably is the *principium individuationis* of Hegel's approach: fashioning an account of civil society's ethicality not in spite of, but because of, its bifurcations.[3] He does not merely formulate a notion of ethical life in specific response to those bifurcations; rather, ethicality properly subsists only in integrating and articulating bifurcation itself. In this regard, Hegel's response to the aporias of civil society exemplifies his claim that thinking 'both inflicts the wound and heals it again' (EL § 24A3). It also comports with the dialectical proclivities of his

[2] Elements of all three approaches are instructively detailed by Axel Honneth in *Freedom's Right: The Social Foundations of Democratic Life*, trans. Joseph Ganahl (New York: Columbia University Press, 2014). For an assessment of Honneth's reception of Hegel in this work, see my 'The Concept of Normative Reconstruction: Honneth, Hegel, and the Aims of Critical Social Theory', in *Reconstructing Social Theory, History and Practice: Current Perspectives in Social Theory* 35 (2016): 57–88.

[3] For an alternative, tradition-oriented view of the positive significance Hegel assigns to bifurcation in his account of civil society, see Joachim Ritter, *Hegel and the French Revolution: Essays on the 'Philosophy of Right'*, trans. Richard Dien Winfield (Cambridge, MA: MIT Press, 1982), 35–123, especially 62–81 and 118–119. The understanding of bifurcation proposed in the current essay bears affinities to that advanced by Albrecht Wellmer in 'Models of Freedom in the Modern World', in *Endgames: The Irreconcilable Nature of Modernity: Essays and Lectures*, trans. David Midgley (Cambridge, MA: MIT Press, 1998), 3–37. However, by accentuating the connection between bifurcation and *negative* freedom, Wellmer presents an account of ethicality based on an excessively static relationship of individual and community. In contrast, the reading offered here, which is focused on *subjective* freedom, fashions a view of ethicality achieved through a formative process in which conceptions of individual and community are reciprocally transformed and enlarged. For a contemporary appropriation of Hegel's social theory that builds on the constitutive status he assigns to bifurcation, see Bernd Ladwig, 'Moderne

thought, whose basic effort is to construe 'opposites in their unity or … the positive in the negative' (SL, 56). And it is consonant with his immanent conception of philosophical criticism, directed as it is to confronting a state of affairs on its own terms.

In proposing this account, I emphasize the concept of *Bildung*, variously translated as education, cultivation or formation. In Hegel's usage, *Bildung* denotes processes equally of individual and societal cultivation. It is important in this context because of its centrality to civil society and because it instantiates the bifurcated structures of civil society itself.[4] Hegel's deployment of the concept is also significant as it undergoes, in his developmental depiction of the stages of civil society, a cultivation process of its own. In the evolution from the System of Needs through the Administration of Justice to the Police and Corporation, *Bildung* articulates an account of the relationship of individual and community that is increasingly adequate to realizing a notion of ethicality appropriate to the requirements of modern society. Especially with the Corporation, this *Bildungsprozess* facilitates how '*the ethical returns* to civil society' (PR § 249).

This point sheds light on Hegel's unique supersession of the aporias of modern society. While Hegel anticipates subsequent thinkers in questioning the rationality of modern market societies, and while he argues that an account of societal rationality is achievable only by transforming modes of sociality endemic to such societies, he claims that the tools to effectuate such transformation are contained in civil society itself. In this regard, his response to modern aporias remains within the ambit of a theory of immanent critique, but in a way specific to his particular conception of reason. Immanent critique is not just the process by which a theoretician confronts a problematic state of affairs with its own norms of rationality. Invoking instead the model, proper to the idea of Spirit, of a substance becoming subject to itself, Hegel construes immanent critique as the activity by which a community constitutes and first establishes its own rationality as it addresses the maladies confronting it.[5]

Sittlichkeit. Grundzüge einer "hegelianischen" Gesellschaftstheorie des Politischen', in Hubertus Buchstein and Rainer Schmalz-Bruns (eds.), *Politik der Integration. Symbole, Repräsentation, Institution* (Baden-Baden: Nomos Verlagsgesellschaft, 2006), 111–135.

4 In detailing the background for the *Phenomenology of Sprit*, Rüdiger Bubner notes the unique connection Hegel draws between *Bildung* and bifurcation in his early writings. See 'Hegel's Concept of Phenomenology', in *The Innovations of Idealism*, trans. Nicholas Walker (Cambridge: Cambridge University Press, 2003), 123–126.

5 See my *Dialectics, Politics, and the Contemporary Value of Hegel's Practical Philosophy* (New York and London: Routledge, 2011), 9–14.

My consideration of Hegel's position has four parts. The first part recapitulates basic elements of the doctrine of civil society, focusing on ways it does and does not articulate ethical life. The second part sketches the general parameters of Hegel's supersession of the pathologies of modern society, noting how bifurcations responsible for the loss of ethicality also supply tools for an account of ethical life that counters that loss. The focus here is on *Bildung*, a concept which is specific to the theory of civil society and which itself undergoes a formative process in the course of the theory's elaboration. The third part examines that process's culmination in the theory of the Corporation, where, with a commensurate conception of *Bildung*, Hegel proffers an account of ethical life that draws on the bifurcating structures that otherwise undermine ethicality. The fourth part concludes with some observations about Hegel's project and the modern conception of ethical life emerging from it.

Civil Society and Its Vicissitudes

We begin by recapitulating elements of Hegel's account of civil society and its multivocal status as a sphere of ethicality. At the outset, civil society, which encompasses his view of modern market societies, appears to connote the clear absence of ethicality. According to 'one principle' (PR § 182), civil society is that social domain where individuals are recognized as private persons possessing particular needs and interests. Crucial as the principle of particularity is to modernity and to what Hegel presents as the realization of subjective freedom, it underwrites a 'system of atomism [*Atomistik*]' (PM § 523) in which individuals, often gratuitously and without limit, focus exclusively on pursuing private self-interest. From this perspective, civil society is comprised of utility-maximizers who display little concern for the common well-being central to ethicality. While the family and the state variously concretize ethical union, civil society – 'the stage of *difference*' (PR § 181) or the 'level of division' (*Entzweiung*) (PR § 186) – instantiates a bifurcated relation of individual and community.

Yet civil society is not thereby a site of perpetual conflict in the sense, say, of Hobbes's state of nature (PR § 289R). As expressed in its 'second principle', it also connotes the systematic interdependence of individual and community (PR § 182). Invoking theories of political economy associated with 'Smith, Say, and Ricardo' (PR § 189R), Hegel, in the 'System of Needs', claims that modern industrial societies, shaped by commodity exchange and the increasing division of labour, operate according to a logic for which the satisfaction of one individual's immediate needs is inextricably intertwined with the need-satisfaction of others. Civil society expresses a 'dialectical movement' (PR § 199), wherein the private pursuit of particular well-being affirms the welfare of all. Nor is this 'conciliatory element' (*das Versöhnende*) merely the product of an invisible hand operating behind the self-interested actions of individual wealth maximizers (PR § 189). Instead, the system of mutual interdependence shaping civil society occasions, *inter alia*, attitudes of cooperation and mutuality, support for public institutions, modes of moral conduct expressing norms of individual and communal well-being, and an 'ethical disposition' (PR § 207) rooted in the circumstance that individuals 'can attain their end only in so far as they themselves determine their knowledge, volition, action in a universal way and make themselves *links* in the chain of this *continuum*' (PR § 187). In these respects civil society articulates elements of ethical life itself: 'the unity of the universal which has being in itself with subjective particularity' (PR § 229).

Yet if civil society does denote 'the *world of appearance* of the ethical' (PR § 181), it cannot be deemed an account of ethicality itself. Genuine ethicality depends on individuals who understand and actively will their commonality. But what typifies the reality of civil society is the absence of just such explicit knowledge and will. Members of civil society may deliberately shape their actions 'in a universal way', yet only because they appreciate that their private ends are best realized by means of social structures and socially acceptable practices. Thus they lack a commitment to the universal as something intrinsically desirable and an appreciation that their particular well-being is properly cultivated only in relations of commonality. They may orient themselves to what is common, but only as is appropriate to a system based on need and want (*Not*): as a matter of necessity (*Notwendigkeit*). What is lacking is the *consciousness of freedom* whereby individuals will the conditions of universal mediation itself and do so on the understanding that the latter conditions their freedom and well-being (PR § 186). While it does give expression to the principle of mutual interdependence as well as that of particularity, civil society, *qua* stage of difference, accommodates only the disjunctive relation of those principles. It does not promote a 'complete interpenetration' (PR § 1A), where community subsists in its explicit affirmation by community members, just as particularity is fully realized only in individuals' self-conscious affirmation of their commonality. If civil society represents the manifestation (*Erscheinung*) of ethicality, it is only as semblance (*Schein*), not reality.

Hegel's point, though, is not simply that civil society denotes the mere semblance of ethicality; he claims that it is its loss as well. In the absence of explicit commitment on the part of members to the conditions of their commonality, civil society generates a host of pathologies that undermine even the appearance of ethicality. Hegel thus rejects the view of Adam Smith, for whom societal well-being is attainable through the invisible hand of the market and its supposed mechanisms of self-regulation and self-adjustment.[6] While market mechanisms may suggest the appearance of an overarching harmony, the reality is disharmony.

In his treatment of civil society, Hegel details multiple ways in which market societies contribute to a loss of ethicality. These include the subordination of individual autonomy to the dictates of fashion, the physically and psychologically debilitating regimentation of work, and the tendency to replace workers with machines. Yet Hegel's most wide-ranging statement of the travails of modern market societies is presented in his account of poverty, which he contends is a by-product of the normal and 'unrestricted' functioning of market economies (PR § 243). Propelled by the actions of wealth-maximizing individuals, market societies give rise to boom–bust cycles where overproduction leads to lay-offs and underemployment. These in turn occasion the emergence of an impoverished underclass, one that acquires a measure of permanence, since the poor, deprived of economic resources and no longer able to draw support from the extended economic family structure of traditional societies, have limited opportunity to acquire skills to (re)gain a place in the economic life of society (PR § 241). But Hegel's understanding of this penurious rabble, as he terms the underclass, is focused principally not on material deprivation but on the associated psychology of humiliation and alienation. Poverty robs the poor of self-respect and self-esteem. Not only does the loss of work deprive individuals of the sense of self-reliance central to the membership ethos of modern societies, but also the poor know that they lack the social recognition central to an order predicated on performance and the marketability of individual effort. Furthermore, aware of their lack of recognition, the poor withdraw their own recognition of society, not only through envy and resentment, and not only through anger directed at the wealthy, but in an adversarial relation to society generally, be it in rejection of work and the achievement principle or in opposition to the social order itself.

6 For an extended examination, see Lisa Herzog, *Inventing the Market: Smith, Hegel, and Political Theory* (Oxford: Oxford University Press, 2013).

Central to Hegel's analysis of poverty is the experience not just of the penurious rabble but also of the 'wealthy rabble' (PR 1821/22, § 244). The latter comprises individuals gripped by unlimited acquisitiveness and devoted to conspicuous consumption. In a manner consistent with civil society as a sphere of 'semblance', they are preoccupied with external displays of individual worth.[7] They are motivated by an avarice that contributes to broader material inequities and disparities of wealth. They take advantage of widespread unemployment by offering minimal compensation to their employees, 'which in turn makes it much easier for disproportionate wealth to be concentrated in a few hands' (PR § 244). They also display an insouciant and disdainful attitude towards the poor, which further contributes to the latter's marginalization and rabble mentality.[8]

In responding to the problem of poverty, Hegel invokes the type of regulatory institutions absent in Smith's account of modern market societies. It is the function of the 'Police' or 'Public Authority' to make '[p]rovisions against the contingency which remains present in the above systems' (PR § 188). Yet he also acknowledges that such regulatory measures are of only limited value in addressing the problem of poverty, as they often replicate the problems in question (PR § 245). Elaborate forms of public assistance can rob individuals of their self-reliance, the lack of which is one element in the poor's deficient sense of self-respect. Similarly, efforts to counteract poverty through publicly created employment opportunities would be counterproductive, as they can contribute to the surplus production that first created the problem. Hence the claim that 'despite an *excess of wealth* civil society is *not wealthy enough* – i.e. its own distinct resources are not sufficient – to prevent an excess of poverty and the formation of a rabble' (PR § 245).

But even allowing for the partial value of such measures, Hegel disputes their capacity to contribute to an account of ethical life. Indeed, they reaffirm the oppositions that occasion their need. Proceeding from a view of individuals as self-seeking private persons, such programmes can only mitigate rather than eliminate the force of those oppositions – at best those that contain or balance competing interests.[9] They are unable to forge a union that properly mediates oppositions, one where the particular individuals explicitly will the universal and the universal in turn is actualized through its affirmation by the particulars.

[7] Erzsébet Rózsa, 'Das Prinzip der Besonderheit in Hegels Wirtschaftsphilosophie', in *Hegels Konzeption praktischer Individualität* (Paderborn: Mentis, 2007), 194.

[8] For an extended discussion see Frank Ruda, *Hegel's Rabble: An Investigation into Hegel's Philosophy of Right*, (London: Continuum, 2011), especially Chapters 5 and 6.

[9] Rózsa, 'Das Prinzip der Besonderheit in Hegels Wirtschaftsphilosophie', 199.

Bifurcation, *Bildung* and the Process of Ethical Formation

Articulation of a proper account of ethicality thus mandates moving from the domain of civil society to the state, 'the actuality of the ethical Idea' (PR § 257). The site of political community proper, the state – or polity – is the domain of citizens rather than the bourgeoisie. As against the merely apparent ethicality incidentally achieved in individuals' pursuit of private gain, the ethicality proper to a polity is the product of their explicit knowledge and will – ethical life as it is not only in itself but for itself as well. While individuals in civil society do make the conditions of their commonality an object of will, those in the political realm do so for its own sake rather than as a means to secure private interest (PR § 258). Accordingly, politically realized ethicality denotes the objectification of freedom rather than necessity. It also realizes subjective freedom and even the principle of self-subsistent particularity, as individuals come to recognize that their particular identities are best achieved in community and in intersubjective relations (PR § 260).

At the same time, however, cultivating ethicality does not mandate jettisoning civil society in favour of the state. Elements of this view may be found in Hegel's early writings, where he champions a notion of civic religion unsullied by economic considerations. In the *Philosophy of Right*, however, and in fact in writings since the early-1800s Jena period, Hegel maintains that civil society, its aporias notwithstanding, itself contributes to a proper account of ethical life. Indeed, his distinctive position is that this account is possible only by employing tools specific to civil society. The forms of bifurcation conducive to the latter's loss of ethicality are also those that forge a modern account of ethicality.

A central element in this effort is the concept of reflection. For Hegel, ethicality is understood in terms of the interpenetration and thoroughgoing mediation of individual and community. What defines that mediation, however, is not simply the fact of mediation but the reflective practices through which individuals consciously, if also habitually, promote their commonality. Ethicality for Hegel is reflective ethicality, one 'which has its knowledge and volition in self-consciousness, and its actuality though self-conscious action' (PR § 142). Rooted in a notion of *Geist* understood as substance that is subject to itself, ethical life depends on the capacity of individuals, singly and in concert, to objectify themselves cognitively – to construe themselves and their relations as objects of reflection. This capacity is facilitated by civil society. As the sphere of division, difference and opposition in Hegel's practical philosophy, it is also the domain of 'reflection', the 'relation of reflection' (PR § 181) and 'reflected reality' itself (PR § 263). By virtue of its bifurcations, civil society furnishes the modes of reflective objectification and self-objectification required of a properly differentiated account of ethical life, one comprised of individuals who understand the relationship of their own well-being to that of community and who act accordingly. Civil society houses an 'ethical root of the state' in part because its bifurcations generate the '*internally reflected* particularity' central to 'a knowing and thinking ethical life' (PR § 255, 255A; translation modified). Even if the specifics of his reading may be questioned, Albrecht Wellmer has captured the general thrust of Hegel's position. Hegel's reception of natural-law individualism represents, for Wellmer, 'the articulation of one basic dimension of freedom, namely, a negative freedom which, by disrupting the bonds of solidarity between individuals, is at the same time a precondition for that reflective … restoration of the solidarity which is the only one adequate for the modern state'.[10]

To appreciate Hegel's supersession of the bifurcations of modern civil society, however, it is not enough simply to reference his theories of reason, reflection, spirit or subjectivity. No less important is how oppositions are to be constructively superseded through the conscious agency of affected individuals themselves. Central here is the concept of education, cultivation or formation (*Bildung*), defined as the 'cultivation of the universality of thought' (PR § 20). It is *Bildung* that induces members of civil society to alter the one-sidedness and 'misapprehension' (*Irrtum*) in views regarding their relationship to others and community generally (PR § 181A). And it is *Bildung* – further characterized as 'the absolute transition to the infinitely subjective substantiality of ethical life' (PR § 187R) – that cultivates in individuals the ethical sentiment enabling them to integrate into their own self-conceptions appreciation of the intersubjective conditions of their freedom and well-being.[11]

In appealing to *Bildung*, however, Hegel does not confront modern society with external norms and expectations. He is not countenancing the practice proscribed in the Preface to the *Philosophy of Right*: instructing the world on how it ought to be. Instead he calls on resources inherent in civil society itself.[12] This is fitting, as he characterized civil society as both 'the stage of *Bildung*' (PR 1819/20, 148) and 'the stage of difference'. In this

[10] Wellmer, 'Models of Freedom in the Modern World', 22.

[11] Rózsa, 'Das Prinzip der Besonderheit in Hegels Wirtschaftsphilosophie', 201.

[12] For an account of civil society as a learning/cultivation community (*Bildungsgemeinschaft*), see Klaus Vieweg, *Das Denken der Freiheit. Hegels Grundlinien der Philosophie des Rechts* (Munich: Wilhelm Fink, 2012), 293–296.

formulation *Bildung* is distinct from *Erziehung*, the family-based upbringing predicated on 'the form of immediate feeling which is still without opposition' (PR § 175). Instead, *Bildung* gives expression to the forms of bifurcation exemplifying civil society. It proceeds from the experience of self-subsistent persons, fosters subjective freedom, takes the form of '*hard work*' directed towards transforming natural immediacy (PR § 187R), subsists in the ongoing tension between particular and universal, affirms the universal reflected in thought, and instantiates the dichotomous relations of reflection that infuse civil society generally.

Hegel's account of *Bildung* in civil society is further distinguished by its dynamic quality. Indeed, the presentation of *Bildung* here takes the form of a developmental learning process of its own. Two points can be made about this process, which charts the evolution from the System of Needs through the Administration of Justice to the Police and Corporation. Both link a socio-cultural learning process to the phenomenon of bifurcation. First, the process is fuelled by a progressive effort to address and rectify the maladies afflicting civil society. Second, it takes the form of an evolving (re)calibration of how the modes of bifurcation that structure *Bildung* shape what is to count as *Bildung*. While *Bildung* in the first stage empowers the utility-maximizing strategies inimical to the ends of ethicality, and while *Bildung* in the second stage lends support to a notion of formal justice that addresses problems encountered in the System of Needs while introducing new ones, *Bildung* in the final stage – especially in the Corporation – actualizes the complex mediation of individual and community required of a genuine account of ethical life. It does so, moreover, through constructively appropriating those tools of bifurcation that so far have impeded ethical life. Indeed, *Bildung* at this stage articulates spirit itself: 'Spirit attains its actuality only through internal division [*daß er sich in sich selbst entzweit*], by imposing this limitation and finitude on itself ..., and, *in the very process of adapting itself to these* limitations [*sich in sie hineinbildet*], by overcoming them and gaining its *objective* existence' (PR § 187R). The next section of this essay examines *Bildung* as expressed in this final and 'true' form (PR § 187A). The remainder of the current section considers *Bildung* as elaborated in the prior two stages.

In his account of civil society Hegel delineates ways in which *Bildung* 'works away', eliminates and transforms given immediacy in the process of cultivating subjectivity, a core principle of modern societies. In the System of Needs this takes the forms of theoretical and practical *Bildung*, both of which are directly tied to fostering conditions for effective participation in modern commercial society. Theoretical *Bildung* teaches the abstract reasoning skills needed to pursue a livelihood in complex, differentiated and growth-oriented societies, including the ability to think 'in a rapid and versatile manner, to grasp complex and general relations, etc.' (PR § 197). Practical *Bildung* cultivates mastery of the technical and social skills as well as the behavioural habits needed for effective performance in market economies. Both articulate the general idea of *Bildung* – cultivating in individuals appreciation of the universal. In both cases, however, this entails an instrumentalism for which the universal is acknowledged largely as a strategy for advancing private needs and objectives.

The Administration of Justice gives voice to a higher form of *Bildung*. Here, too, *Bildung* cultivates a consciousness of the universal and what is common, yet no longer in order just to maximize utility preferences. Instead, cultivated consciousness assumes a more reflexive form, understood as a *consciousness of right* predicated on supporting and upholding the legal structures that facilitate the functioning of modern commercial societies.[13] Included here is support for a fair, impartial and formally codified system of justice. Included as well is a consciousness of *rights* in which individuals recognize one another *as* equal bearers of rights – as persons to be respected as such, i.e. in virtue of their humanity rather than for particular status considerations. It is through *Bildung* – '*thinking* as consciousness of the individual in the form of universality' – that '[a] *human being counts as such because he is a human being*, not because he is a Jew, Catholic, Protestant, German, Italian, etc.' (PR § 209R).

Bildung cultivates this sentiment, moreover, without the abstract appeal to universal human rights Hegel associates with cosmopolitanism. The mentality focused on individuals as bearers of equal rights is part of a socio-historical learning process linked to an economic order in principle predicated on the meritocratic valuation of performance and accomplishment. In this sense the reflexive capacity of individuals to treat one another as persons is not the product of a specific insight or abstract cognition but a function of membership in a culture in which as a matter of everyday practice individuals are disposed to regulate their 'will according to a universal principle' (PR § 209A). In modern societies, a reflexive consciousness of right becomes a matters of customary practice, just as custom itself, deemed by Hegel – opposing the historical school of law – to 'contain the moment of being *thoughts* and being *known*' (PR § 211R), is shaped by this reflexivity.

[13] See Vieweg, *Das Denken der Freiheit*, 307–308.

Hegel's point, though, is not that a cultivated rights-consciousness simply provides the cultural resources needed to support a modern system of law. He contends as well that this system properly attains reality only through such consciousness. Understood as the realization of self-conscious freedom, a system of right depends on the capacity of its addressees to know and endorse that system as it relates to and articulates the circumstances of their everyday lives. While the life-practice of modern individuals is shaped by the general principles embodied in modern legal structures, the system of right acquires 'validity and objective actuality' only when 'recognized, known and willed' by those to whom it applies (PR § 209).

On multiple counts, then, the section on the Administration of Justice articulates an account of the relationship of individual and community that is richer and more ramified than is the case with the System of Needs. At the same time, however, the resources available through the Administration of Justice cannot properly accommodate ethicality itself. Two related problems must be noted, both of which bear on how *Bildung* at this stage fails to mediate universal and particular.

First, the Administration of Justice provides recognition only for an abstract notion of justice, one directed to the general notion of universal rights and to the recognition of each particular individual in terms of a shared humanity. It fails to address a central concern of ethicality and civil society alike: general welfare addressed to the particular individual *as* particular. This failure is especially evident with reference to the phenomenon of modern poverty, which reveals how the actual operation of civil society – reflected in the boom–bust cycles of market economies – effectively undermines for many the basic rights to which all are formally entitled as societal members.[14] Poverty calls into question the availability of 'negative'

[14] Here I cannot deal in any detail with the rights individuals possess by virtue of membership in civil society. It is perhaps enough to note that in Hegel's account of realized freedom membership in civil society itself entails a range of individual rights, and in ways not previously thematized in the *Philosophy of Right*. Given that individuals in complex industrial societies can pursue a livelihood only through membership in society, those societies must in turn ensure that individuals have the opportunity to do so. '[I]f a human being is to be a member of civil society, he has rights and claims in relation to it ... Civil society must protect its members and defend their rights, just as the individual owes a duty to the right of civil society' (PR § 238A). These rights include not only negative liberty rights and some level of rights to political participation but also the positive social or welfare rights. The system of interdependence constituting civil society is such that 'the livelihood and welfare of individuals should be *secured* – i.e., that *particular welfare* should be *treated as a right* and duly *actualized*' (PR § 230). Yet Hegel also maintains that the system of rights typically realized in modern societies remains significantly formal, oriented to universal principles of justice and equality unable to address adequately the material inequities and forms of 'rightlessness' linked to vast disparities in wealth and to the dislocations and insecurities associated with market dynamics.

liberty rights. Rights that protect individuals against violations of person and property have little meaning for the poor and unemployed, who, owing to the actual operation of market societies, lack not only property but tendentially personhood itself, which for Hegel – rejecting Kant's distinction between persons and things (PR § 40R) – is dependent in part on property and the conditions of work needed for its acquisition (PR §§ 41, 241). In addition, poverty calls into question protections provided by 'positive' welfare rights, since the poor are in fact commonly deprived of work, health, subsistence and even life itself (VNS § 118). Furthermore, the poor cannot avail themselves of political rights: without necessary capital and resources (education, skills, clothing and health), they are effectively barred from participating in fora for the collective shaping of political life. Nor do the poor evidence that consciousness of rights Hegel associated with the membership culture of modern society. Not only do they perceive themselves as lacking rights to which they are formally entitled; not only do they see themselves as deprived of membership rights in a society culturally defined by a commitment to principles of economic self-reliance; inasmuch as they are not recognized as full members in a society for which membership is tied to possession of rights, they exhibit a 'feeling of rightlessness' (PR 1821/22, § 244), an internalized sense of social disenfranchisement.

But – this is the second problem with *Bildung* at this stage – even for those who experience it, the rights-consciousness present here remains distinct from ethical sentiment proper. Such consciousness takes the form of *rectitude*, the conscientious support by community members of institutions and practices that protect rights and the pursuit of individual need satisfaction (PR § 207). As such, rights-consciousness remains tied to the concerns of the bourgeois private person. It is not ethical consciousness itself – the mentality of those who know, and act on the understanding, that their identity and well-being are constituted intersubjectively and under conditions of communal well-being.[15]

Hegel responds to these issues with his theory of the Police and Corporation, both of which represent more comprehensive mediations of particular and universal concerns. The Police denotes the centralized public authority already referenced, that charged with regulating commerce,

See further my 'Hegel, Human Rights, and Political Membership', *Hegel Bulletin* 34(1) (2013): 98–119. See also Klaus Vieweg, *Das Denken der Freiheit*, 309–336.

[15] For the relationship of rectitude and ethical sentiment, see my 'Hegel's Concept of Virtue', in *Dialectics, Politics, and the Contemporary Value of Hegel's Practical Philosophy*, especially 163–166.

maintaining resources enabling individuals to function in market societies and providing assistance to the poor and needy. The Corporation denotes self-organizing professional and work-related associations dedicated to promoting the well-being of their members. From the perspective of realizing ethicality the Corporation is the preferred alternative, as it represents an 'immanent' rather than merely 'external' mediation of individual and common concerns. Indeed, the Corporation is the site where '*the ethical returns* to civil society' (PR § 249). Hegel's position is reflected in the distinctive role played here by *Bildung* and how the latter contributes to the realization of a notion of ethicality responsive to the exigencies of civil society.

The Corporation and the Idea of Ethical (*sittlicher*) *Bildung*

We begin by noting how corporate membership affirms the well-being of the particular individual. One way is through worker training programmes and material assistance for those adversely affected by the dynamics of market societies. Another is through attention to the psychological maladies – feelings of humiliation and diminished self-worth – experienced by those who are adversely affected by market forces. Corporate bodies address these maladies, as they are structured to recognize and value individuals for the unique skills, talents and capabilities they possess by virtue of corporate membership. If membership in civil society can make the individual feel like a 'nobody' – at best a legal person formally indistinguishable from others, the corporation recognizes him or her as '*somebody*' (PR § 253).

Such recognition takes the form of the 'honour' an individual possesses through corporate or 'estate' membership (PR § 253). Hegel asserts that, while honour is more commonly associated with traditional societies, his use of the term is appropriate to modern societies and their systems of mediation (PR 1819/20, 205). In his view, an individual merits esteem or honour not by virtue of some inhering property or quality, but through the recognition he or she receives from fellow members of the corporation. What counts, however, is not the recognition itself but the 'representation' (*Vorstellung*) informing it. A corporate member acquires honour in being recognized as possessing the general talents and capabilities understood by members to define membership itself. In Hegel's terms, he or she is honoured when recognized not as an individual but as the embodiment of a universal (PR 1819/20, 204–206). It is through such 'mediated representation' – acknowledgement by others according to general norms

– that the person is recognized in ways otherwise absent in civil society: for his or her unique particularity (PR 1819/20 Ringier, 151).

Hegel identifies corporate honour with the concept of *Bildung*, 'the cultivation of the universality of thought'. As elsewhere, it is this capacity to regard individuals as embodying universal categories that constitutes the 'corporate spirit' and the cultivated consciousness of a corporate community (PR § 289). But it is important to appreciate what is distinctive here. Already in the Administration of Justice Hegel noted how *Bildung* inculcates in community members consciousness of the universality needed for the societal affirmation of the equal rights of persons. Yet whereas the legal system construes universality with reference to an individual's general humanity, the corporate community does so with regard to his or her personal particularity. The 'reflexivity of *Bildung*' associated with corporate honour attends to 'individuality in all particularity' (PR 1819/20, 205). It is in this 'rooting of the particular in the universal' (PR § 289) that the corporation accommodates a notion of *Bildung* committed to the mediation of universal and particular. It also facilitates realization of a notion of ethicality predicated on such mediation.

Hegel's point, however, is not simply that corporate membership entails a cultivated community committed to recognizing the worth of the particular individual. His point is also that the corporate community has as its 'purpose' the cultivation of the individual (VRP 3: 710). As a 'somebody' recognized simply for whom he or she is, a corporate member can dispense with the practice, characteristically unrestricted in market societies, of seeking recognition through external manifestations of success. A 'man of honour' instead exhibits a sovereign self-mastery largely unaffected by the concerns of wealth and power that preoccupy the 'uncultivated'. Calling it the 'highest form' of *Bildung* (VNS § 91), Hegel accentuates the 'simplicity' (*Einfachheit*) of such undistracted individuals. In doing so, however, he does not promote, in the manner of Rousseau, a view of individual cultivation focused on solitary self-reliance (PR § 153A). This is precluded by his contention that sovereign selfhood depends on recognition provided by community members. It is precluded as well by civil society itself, where individual existence and identity are inextricably tied to the fate of society as a whole. In championing simplicity, Hegel's point is not to deny those entanglements but to cast them in a new light. It is to conceive the relationship of individual to community, self to other, not in the instrumental way common in modern market societies, but as one in which the identity of individuals is fully constituted only in those relations. It is in this recognition that individual

PRECLUDE – RULE OUT IN ADVANCE
TO MAKE IMPOSSIBLE BY
NECESSARY CONSEQUENCE
PREVENT

identity obtains, not 'atomistically', but through communal affiliations that genuine personhood – the 'organically cultivated particularity' (VRP 4: 622) – is first established. Such relations of intersubjective mediation are also what accounts for the simplicity of cultivated individuals.

Appreciation of how corporate existence contributes to the ethical cultivation of the individual must also consider the reflective nature of the individual's relation to community. As with *Bildung* generally, that experienced by a corporate member takes the form of 'knowledge' or 'insight' regarding his or her relationship to what is common (PR 1819/20, 202). Such reliance on reflection flows from the fact that, as members of civil society, individuals understand themselves first and foremost in terms of their particularity, and thus need to grasp the relation of their 'private' to their 'substantial' selves. In addition, such 'genuine consciousness' (PR 1819/20, 207) is needed to correct the 'misapprehension' bedevilling most members of civil society, for whom explicit attention to the conditions of their mutual well-being is irrelevant to their personal well-being (PR § 181A). And such reliance on reflection is required by ethical life itself, for which the interpenetration of individual and community it connotes must be evident not just to third-person analysis but to the participants themselves.

But reflection does not thus take the form of processes of abstract cognition removed from the flow of everyday life. Part of the simplicity fostered by cultivation is its fashioning of wider normative commitments as matters of custom and habit (PR 1819/20 Ringier, 152). A cultivated person is 'present in everything he does' (PR § 107A). Yet appeal to habit does not gainsay the centrality of thought in Hegel's account of ethical *Bildung*. His point is simply that in the corporate community reflective commitment to communal well-being is now part of the everyday practice of particular persons. A constitutive feature of the 'organically cultivated' personality is the habitual appreciation of the co-dependence of his or her own ends and those of community.

These considerations bear on the republican dimension of corporate membership. Inasmuch as an individual recognizes that his identity is fully constituted in communal relations, he supports as a matter of everyday practice the community and its well-being. In recognizing 'that he belongs to a whole ... he has an interest in, and endeavours to promote, the less selfish end of this whole' (PR § 253). Hegel's point, to be sure, is not that individuals promote communal well-being only through corporate membership. It is a general, if uncertain, feature of civil society, understood as a system of mutual interdependence, that individuals can contribute to the greater good simply through pursuit of private self-interest. The difference, though, is that in the corporation that which otherwise is an 'unconscious necessity' becomes an explicit object of knowledge and will (PR § 255A). Like members of civil society generally, corporate members focus on the satisfaction of their particular needs. As corporate members, however, they appreciate that not only the satisfactions of those needs but their very particularity as persons is tied to conscious activity in support of the whole.

Underlying Hegel's position is an account of the reflexive nature of ethical agency itself. In acting for the whole, individuals are directed not just to community but to the idea of community itself – the community *as* community (VRP 3: 709). Such reflexivity is the appropriate form of ethical consciousness specific to corporate membership which, proceeding from the fact of bifurcation, is directed not to a pre-existing notion of community but to the general conditions for community as such. But attention to the universal 'as a universal end' (PR § 251) is also a feature of an appropriately cultivated consciousness, where cultivation is understood as commitment to the universal in thought. Here corporate consciousness articulates 'true *Bildung*', that connoting 'true originality'. Expressive of the 'infinite self-determination' of a 'free subjectivity', corporate community consists of individuals who make the idea of community itself an object of knowledge and volition (PR § 187R, 187A). It is in this normatively robust form of self-reflexivity that '*Bildung* is an immanent moment of the absolute, and that it has infinite value' (PR § 187R).

Similarly, Hegel asserts that the ethical union denoted by the corporation is itself reflexively constituted. What counts as corporate commonality is not a shared set of substantive ends or values. This is barred by the bifurcations which motivate corporate communality and by the principle of self-subsistent particularity around which it revolves. Instead, Hegel advocates what instructively has been called a *formal conception of ethical life.*[16] In line with the reflexivity he associates with a cultivated community, the substantive unity of ethical life is simply the practice of community members defining and redefining the conditions of their commonality.

Likewise, the very reality of ethical life is reflexively constituted. Ethicality does not articulate a presumed order of being but subsists in the activity of individuals establishing their commonality. In the corporation 'ethical unity … is generated through the joint effort [*Mitwirkung*]

[16] Axel Honneth, *The Struggle for Recognition: The Moral Grammar of Social Conflicts*, trans. Joel Anderson (Cambridge, MA: MIT Press, 1995), 173.

of the members themselves' (VRP 4: 588). Corporate fellowship *is* engagement for fellowship itself. Granted, such engagement is already shaped and indeed cultivated by existing practices and institutions that promote ethical comportment.[17] Yet, if ethical engagement depends on an existent ethical order, ethical life itself – the actuality of self-conscious freedom – attains reality only in the actions of those committed to the conditions of their ethical commonality. The modes of knowledge and volition central to ethicality may have their 'foundation' in the realm of 'ethical being' (*sittliche Sein*), but ethicality itself acquires 'its actuality [*Wirklichkeit*] through self-conscious action' (PR § 142).

Furthermore, institutions, corporations included (PR § 263), are themselves reflexively constituted totalities. In Hegel's specific understanding, institutions are not structures or practices that supervene on agential conduct. As elements in the general realization of freedom, corporate institutions properly exist in and through the conscious activity of individuals and the mediating substructures that express their will.[18] Like the constitution, whose morphology they replicate, institutions are linked to the 'essential self-consciousness' of particular persons and their 'activity directed towards a universal end' (PR § 264). What Hegel says of the state generally obtains equally for the corporation, the 'smaller state' (VRP 4: 621): 'It is the self-awareness [*Selbstgefühl*] of individuals which constitutes [its] actuality' (PR § 265A).

None of this is to suggest that Hegel presents corporate membership as the full realization of ethical life. As a final articulation, it is deficient in several respects. It attends only to membership in a particular vocational entity, not society generally. It counts as members principally trade professionals, thus excluding many affected by poverty. And its notion of commonality derives from the 'inherent likeness' (PR § 251) of members, thereby failing to accommodate the societal differentiations required of a genuine polity. In this regard, a full account of ethicality mandates transition to the explicit theory of political community represented for Hegel by the state.

Appreciation of this point, however, does not detract from the centrality of corporations to a system of ethical life. If the latter attains full expression in political community, political community, owing to its status as a

[17] Honneth, *Freedom's Right*, Part 1, Section 3: 'Social Freedom and the Doctrine of Ethical Life', 42–62.

[18] For a related treatment of Hegel's institutional theory, see Elisabeth Weisser-Lohmann, *Rechtsphilosophie als praktische Philosophie. Hegels 'Grundlinien der Philosophie des Rechts' und die Grundlegung der praktischen Philosophie* (Munich: Wilhelm Fink, 2011), 228–231.

differentiated totality, remains dependent on corporate bodies. Inasmuch as a polity is constituted in the mediation of universal and particular, it depends on a developed account of particularity and the particular individual, whose explication is the task of the theory of civil society and, quintessentially, the corporation. In addition, reliance on corporations is entailed by a polity's status as an institutionally differentiated totality – 'an articulated whole whose parts themselves form particular subordinate spheres' (PW, 263). As such, a polity depends on corporations – with the family one of 'the pillars on which public freedom rests' (PR § 265).

Similarly, corporations help constitute the reflective ethicality that acquires full elaboration in the state. Economically conceived corporate entities nurture the ethical consciousness required of a polity – that based on appreciating the connection between one's personal well-being and that of the community. In addition, the corporation, in Hegel's institutionally differentiated polity, instantiates the forms of intermediate association needed to foster ethical sentiment in political communities the size, scale and complexity of modern states. Indeed, it is owing to their capacity to cultivate ethical consciousness under modern conditions that Hegel terms corporations 'the secret of patriotism' (PR § 289R). Moreover, a corporate community is the site where individuals, responding to the maladies of market societies, first develop a reflexively conceived ethical consciousness, one directed to the conditions of their shared commonality. And the sheer plurality of corporate communities cultivates appreciation for that sense of *shared* identity central to a notion of ethical community appropriate to an internally differentiated polity.

Conclusion: The Concept of a Modern Ethical Life

In this essay I have sought to clarify Hegel's understanding of ethical life in civil society. Clarifying his position is important because civil society, while a component in the *Philosophy of Right*'s general account of ethical life, is also the domain representing the pervasive loss of ethicality. Focusing on the bifurcations that fuel this loss, I have argued that Hegel, consonant with the general aims of his dialectical theory, fashions an account of civil society's ethicality not in spite of, but because of, its bifurcations. I have given special attention to the concept of *Bildung*, which is not only central to the theory of civil society but also illustrative of its bifurcations. Hegel's use of *Bildung* is noteworthy, as it itself undergoes a *Bildungsprozess* – from the System of Needs through the Administration of Justice to the Corporation. I emphasized the role played by *Bildung* in the Corporation, for it is here that Hegel not only proffers an account of civil society's ethicality but does so by constructively appropriating the bifurcating structures that otherwise undermine ethicality. In presenting this account as the product of an internal *Bildungsprozess*, I have also sought to show that Hegel, consonant with his approach to immanent normative analysis, advances a critique and correction of modern social pathologies understood not as external operation but as the work of affected individuals.

The conception of ethicality that emerges from Hegel's theory of civil society has a decidedly modern character. Unlike those that might appeal to Aristotle and classical Greek thought, it is not based on a philosophical anthropology or a political understanding of human nature. This is precluded by the priority Hegel assigns to the modern principle of self-subsistent particularity and the social bifurcations associated with it. A modern account of ethicality is instead a differentiated and reflexively mediated one, predicated on reconstructing modern notions of individuality and community. On the one hand, Hegel advances a notion of ethical consciousness based on recognition by persons that their individual interests are best pursued in community, that their particularity is properly constituted in intersubjective relations, that community has intrinsic as well as instrumental value, and that it is to be supported *as* community – normatively desirable as well as empirically existent. On the other hand, he promotes a notion of ethical life that eschews appeal to a pre-existing set of values or a presumed order of being. Responding to a bifurcated social reality comprised of diversely situated groups and individuals, modern ethicality takes the form of a community whose 'substance' consists in the activity of members' clarification, definition and establishment of the conditions of their communality. Similarly, a community shaped by its members' consciousness of their interdependence is also one in which individuals are attentive to each other's material well-being and to a notion of individual worth that is only minimally concerned with the external signs of success reflected in the 'spectacle' that otherwise is civil society. Again, ethicality denotes a community that is established and maintained in its members' cognitive and volitional affirmation of their mutuality and commonality, something which is itself facilitated through participation in the various sub-political domains comprising a modern polity. And, for a diversely constituted polity shaped and sustained in the mediation of universal and particular, ethical life reposes on ongoing processes of renewal and recalibration, something mandated further by the necessary incompleteness in a community's capacity to subject itself to definitive self-reflection. For Hegel, modern societies foster a decidedly modern notion of ethicality, one cultivated and sustained through the modes of differentiation and reflexivity specific to civil society itself.

Many questions can be raised about this conception of ethical life. Is the notion of a corporatistically conceived ethicality truly reflective of trends and possibilities inherent in modern market societies or does it rely on assumptions inconsistent with an immanently conceived reconstruction of those societies? Can economic cooperatives indeed underwrite an account of ethical life adequate to the addressing of modern social pathologies? Do contemporary societies accommodate, even reconstructively, the processes of individual and collective learning required of a modern ethicality? Has Hegel adequately integrated the force of modern bifurcations in his constructive appropriation of those bifurcations? How does the union of universal and particular articulated with the Corporation comport with the monarchical version elaborated later in the *Philosophy of Right*? Can a corporatistically conceived ethicality address the maladies associated with the operation of market mechanisms at the global level?

These questions cannot be addressed here. What I have attempted to do instead is shed some light on Hegel's complex claims regarding the ethicality of civil society. Rather than advancing a notion of ethicality fashioned against the bifurcating pathologies he so acutely depicted, Hegel, I have argued, presents one generated through the constructive deployment of bifurcations. I thereby detailed Hegel's decidedly modern notion of ethicality, a differentiated and reflectively mediated sort that harnesses the oppositions shaping modern society. I have also explicated Hegel's distinctive response to the challenges posed by modern society, one dedicated to 'looking the negative in the face, and tarrying with it' (PhG, 19). Further, by focusing on a concept of *Bildung* directed to cultivating subjective particularity, I have affirmed his distinctive challenge to modern subjectivity, one that engages the resources of subjectivity itself. And by focusing on Hegel's appeal to norms and practices endemic to modern societies themselves, I have sought to make clear the immanently transcendent character of his supersession of the aporias of social modernity. All are features of Hegel's critical reconstruction of modern society, and all arguably continue to speak to us today.

CHAPTER 7

Why Ethical Life is Fragile: Rights, Markets and States in Hegel's Philosophy of Right

Hans-Christoph Schmidt am Busch

In his main work of social and political philosophy, *Elements of the Philosophy of Right*, it is Hegel's declared intention to show that a form of the state is being established in Europe that realizes what he calls 'the Concept' and which is therefore 'rational'. States exhibiting this type of rationality are, both in their character and in their functioning, not only fully comprehensible but also entities which allow citizens to be 'at one with themselves' (*bei sich selbst*) (PR § 7A; see also § 268) in their everyday and political lives.[1] In Hegel's view, they therefore enable citizens to lead an ethical life (*ein sittliches Leben*)[2] in which freedom is realized and reconciliation with the social and political world achieved.[3]

More precisely, Hegel explicitly claims that states must have a specific basic structure in order to realize this type of rationality.[4] This structure is comprised of two ethical 'spheres' (PR § 261), the 'family' and 'civil society', wherein people have a legally secured space to cultivate and maintain private relations and to pursue economic activities of their own free will. Hegel likewise understands the political state[5] as an ethical sphere, one which functions to give citizens the possibility of identifying with

[1] See, for instance, Robert Pippin, *Hegel's Practical Philosophy: Rational Agency as Ethical Life* (Cambridge: Cambridge University Press, 2008); Ludwig Siep, *Der Staat als irdischer Gott. Genesis und Relevanz einer Hegelschen Idee* (Tübingen: Mohr Siebeck, 2015); and Klaus Vieweg, *Das Denken der Freiheit. Hegels Grundlinien der Philosophie des Rechts* (Munich: Wilhelm Fink, 2012).

[2] Throughout the present essay, I use the phrase 'ethical life' to translate Hegel's term *Sittlichkeit*. Accordingly, I use the word 'ethical' in the sense of *sittlich*.

[3] See Frederick Neuhouser, *Foundations of Hegel's Social Theory: Actualizing Freedom* (Cambridge, MA: Harvard University Press, 2000) and Michael Hardimon, *Hegel's Social Philosophy: The Project of Reconciliation* (Cambridge: Cambridge University Press, 1994).

[4] This has not been taken into account by critics who believe Hegel's thought is totalitarian. See, for instance, Karl Popper, *The Open Society and its Enemies, Volume II, The High Tide of Prophecy: Hegel, Marx, and the Aftermath* (London: Routledge & Kegan Paul, 1945).

[5] Hegel uses the word 'state' in both a narrow and a broad sense. In the narrow sense 'state' designates the branches of government and their administration; in the broad sense it refers to the polity as a whole, which includes the spheres of the family and civil society.

the polity as a 'whole' (PR § 253) and to obtain thereby a 'consciousness' (PR § 268) of freedom and reconciliation.

Did Hegel successfully realize the philosophical project outlined above? Was he able to adequately explain how the social and political structures emerging in Europe during his lifetime enabled people to lead an ethical life? This has been repeatedly denied. Numerous critics have charged Hegel with having underestimated the tensions and conflicts which civil societies generate and which endanger ethical life, and with having overestimated the prospects that political states could establish institutions fostering ethical life. This assessment was expressed very early on by Hegel's pupils and the Left-Hegelians,[6] and it promoted the alternative theories of state and society found in Marx, Marxism and contemporary critical theory.

Is the critique justified? Without question, Hegel repeatedly suggests throughout his work that modern states can 'overcome' (*aufheben*) the tensions and conflicts arising from civil society and thereby lead people to live ethical lives[7] – a position which, given the historical developments of the nineteenth and twentieth centuries, is hard to defend. But Hegel's standpoint is in fact far more nuanced than these critics assume. Indeed, Hegel appears to develop ideas in his *Philosophy of Right* that explain why civil societies are ethically ambivalent and why states are unable to offset the ethically negative effects of such societies.[8] If this reading is justified, then the *Philosophy of Right* may itself be a work that is not free of tensions.

As I will show in what follows, Hegel can be seen as a theoretician of the *fragility* of modern ethical life. In order to develop this perspective I first explain precisely what, according to Hegel, the ethical disposition of members of civil society consists in and why markets structured by civil law (*Privatrecht*) are ethically ambivalent. As Hegel believes that markets are necessary to secure institutionally the ethical disposition of civil society, this raises the question of whether modern states can either mitigate the ethically corrosive effects of markets or foster an independent form of ethical life that is open to all citizens. If one closely tracks Hegel's remarks

6 See Michael Quante and Amir Mohseni (eds.), *Die linken Hegelianer. Studien zum Verhältnis von Religion und Politik im Vormärz* (Paderborn: Wilhelm Fink, 2015).

7 To mention only one such instance, see PR § 260.

8 Shlomo Avineri has rightly emphasized that Hegel has 'no solution' to 'the problem of poverty'. See his illuminating discussion in *Hegel's Theory of the Modern State* (Cambridge: Cambridge University Press, 1972), 147–154. As we shall see, the ethical ambivalence of the market we seek to explain affects not only the poor, but the other members of modern societies as well.

on this topic, it appears that *neither* possibility is open to states. Hegel's reflections therefore yield the conclusion that ethical life in the modern world is irrevocably fragile.

The Ethical Disposition of Members of Civil Society

Hegel believed that in Europe, within his lifetime, a new type of society was forming: 'civil society' (*bürgerliche Gesellschaft*). The origins of civil society lead him back to the political and economic upheavals of the late eighteenth and early nineteenth centuries, notably the French Revolution and the spread of industrialization from England. As Hegel emphasizes in the *Philosophy of Right*, civil societies differ from other types of society not only in institutional terms, but also in that their members have a specific 'ethical disposition' (*sittliche Gesinnung*) which distinguishes them from members of other societies:

> The ethical disposition ... is therefore ... that each individual, by a process of self-determination, makes himself a member of one of the moments of civil society through his activity, diligence, and skill, and supports himself in this capacity; and only through this mediation with the universal does he simultaneously provide for himself and gain recognition in his own eyes [*Vorstellung*] and in the eyes of others. (PR § 207)[9]

How is this argument to be understood? With regard to the meaning of individual expressions, the following must first be established: when Hegel talks about a man[10] who makes himself 'a member of one of the moments of civil society', someone who 'provides for himself ... only through this mediation with the universal', he means that the person in question secures his livelihood by manufacturing goods or offering services which other members of society can use, all of which lies within the framework of a social division of labour. But why does Hegel say that the individual in a civil society has an '*ethical* disposition' to learn and exercise a profession and to secure his livelihood by helping to secure the livelihood of others? And why does the individual thereby 'gain recognition

[9] For the sake of clarity and consistency, I have occasionally altered H. B. Nisbet's translation of Hegel's *Grundlinien der Philosophie des Rechts* (*Elements of the Philosophy of Right*). Changes to Nisbet's translation are not noted.

[10] In keeping with the spirit of his times, Hegel assumed that only male members of civil societies took part in the division of labour described above (see on this point PR § 238). When quoting and paraphrasing Hegel, this usage is sometimes retained here. However, the applicability of Hegel's argument both to men and to women should be borne in mind.

in his own eyes and in the eyes of others'?[11] As I would like to show, the ethical disposition of members of civil society can be characterized on the basis of six elements. These elements can be described as follows.

E-1: For any given member of a civil society, A, it is important that he learns and exercises a profession through his own self-determination and activity, and that he thereby not only secures his own livelihood but also helps to secure the livelihood of others.

Or, slightly formalized: for any given member of a civil society, A, it is important to do X.

E-2: A has the conviction that doing X is also important to other members of society, B, C, etc.

E-3: A, B, C, etc. take the view that they should each do X, insofar as it is possible.

E-4: When A does X, it is important for A to be recognized by B, C, etc. for doing so.

E-5: When B, C, etc. do X, then A is willing to recognize them for doing so.

E-6: A, B, C etc. take the view that each of them should be recognized by the others when he does X.

For A doing X is an activity that figures in his conception of a good life; if A could not do X, he would think that his life was incomplete. But why is this so? A lives in a society where the division of labour is such that no one person alone can produce the goods they need to secure their livelihood. On the contrary, almost all the goods A needs are produced by other members of society. In this situation, it is important for A to acquire the goods he needs to secure his livelihood *in exchange for* goods which he has produced and which will help other members of society to secure their livelihood. Now the activity which enables A to do what is important for

[11] Many authors have recently discussed Hegel's theory of recognition. To the best of my knowledge, however, very little attention has been paid to the passage from the *Philosophy of Right* cited above. On Hegel's theory of recognition see, for instance, Axel Honneth, *The Struggle for Recognition: The Moral Grammar of Social Conflicts*, trans Joel Anderson (Cambridge, MA: MIT Press, 1995); Axel Honneth, *Freedom's Right: The Social Foundations of Democratic Life*, trans. Joseph Ganahl (New York: Columbia University Press, 2014); Heikki Ikäheimo, *Anerkennung* (Berlin and Boston, MA: de Gruyter, 2014); Michael Quante, *Die Wirklichkeit des Geistes. Studien zu Hegel* (Berlin: Suhrkamp, 2011); Ludwig Siep, *Anerkennung als Prinzip der praktischen Philosophie. Untersuchungen zu Hegels Jenaer Philosophie des Geistes*, 2nd edn (Hamburg: Felix Meiner, 2014); and Andreas Wildt, *Autonomie und Anerkennung. Hegels Moralitätskritik im Lichte seiner Fichte-Rezeption* (Stuttgart: Klett-Cotta, 1982).

him is X. This is why A views doing X as an essential element of the kind of life he wishes to live.

It follows that A does not merely take up an occupation to have money for his own use. What is *also* important for him is to engage in an activity that helps other members of society to satisfy their needs and secure their livelihood. For this reason A would not view gifts or donations from other people or the state as equivalent to the money earned through work within the framework of the social division of labour.

As these considerations show, A has an *evaluative* and *volitional-practical* attitude that helps him to structure his own life. This attitude allows him, for instance, to assess the wishes he might have, to accept or reject them, and to judge possible acts as either appropriate or inappropriate in accordance with the requirements of doing X. This attitude has a significant impact on A's self-understanding and practical identity.

In a civil society, it is not merely important for A to do X; A also assumes that doing X is important for the other members of society. He would be surprised, even amazed, if he were to discover that B or C had absolutely no interest in doing X. Moreover, A – as well as B and C – thinks that it is *normatively* right that each of them, if possible, performs X. A – along with B and C – is thereby equipped with a standard which allows him to classify his own behaviour and that of others as either good or bad, as praiseworthy or blameworthy – depending on whether it fulfils or degrades the norm in question. It is noteworthy here that this norm claims that every member of society should do X, *provided that they are able to do so*; persons for whom it is impossible to do X (for instance, as the result of a disability) do not degrade the norm if they do not do X.

As noted above, members of civil society are ready to recognize each other for doing X, and they consider it appropriate or normatively right that people who do X are to be recognized for doing so. Moreover, it is important for them to be recognized if they do X. These elements (E-4, E-5 and E-6) of the attitude held by members of civil society must relate to an activity that is achieved only through significant effort. If, for instance, doing X merely consisted in greeting work colleagues each morning, it could not – at least under normal conditions – be a fitting basis for recognition. Rather, doing X involves learning and practising a profession to secure one's own livelihood by helping to secure the livelihood of other people. Doing X therefore consists in an extended and complex activity whose success requires effort and determination. As such, doing X constitutes a suitable basis for recognition, a recognition that can be grounded in various aspects of the activity in question (such as the technical skills needed to carry it out or its particular usefulness for other members of society).[12]

To sum up: when Hegel talks about the 'ethical disposition' of members of civil society he refers to an attitude that can be characterized by the elements mentioned above. As explained, such an attitude contains evaluative, normative and volitional-practical aspects, as well as convictions relating to the existence of these elements (in oneself and other persons). As is evident from the preceding reflections, such an attitude has considerable influence on people's self-understanding, their way of life and the social relations they entertain with one another.

In view of the aims we are pursuing, we need to consider what it means for an individual to engage in 'a process of self-determination' when becoming and remaining a member of a 'moment', or professional sector, of civil society. Alongside Hegel's statement analysed above, another passage from the *Philosophy of Right* sheds light on this question. In a civil society,

> [t]he ultimate and essential determinant is subjective opinion and the particular arbitrary will, which are accorded their right, their merit, and their honour in this sphere. Thus, what happens in this sphere through inner necessity is at the same time mediated by the arbitrary will, and for the subjective consciousness, it has the shape of being the product of its own will. (PR § 206)

What must be in place for a person A to become and remain a member of a 'moment' of civil society through 'a process of self-determination'? For a start, there has to be a decision-making situation in the first place – the prevailing social situation cannot be one wherein who does what job is determined by factors like background or ethnicity. It also cannot be the case that another person or institution either decides what work A must carry out, or compels him to agree to undertake certain work. In fact, A must be *entitled* to become a member of any of the various and distinct 'moments' of civil society – a provision that is satisfied if there are no laws or customs prohibiting A from pursuing specific professional activities. Moreover, A must be *entitled* to act on specific vocational choices in accordance with his 'opinion' and preferences – what Hegel calls his 'particular arbitrary will' (PR § 206) – and *not be obliged* to have his reasons for or against a professional activity disclosed, discussed or subjected to scrutiny.[13]

[12] On this point, see my discussion in *'Anerkennung' als Prinzip der Kritischen Theorie* (Berlin and New York: de Gruyter, 2011).

[13] Of course, this does not prevent A from choosing to divulge his reasons.

Only if these conditions are met can A and his fellow citizens ground the conviction that the specific professional activity by which A becomes and maintains himself as a member of a 'moment' of civil society is 'the product of [his] own will' (PR § 206). And only then will they be of the conviction that, for any individual A, the activity in question is one that he exercises 'by a process of self-determination'.

Why Markets Are Ethically Ambivalent

For Hegel, ethical dispositions are components of institutional practices. They have elements that can be secured only through social or state institutions; as psychological phenomena, they can only endure in a fitting institutional context. This is why Hegel takes institutional arrangements to be the 'true ground' (PR § 268R) of ethical dispositions.

What are the institutional requirements of the ethical dispositions held by members of civil society? Can these requirements be met? If so, how? In the course of discussing these issues, Hegel first examines whether the dispositions in question can be appropriately ensured by *markets*. The reflections he puts forward in this context are highly instructive and will therefore be reconstructed in the present section. In order to do this it is first necessary to clarify the type of social reality Hegel means to refer to when using the term 'market' (PR 1821/22, § 235). Hegel's *Philosophy of Right* and the notes and transcripts associated with his lectures on this material provide a suitable exegetical basis for insight into this topic. Moreover, as a matter of theoretical coherence it is noteworthy that, at certain points throughout these materials, Hegel appears implicitly to draw upon thoughts that he had already developed in his Jena period. We can therefore characterize his 'mature' understanding of the market as follows.

(1) Markets are places where people who do not provide for themselves (see PR § 183) exchange diverse goods – for instance, consumer goods, productive goods, labour or money (see PR § 80).
(2) In markets these goods are offered 'not so much to a particular individual as such as to the individual in a universal sense, i.e. to the public' (PR § 236). Thus markets are not places where face-to-face relationships operate.
(3) People who exchange in markets 'recognize' one another 'as persons and owners of property' (PR § 71). By virtue of this type of recognition, they take each other to be entitled to decide as 'individuals'

(*Werke* 7: 109), that is, independently of one another, whether and on what terms they would like to offer for sale those things or services that fall within their private property, and whether and on what terms they would like to buy things or services that belong to other market participants.

(4) The legal 'powers' (PR § 38) and duties which market participants have as persons and owners of property are specified and secured through an institutional complex which Hegel calls 'abstract right' (and which comprises legislative, executive and judicial organs).

(5) The goods exchanged in markets have prices that are determined by the market participants, not by the government.

(6) The prices of goods exchanged in markets depend on the overall demand for goods and the overall supply of goods (see PR § 236). Prices result from decisions that market participants make – at least in principle – independently of each other, namely, to offer or demand specific goods at certain rates. In this sense, the prices of goods in markets are formed 'atomistically' (SEL, 168).

(7) The prices of goods exchanged in a market fulfil an informational function: they show market participants which costs arise in the production of specific goods (at the time in question) and what revenues may be generated with the sale of them (at the time in question). They thus allow for knowledge about 'whether the production of such a surplus is [equivalent to, SaB] the possibility of meeting the totality of needs, whether a man can subsist on it' (SEL, 168).

(8) By means of a price mechanism, markets tend 'on the whole' to 're-establish' the 'correct relationship' between the supply and demand of goods (PR § 236). When there is an oversupply of goods of a certain type (A), the price of each of them will eventually become so low that not all producers will be able to subsist; in such a situation, some of them will cease to produce goods of this type, and this will continue until those who remain in the business 'can live off it' (SEL, 169). Likewise, when there is too much demand for goods of a certain type (B), the price of each of them is so high that additional market participants will begin to produce goods of this type; in such a situation, the price of each good B will fall, and this will continue until those in the business can simply make their living through this activity. In that way, 'by a process of unconscious necessity' (PR § 236R), markets tend towards an 'equilibrium' of supply and demand.

It follows that, when Hegel uses the term 'market', he is referring to *a market economy structured by civil law*, in which the price of each good depends upon the price of all other goods. As he himself notes, his understanding of the market is a *modern* one: it is influenced by 'one of the sciences which have originated in the modern age as their ground [*Boden*]': classical economics as it exists in the writings of 'Smith, Say [and] Ricardo' (PR § 189R).[14]

Is such a market system able to fulfil the institutional requirements of the ethical dispositions that characterize the members of civil society? In Hegel's opinion, no positive answer can be given to this question. As we shall see, he is convinced that such a system is, in ethical terms, *ambivalent*. In his view, the market has qualities that promote the formation or maintenance of the ethical dispositions held by members of civil societies, but it simultaneously has properties that endanger the formation or maintenance of those dispositions as well. Hegel believes that this ambivalent quality stems from the legal framework of markets as well as from the way in which markets typically function. We will deal with these elements of his theory in the remaining part of this section.

On the one hand, *recognition effectively takes place in markets*.[15] As a market participant an individual is recognized by other participants and social institutions as a person and an owner of property (see PR § 71). This can be developed from points (3) and (4) above.

People who perform exchanges in markets take each other to be entitled to make decisions independently of one another regarding whether and on what terms they wish to buy or sell the things that they own. They also take each other to be entitled to make decisions independently of one another regarding whether and on what terms they wish to offer services to, or demand services from, other market participants. Moreover, they do not take themselves to be obliged to divulge the reasons for their respective decisions. Because this is the case, the exchange of goods or services in markets takes place when the participating parties want it to take place. Only when they reach an agreement does such an exchange actually come about. Such an event is thus accompanied by the *experience* of

[14] On Hegel's economic theory and its relation to classical economics, see Sven Ellmers, *Freiheit und Wirtschaft. Theorie der bürgerlichen Gesellschaft nach Hegel* (Bielefeld: Transcript, 2015); Lisa Herzog, *Inventing the Market: Smith, Hegel, and Political Theory* (Oxford: Oxford University Press, 2013); Birger Priddat, *Hegel als Ökonom* (Berlin: Duncker & Humblot, 1990); and Norbert Waszek, *The Scottish Enlightenment and Hegel's Account of 'Civil Society'* (Dordrecht: Kluwer, 1988). The writing of the present essay was well under way when the book *Hegel and Capitalism* (Albany, NY: SUNY Press, 2015) edited by Andrew Buchwalter appeared. That book could therefore not be taken into account here.

[15] A terminological remark: when we speak of *the market* or of *markets*, we mean a market economy of the type described above, that is, one structured by civil law.

being recognized by one's contracting partners as a person and an owner of property.

At the same time, people who carry out exchanges with one another in markets are recognized institutionally. The organs of 'abstract right' give a *legal* form to the 'powers' which market participants grant each other, as well as to the corresponding 'prohibitions' (PR § 38).[16] These institutions solve disputes between market participants by legal means and ensure that contractual agreements are adhered to. By exercising these tasks, the organs of 'abstract right' ensure that market participants have, as persons and property owners, 'valid actuality' (PR § 208). This is why people who exchange in markets can be said to be recognized by the institutions of state and society.[17]

Markets thereby strengthen *one element* of citizens' ethical disposition: the 'self-determination' with which professional activities are pursued. That is, as market participants, people know that they are entitled to be members of the different 'moments' or professional sectors of civil society and that they can act with respect to specific professional options in accordance with their own 'opinion[s]' and preferences ('particular arbitrary will') without having to disclose the reasons for their respective decisions.[18] In this sense, markets are institutions that can make *positive* contributions to the formation or maintenance of the ethical disposition characteristic of members of a civil society.

On the other hand, Hegel thinks that a market economy of the type described above also has properties that endanger the formation and maintenance of citizens' ethical dispositions. This claim may surprise some readers. For, as we have seen, such a market system signals to an individual (via the prices of traded goods and services) which professional activities make it possible for him to contribute to the satisfaction of the needs of other market participants and to secure simultaneously his own livelihood. It provides, moreover, the legal freedom for him to engage in these activities. For this reason a market economy appears to be an institutional complex that enables members of civil society to do what they take to be important and what they also believe they *ought* to do – namely, '[b]y

[16] Hegel is thus well aware of the distinction, emphasized by H. L. A. Hart, between legal norms prohibiting actions and legal norms conferring powers. See Hart, *The Concept of Law*, 2nd edn (Oxford: Oxford University Press, 1997), 27–42.

[17] For an in-depth analysis of Hegel's theory of abstract right, see Amir Mohseni, *Abstrakte Freiheit. Zum Begriff des Eigentums bei Hegel* (Hamburg: Felix Meiner, 2014).

[18] Without these entitlements, the price mechanism described above could not be in place. See point (8) above.

a process of self-determination', make themselves 'a member of one of the moments of civil society through [their] activity, diligence, and skill, and support [themselves] in this capacity'. Why, in Hegel's view, is this impression about the enabling nature of the market economy false and misleading? The following five reasons are suggested by Hegel's *Philosophy of Right* along with the associated lectures and notes that implicitly draw upon his earlier Jena writings.

(1) A market-economic system cannot ensure that each person *in fact* can 'make himself a member of one of the moments of civil society through his activity, diligence, and skill, and support himself in this capacity'. For Hegel, the absence of this assurance stems from several possibilities: market participants may simply lack and be unable to acquire the requisite qualifications for particular professional occupations (PR § 237); changes in the demand for goods and services may cause great fluctuations in prices and, at least temporarily, lead to unemployment (PR § 236); and technological innovation may cause long-term reductions in employment levels within particular sectors (PR § 243). In addition, Hegel believes that in the long run a market-economic system favours the emergence of monopolies, i.e. businesses that are not subject to the competitive economic price-formation mechanism outlined above. Such monopolies have the power to reduce the supply of goods and jobs in accordance with their own interests. 'Circumstances' (PR § 241) like these can make it impossible for members of a civil society to practise a given professional activity and to live in accordance with their ethical disposition.

(2) Market-economic relations cannot ensure that persons who pursue professional activities can thereby earn an income with which to secure their livelihood. For Hegel this assessment follows directly from his reflections on price-formation processes. The fact that markets tend, 'by a process of unconscious necessity', towards an 'equilibrium' of the supply of and the demand for goods implies that there are periods in which such an 'equilibrium' (PR § 236) does *not* exist. This entails that producers of goods may not always be able to secure their livelihood through professional activity. In the present context these possibilities are relevant because the ethical disposition characterizing members of civil societies requires that the individual 'provides for himself ... only through this mediation with the universal', that is, through his professional activity. If Hegel's speculations are

correct, then markets may not always meet this requirement even when people are employed.

(3) A market economy cannot ensure that professional activities *as such* possess the types of qualities that make possible and sustain the relevant ethical dispositions among members of civil society. Certainly, a great deal of work that generates market prices can be exercised only by persons with specific professional qualifications and judgment ('skill'); however, there are also paid jobs with undemanding content that require little to no decision-making from employees. Hegel himself makes this clear in his treatment of 'factory work' (SEL, 246–247), which consists in the continual performance of simple manual movements. In his judgment, such work simply cannot give the worker a basis for the consciousness that he is making himself into a member of civil society through 'his own activity' and 'skill'. On the contrary, the 'limitation' (PR § 243) of such a job profile encourages self-perceptions that are negative in both evaluative and normative terms. In Hegel's view, persons in such employment tend to regard themselves as subordinate and dependent, and even in some cases start to develop 'an inability to feel and enjoy the wider freedoms and particularly the spiritual advantages of civil society' (PR § 243).

(4) A market economy cannot ensure that a professional can *intentionally* 'make himself a member of one of the moments of civil society through his own activity, diligence, and skill', nor that he can *intentionally* 'support himself in this capacity'. As noted above, a member of a civil society lives in accordance with his disposition when he acts upon his decision to acquire economically relevant qualifications and to apply these in the context of a professional activity (see the section on 'The Ethical Disposition of Members of Civil Society' above). But what if, even with respect to the near future, one simply cannot foresee the qualifications that will be relevant? In that case it would, strictly speaking, be impossible for a person, by acquiring certain qualifications, to 'make himself a member of one of the moments of civil society through his own activity, diligence, and skill' and to 'support himself in this capacity'. Granted, he may decide to acquire specific skills, and if it turned out that these qualifications became socially superfluous he could always try to acquire other job-related skills; but under these circumstances he would not be able to form *long-term* career plans, which relate to the acquisition *and* exercise of qualifications within the context of a given professional activity. His professional life would thus run the

risk of being so fragmented[19] that it would fail to meet the requirements of the relevant ethical dispositions among members of civil society.

In Hegel's view, markets can develop in such a way that they make professionals into a plaything of price developments that can hardly be foreseen. But if people, when they decide to acquire professional skills, find themselves in 'the position of a gambler [*Spieler*]', they cannot regard any professional success they might have as *merited*, but rather only as a mere 'coincidence' (PR 1821/22, § 253). In that case, however, it will be impossible for them to realize the structure of recognition characteristic of the ethical disposition held by members of civil society (see elements E-4, E-5 and E-6 above). For this reason, markets may create circumstances in which professionals cannot – no matter what they earn – live in accordance with the salient ethical dispositions.

(5) A market system cannot prevent the formation of positions of power that in turn affect its functioning and legal framework in a way that undermines the ethical dispositions analysed above. As has already been noted, Hegel thinks that, in the long run, such a system encourages the emergence of monopolies. Such monopolies pose a danger that the equality of market participants before the law will no longer be a given. This would have severe repercussions for the ethical dispositions in general. In his lectures on the philosophy of right from the years 1821 and 1822 Hegel uses drastic words: 'The rabble [*Pöbel*] need not solely be on the side of the poor, as is usually supposed, but can also be on the side of the rich, who can be just as mob-like. There is a rich rabble. Because wealth is a power, and this power of wealth easily becomes a power over the law – the rich can get away with a great deal that would bring shame to anyone else ... One can call this depravity, that the rich take everything to be permissible' (PR 1821/22, § 244).[20]

Hegel draws the following conclusion from these reflections: sooner or later, in any market economy structured by civil law, there will occur developments which make it impossible for many citizens to live in accordance with their ethical dispositions. Some will even lose these dispositions altogether. In such a scenario, society is faced with people with

[19] As is well known, Richard Sennett termed persons who work under such conditions *drifters*: going from job to job, from employment to employment, never having any coherent vocational- or life-history. See Sennett, *The Corrosion of Character* (New York: W. W. Norton, 1998).

[20] On Hegel's theory of the rabble, see the recent publications by Louis Carré, 'Populace, multitude, populus. Figures du peuple dans la *Philosophie du droit* de Hegel', *Tumultes* 40 (2013): 89–107 and Frank Ruda, *Hegel's Rabble: An Investigation into Hegel's Philosophy of Right* (London: Bloomsbury, 2011).

no prospect of employment, who cannot make a living from their work, who are engaged in monotonous and deadening labour, and who have no chance of forging a career but instead drift from one job to the next. These people will not perceive themselves as living in a society where individuals can make themselves 'a member of one of the moments' of that society and 'support [themselves] in this capacity' through *their own* 'activity, diligence, and skill'. On the contrary, such people are likely to believe that the distribution of jobs and incomes boils down to *mere coincidences* or *arbitrary decisions*. This then makes it impossible for people who secure their livelihood with their work to 'gain recognition in [their] own eyes and in the eyes of others' (PR § 207). Consequently, they will develop an attitude that is different from the disposition characteristic of members of civil society and which may, as Hegel suspects, extend to 'inward rebellion against the rich, against society, the government, etc.' (PR § 244A).

Two Options

That markets are, in ethical terms, *ambivalent* is for Hegel a discovery of enormous social and philosophical consequence. If one wants to understand why this is so, one must recall that in the *Philosophy of Right* Hegel holds fast to the following two theses.

(Th-1) The self-determination with which people pursue professional work is an *essential* component of the ethical disposition of members in a modern society.

(Th-2) The self-determination with which people pursue professional work can, in institutional terms, be secured *only* through a market economy structured by civil law.

For present purposes it will suffice to show *that* Hegel defended these two theses.[21] In the light of the discussion in the section on 'The Ethical Disposition of Members of Civil Society', it is unsurprising that Hegel, who takes civil society to be modern, adheres to thesis Th-1 and declares that '[w]hatever an individual wants to undertake in our civil society, whichever way he wishes to benefit society, it must have a form dependent

[21] For more on these issues, see my discussion in 'Personal Respect, Private Property, and Market Economy: What Critical Theory can Learn From Hegel', *Ethical Theory and Moral Practice* 11(5) (2008): 573–586 and 'Personal Freedom without Private Property? Hegel, Marx, and the Frankfurt School', *International Critical Thought* 5(4) (2015): 473–485.

on his subjective freedom' (PR 1821/22, § 237). Moreover, Hegel thinks that the self-determination with which people pursue their work can only be secured institutionally through a market economy structured by civil law (Th-2). In the first part of the *Philosophy of Right*, where he analyses 'abstract right', Hegel remarks that 'reason makes it just as *necessary* that human beings should enter into contractual relationships – giving, exchanging, trading, etc. – as that they should possess property' (PR § 71R). In the subsequent development of his theory of 'civil society' he criticizes the idea of a state-controlled economy with the remark that work 'mediated by [a man's] particular arbitrary will and particular interest' is to be secured by 'the freedom of trade and commerce' (PR § 236R). These statements make it clear, I believe, that Hegel holds fast to the theses laid out above.

Theses Th-1 and Th-2 explain why the ethical ambivalence of markets reconstructed above is so significant for Hegel: he is confronted with the question of whether or not a modern polity can ground a stable form of ethical life accessible to all citizens. In the light of the market's ethically problematic effects it seems that such a form of ethical life can be realized only if at least one of the following two options is available to a modern state.

(O-1) A modern state can establish an ethical practice that is robust and within which participation is possible even for people who have distanced themselves from the ethical disposition characteristic of members of civil society (for instance, due to the experiences they have had as market participants).

(O-2) A modern state can establish institutions which ensure that, in ethical terms, markets have no significant corrosive effects and thus do not jeopardize the formation and maintenance of the ethical disposition of members of civil society.

If neither option is available then it seems a modern state simply *cannot* be an ethical sphere *for all citizens*. It would rather be a place of *fragile ethical life*: people's ability to live in accordance with their ethical dispositions as well as these dispositions themselves would be dependent on market developments which cannot be controlled politically.

The Ethical Disposition of Members of a Well-Ordered State

Is the first option (O-1) available? Can a modern state establish an ethical practice that is robust and within which participation is possible even for people who have distanced themselves from the ethical disposition characteristic of members of civil societies? Following the *Philosophy of Right*, a modern *state*, insofar as it is well ordered, grounds *a specific ethical practice.* This practice goes hand in hand with an ethical disposition on the part of its citizens (*Staatsbürger*) that Hegel sometimes calls 'the political disposition' or 'patriotism in general' (PR § 268). Does this ethical practice have the relevant properties for the first ameliorative option to be available? Is such a practice robust and open to all, even to those who cannot or do not accept the ethical disposition characteristic of members of civil societies? An answer can be found in the following passages from the *Philosophy of Right.* A modern state, writes Hegel, has its 'principle' (PR § 260), its 'essence' (PR § 260A) and its 'strength … in the unity of its universal and ultimate end with the particular interest of individuals, in the fact that they have duties towards the state to the same extent as they also have rights' (PR § 261).

Hegel adds that

> [i]n the process of fulfilling his duty, the individual must somehow attain his own interest and satisfaction or settle his own account, and from his situation within the state, a right must accrue to him whereby the universal cause [*Sache*] becomes his *own particular* cause. Particular interests should certainly not be set aside, let alone suppressed; on the contrary, they should be harmonized with the universal, so that both they themselves and the universal are preserved. The individual … finds that, in fulfilling his duties as a member of the state, he gains protection for his person and property, consideration for his particular welfare, satisfaction of his substantial essence, and the consciousness and self-awareness of being a member of a whole. And through his performance of his duties as services and tasks undertaken on behalf of the state, the state itself is preserved and secured. (PR § 261R)

Accordingly, Hegel takes 'the political disposition, patriotism in general' to be 'trust (which may pass over into more or less educated insight), or the consciousness that my substantial and particular interest is preserved and contained in the interest and end of an other (in this case, the state), and in the latter's relation to me as an individual' (PR § 268).

We can now see what the ethical disposition of members within a well-ordered state involves.[22] Without claiming to provide an exhaustive account, we can say that this disposition contains the following elements.

[22] Another terminological remark: I use expressions such as 'member of a state' or 'member of the state' to translate the world *Staatsbürger* (*citoyen*); likewise I use expressions such as 'member of civil society' to translate the word *Bürger* (*bourgeois*).

(E-7) For a member of a well-ordered modern state, A, it is important that he is effectively recognized ('protected') as a 'person' and 'property' owner by social and state institutions.
(E-8) For A it is important that his 'particular welfare' be taken into account by social and state institutions.
(E-9) For A it is important that he has the 'consciousness and self-awareness' of being a 'member' of the state as a 'whole'.

If one adopts Hegel's terminology, then elements E-7 and E-8 represent A's 'particular interest' while element E-9 represents his 'substantial interest'.

Moreover, as can be inferred from the passages cited in this section, A's 'disposition' has the following elements.

(E-10) A believes himself to have a normatively justified claim ('a right') that social and state institutions be such that his 'particular interest' and his 'substantial interest' are fulfilled or can be fulfilled by him.
(E-11) A believes that social and state institutions are such that his 'particular interest' and his 'substantial interest' are fulfilled or can be fulfilled by him. (In Hegel's words, A believes that his 'interest is preserved and contained in the interest and end' of the state as a 'whole'.)
(E-12) A believes that the legal 'duties' which he has as a member of the state are legitimate.
(E-13) A is willing to fulfil the legal 'duties' which he has as a member of the state.

According to Hegel, the ethical disposition in question is part of an institutionalized practice through which A, in fulfilling his civic duties, not only consciously contributes to the 'preservation' (*Erhalt*) of the state but also comes to perceive that his 'particular' and 'substantial' interests are satisfied. For this reason Hegel claims that, in a well-ordered state, the 'universal end' – namely, the continued existence of the state in its institutional structure – and the 'interest[s] of the individual' form a 'unity'.

What is the conceptual relation between the ethical disposition of members of the state and the ethical disposition of the members of civil society? Can people who have distanced themselves from *this* disposition – for instance, as a result of experiences they have had in markets – develop or maintain the ethical disposition characteristic of members of a well-ordered state? Is this even possible?

Hegel's answer to this question is unequivocal. It comes to light when one realizes precisely what the 'particular welfare' of a member in a modern state involves. If one follows Hegel's own account (see PR §§ 260–268), then what we have analysed above as 'doing X' forms *an essential component* of this kind of welfare. In other words, that which is important to people as members of a civil society, that which they believe they should do in virtue of being such members, is also something that is an intrinsic part of their 'welfare' as members of the state. On the basis of this finding, we can derive from elements E-8, E-10 and E-11 the following constituents of the ethical disposition among state members.

(E-8′) For A it is important to do X.
(E-10′) A believes himself to have, in normative terms, a claim that social and state institutions should be such that he can do X.
(E-11′) A believes that social and state institutions are such that he can do X.

From these considerations, two conclusions may be drawn.

(1) People who have distanced themselves from the ethical disposition characteristic of members of civil society *cannot* develop or maintain the ethical disposition that characterizes members of a well-ordered state. From their perspective, they simply do not find importance in something that is highly important for those who have the ethical disposition of state members: doing X or, to quote Hegel again, '[b]y a process of self-determination', making themselves a member of a moment of civil society through their 'activity, diligence, and skill', and supporting themselves in this capacity.[23] People who, as a result of their experiences in markets, reject the ethical disposition found among members of civil societies thus cannot participate in the ethical practice of the modern state because they lack its accompanying disposition.
(2) Whoever has the ethical disposition characteristic of members of a well-ordered state is convinced that social and political institutions are such that he can do X (E-11′). Cases of deception aside, this conviction can exist only if social and state institutions *actually*

[23] Or, put differently, E-1 = E-8′. And: whoever has distanced himself (completely) from the ethical disposition of a member of civil society rejects E-1/E-8′, and whoever shares the ethical disposition of a member of a well-ordered state adheres to E-1/E-8′. Therefore, those who have distanced themselves from the ethical disposition of a member of civil society cannot share the ethical disposition of a member of a well-ordered state.

have the required shape. Now this condition, as explained above, is only very inadequately fulfilled by markets structured by civil law. If the ethical disposition is to be open to all citizens, it is thus necessary for markets to be stabilized through *additional institutions* so that they do not have any ethically problematic effects. Only then can the ethical practice fostered by the state and the ethical dispositions that go hand in hand with it be robust and resistant to crises.

Hegel himself was fully aware of these considerations. In his view, a modern state cannot prevent citizens who are continually unable to do X from developing an attitude of rejection and indignation – something that can be explained in terms of the frustration of the claim contained in element E-10′. Accordingly, it is within those 'institutions' which enable citizens to secure their 'particular interest' or 'particular welfare' that Hegel sees the 'firm foundation of the state and of the trust and disposition of individuals towards it' (PR § 265). If this foundation is missing, the state will probably founder:

> What matters most is … that my particular end should become identical with the universal; otherwise, the state must hang in the air … It has often been said that the end of the state is the happiness of its citizens. This is certainly true, for if their welfare is deficient, if their subjective ends are not satisfied, and if they do not find that the state as such is the means to this satisfaction, the state itself stands on an insecure footing. (PR § 265A)

This provides an answer to the question posed at the start of this section. If one follows Hegel's thoughts, then the first option (O-1) is *not* available to a modern state since the ethical practice it promotes is *not* open to citizens who have distanced themselves from the ethical disposition characteristic of members of civil society. Hegel's discussion thus raises a question we have already encountered: is option O-2 available to a modern state? Only if it is would the state be able to stabilize the ethical practices and dispositions of citizens as members of both civil society and the state. And only then could it count on their consent and avoid 'stand[ing] on an insecure footing' or 'hang[ing] in the air'.

Markets, Corporations and the Police

Can a modern state establish institutions that ensure that markets have no significantly detrimental ethical effects? In the light of his remarks in the *Philosophy of Right* one can see that Hegel gives a nuanced response to this question. On the one hand, he takes the position that states have the capacity to influence market-economic developments in accordance with the requirements of citizens' ethical dispositions; on the other, he is also convinced that states lack the capacity to solve the ethical problems arising from markets. The reasons Hegel has for adopting this standpoint shall be examined in the remainder of this section.

The institutions through which a modern state can influence market developments are, in Hegel's view, the 'police' and the 'corporations'. It should be emphasized that for Hegel the police is not only responsible for investigating and foiling crimes but also has an economic role: 'regulating' (PR § 236) market relations.[24] In contrast, the corporation is a *company-* or *enterprise-based* institution with a specific form of organization. As Hegel repeatedly makes clear, when he uses the terms 'police' and 'corporation' he is not referring to concrete historical phenomena – for instance, the police and corporate institutions that formed in several European countries during the Middle Ages or the Early Modern period.[25] What then does Hegel mean when referring to the police or corporations?[26]

Corporations, writes Hegel, are institutions which, 'under the supervision of the public authority' of the state, exercise the right 'to admit members in accordance with their objective qualification of skill and rectitude and in numbers determined by the universal context, to protect its members against particular contingencies, and to educate others so as to make them eligible for membership' (PR § 252). Corporations thereby ensure that a 'livelihood' and the 'capability' of achieving it are 'guaranteed' and 'recognized' so that 'the member of a corporation has no need to demonstrate his competence and his regular income and means of support – i.e. the fact that he is somebody – by any further external evidence. In this way, it is also recognized that he belongs to a whole which is itself a member of society in general, and that he has an interest in, and endeavours to promote, the less selfish end of this whole' (PR § 253).

[24] This understanding of the tasks of the police derives from cameralism, one of the main currents in economic thought in central Europe in the centuries before the French Revolution. On changes in thinking about the police during Hegel's lifetime see, for instance, Naoko Matsumoto, *Polizeibegriff im Umbruch. Staatszwecklehre und Gewaltenteilungspraxis in der Reichs- und Rheinbundpublizistik* (Frankfurt am Main: Klostermann, 1999).

[25] See PR § 236A, § 255A and § 290A.

[26] On this topic, see also Thomas Klikauer, *Hegel's Moral Corporation* (Basingstoke: Palgrave Macmillan, 2015).

Thus a corporation is an institution that recruits its members according to their 'skill' or 'capability', on the basis of universal and transparent ('objective') criteria. It operates an insurance system offering members financial protection against 'contingencies' such as illness or accident or age-related disability, and it ensures further professional training and development for its members (to 'make them eligible for membership' and to enable them to remain so). The necessary legal powers for all this are created by the 'public authority', that is, the state.

If one follows Hegel's line of thought, then it is understandable why a corporation enables its 'members' to lead an ethical life. A company constituted as a corporation lets members do what is important to them (see elements E-1 and E-8′) and what they believe they should do (E-3). Moreover, in rendering its recruitment criteria public, the corporation makes it possible for members to be recognized for what they do not only within the corporation but also by members of society outside the corporation. In that way, it not only fulfils a claim which its members have as citizens (E-10′) and makes it possible for them to uphold the corresponding conviction (E-11′), but also strengthens its members' 'interest' in the corporation and gives them reasons to adopt an attitude towards the state which includes elements E-12 and E-13. A corporation, it would thus seem, meets all the requirements of the ethical dispositions analysed above and is thus capable of giving the state a 'firm foundation' (PR § 265).

However, corporations exist in a market landscape. Hegel himself emphasizes this fact when, in the citation above, he points to 'the universal context' in which a corporation finds itself. This implies that a corporation cannot determine the prices at which it buys and sells; both the price of goods which it processes and the price of goods which it produces will depend on the overall demand for goods and the overall supply of goods (see the section on 'Why Markets Are Ethically Ambivalent' above, point 6). Consequently a corporation operates in an environment which it cannot control and where its existence is at risk from a variety of events and developments (for instance, changes in demand, technological innovations which make qualified work superfluous, or competition from companies with non-corporative forms of organization). In other words, as a company that enables its 'members' to lead an ethical life, the corporation *cannot* secure its own survival. This raises the question of whether the state can establish institutions that would perform this function.

It is here that Hegel's discussion of the police comes in. In economic-policy terms, the police has the task, through 'regulating' (PR § 236) market relations, of contributing to people being able to lead an ethical life. Or, as Hegel puts it, '[t]he aim of oversight and provisions on the part of the police is to mediate between the individual and the universal possibility [*allgemeines Vermögen*] which is available for the attainment of individual ends' (PR § 236A).

What powers should the police have in Hegel's view? On the one hand, Hegel is convinced that the police can carry out their aforementioned task only if they are authorized to take measures to improve the infrastructure (PR § 236A), provide tax incentives for companies to relocate (PR § 252R), take precautions to protect consumers (PR 1821–22, § 235), and make provision for preventive health care and schooling (PR § 239A). On the other hand, Hegel makes it clear that he thinks it will be impossible to give a definitive answer to the question of which powers the police should have: 'the more precise determinations will depend on custom, the spirit of the rest of the constitution, prevailing conditions, current emergencies, etc.' (PR § 234).

Can the police regulate the market environment surrounding corporations so that their continued existence is assured? If one follows Hegel closely, it is clear that this is *not* the case. Where markets exist, there exists also the structural possibility that economic developments will occur which the police cannot even roughly predict (see the section on 'Why Markets Are Ethically Ambivalent', point 6). As a result, what Hegel refers to as the 'oversight' exercised by the police is necessarily incomplete. For this reason alone their 'provisions' – that is, what the police do to avert or mitigate problematic economic developments – will always run the risk of being *inefficient*. Because of their limited knowledge – of current economic conditions and the effects of their own actions – the police can thus only secure the ethical life of the people in a way that 'must always be incomplete' (PR § 237). Moreover, if they wanted to render this kind of security 'more complete', the police would have to take measures which would themselves be *ethically problematic* – such as restricting people's aforementioned entitlements (see the section on 'The Ethical Disposition of Members of Civil Society') to the point where they could no longer have a consciousness that they were working from their own 'self-determination' and that they were adequately protected as 'persons and owners of property' (see above, element E-7). For these reasons, the police may well contribute to the continued existence of corporations; but permanently securing their existence is far beyond their power.

All of which goes to show that in Hegel's view the ethical life of members of a modern polity is *fragile*. Even when he does not formulate this view explicitly, it follows directly from the considerations we have reconstructed here. As we have seen, Hegel believes that the requirements of the ethical dispositions of members of civil society and the state can be secured only through markets structured by civil law, while he is also of the conviction that markets have ethically problematic effects which modern states can avert or mitigate only in very limited ways. From a Hegelian point of view, the modern world therefore cannot be a place of institutional stability or ethical perfection. As long as markets are an ethical requirement, they will repeatedly confront us with the task of finding institutional arrangements that – as far as possible – prevent harmful developments and – as far as possible – allow us to live a good life.[27]

[27] Special thanks are due to Max Cherem, David James and Michael Quante for helpful comments on earlier versions of my essay and to Adrian Wilding for his translation of the German manuscript into English.

CHAPTER 8

That Which Makes Itself: Hegel, Rabble and Consequences

Frank Ruda

You have a reputation of being alive, but you are dead.

The Revelation to John, 3:1

A Hegelian Bomb

In § 244 of his *Elements of the Philosophy of Right* Hegel introduces what he refers to as 'the rabble', the *Pöbel*. It is this peculiar, and seemingly and allegedly marginal, 'topic' of Hegel's thought that can ultimately show why an early formulation of Hegel applies to (the late) Hegel himself. At one point between the ages of thirty-three and thirty-six Hegel wrote in his so-called *Wastebook* that 'original, completely wonderful works of education [*Bildung*] resemble a bomb, which falls into a lazy city in which everyone sits in front of their beer-mug and is extremely wise and does not sense that it is their flat well-being that caused the very crash of thunder' (*Werke* 2: 550). In what follows I will argue that Hegel's *Elements of the Philosophy of Right* resembles such a bomb: a bomb whose explosive character derives, at least partially, from the issue of the rabble. How could this be? This has already been argued in a similar vein by Domenico Losurdo,[1] who contended that the *Philosophy of Right* was immediately after its publication perceived as containing some highly explosive material because of Hegel's theory of the corporation. This very theory, as Losurdo reconstructs it, implies the sketch of an organizational model and a conception of a political instrument for the working class in the very historical moment of its formation, a sketch of a proto-trade union that would enable the working class to distance itself from the ossified structures of the mediaeval guild system and to influence economic factors such as working hours, wages and further general factors linked to the workers' interests.

[1] Domenico Losurdo, *Zwischen Hegel und Bismarck. Die achtundvierziger Revolution und die Krise der deutschen Kultur* (Berlin: Akademie Verlag, 1993), 157–234.

This would already be enough – considering the state of Prussia in the 1830s – to justify reading the *Philosophy of Right* as a metaphorical bomb. And it led, for example, Rudolf Haym in his *Hegel and His Time* (1857)[2] to formulate his famous criticism of Hegel for being an apologist of the Prussian state. Yet it is important to remark that Haym was a proponent of the liberal-bourgeois camp that emphasized first and foremost the individual realization of freedom in the sphere of the market and whose domain is economic competition. And it is precisely Hegel's depiction of the practical results of such an interpretation of freedom that allows the explosiveness of Hegel's text to be related to the issue of the rabble. Hegel demonstrates the contradictory and self-destructive outcome of the individualist and liberal interpretation of freedom when realized in and as the world of bourgeois market dynamics, that is, as civil society. And he recapitulates the contradictory nature of this conception of freedom in the following thesis: those societies in which there is a necessary connection between the free inner self-determination of all subjects (an idea historically brought about by the Reformation[3]) and the universal legal equality that provides the very objective conditions for subjective self-determination (an idea whose historical origin lies in the French Revolution[4]), that is, *modern societies, necessarily generate poverty* precisely because of the connection between the aforementioned principles which make these societies modern. Poverty is, as Hegel shows, a phenomenon that therefore has, as much as the societies confronted with it, a distinctively modern quality. It is specifically related to what is modern about modernity, namely the possibility, that is legally guaranteed to everyone, of realizing his or her own freedom in a self-determining manner – at least in the minimal form of earning one's own subsistence through one's own labour in the domain of civil society, the 'system of all-round interdependence' (PR § 183), that is, the market.

As Hegel stated in one of his lectures on the history of philosophy: before Luther 'poverty was considered to stand higher than living

[2] Rudolf Haym, *Hegel und seine Zeit. Vorlesungen über Entstehung und Entwicklung, Wesen und Wert der Hegelschen Philosophie* (Leipzig: Heims, 1973). This is a criticism that has been taken up – in a similarly unconvincing manner – by Ernst Tugendhat, see Ernst Tugendhat, *Self-Consciousness and Self-Determination*, trans. Paul Stern (Cambridge, MA: MIT Press, 1989), and even by Adorno, who considers the *Philosophy of Right* to be 'awkwardly ideological'. See Theodor W. Adorno, *Hegel: Three Studies*, trans. Shierry Weber Nicholsen (Cambridge, MA: MIT Press, 1993), 131.

[3] See Joachim Ritter, 'Hegel und die Reformation', in *Metaphysik und Politik. Studien zu Aristoteles und Hegel* (Frankfurt am Main: Suhrkamp, 2003), 310–320.

[4] See the best book on Hegel and the French Revolution, Rebecca Comay, *Mourning Sickness: Hegel and the French Revolution* (Stanford, CA: Stanford University Press, 2010).

from the labour of one's own hands but now [after the Reformation and also in modernity *tout court*, FR] it is known that poverty is an aim that is not more ethical than labour. Rather, it is *more* ethical to live from one's labour and to be happy about what one brings before oneself' (*Werke* 20: 49). And this is why it can be stated that 'The important question of how poverty can be remedied is one which agitates and torments modern societies especially' (PR § 244A). Poverty agitates and torments the moderns and it outrages all those who do not want to hear and accept it – and this is one aspect of the *Philosophy of Right*'s explosiveness. It angers those who believe, as Hegel once smugly remarked, that the 'most direct means of dealing with poverty' is 'to leave the poor to their fate and direct them to beg from the public' (PR § 245R). It is not overly difficult to attribute this position to the liberal bourgeoisie of Hegel's time, which was then in the process of formation. But, unlike this liberal bourgeoisie, Hegel does not shy away from confronting the contradictory nature of modernity and modern societies. He even explicitly demonstrates that modern civil society from a certain historical moment of its own economic development onwards is not able to uphold its own principle without giving rise to a contradiction.

Although civil society holds that each of its members ought to gain his or her subsistence through the investment of his or her own labour power – this is a principle of civil society – Hegel's conceptual diagnosis shows that civil society produces the contradiction that all *ought* to subsist in this way at the same time as it makes it impossible that all *can* actually subsist in this way.[5] For civil society produces poverty, which Hegel defines as a state in which all the advantages of civil society are lost, but all the desires generated by it persist. Although Hegel discusses a series of solutions to the problem of poverty,[6] he clearly indicates that none of them is really able to overcome this problem. Rather, an even greater problem is generated, one that for Hegel goes under the name of the 'rabble'. One can thus see that the explosive character of Hegel's conceptual elaboration of the nature of civil society is directly linked to the unmasking of a fundamental problem of modernity (poverty) and its consequence, namely the rabble.[7]

[5] Another manner of putting this in very profane terms is to say that civil society necessarily produces unemployment – whatever its current historical rates, it is a systemic effect.

[6] He discusses redistribution of wealth, colonization, public begging, civil society taking care of the poor, the right of necessity (*Notrecht*), the corporation and the police. I will return to some of them.

[7] Hegel does not therefore – as Shlomo Avineri has argued – simply leave the problem of poverty unresolved; rather, he shows that modern civil society can offer no solution to the problem of poverty and this is why it is a real and tormenting problem. See Shlomo Avineri, *Hegel's Theory of the*

Rabble, *sui generis*

How tormenting the problem of poverty and its consequences are becomes intelligible when one takes into account one of the options that Hegel considers for dealing with this problem, namely, to leave the poor to their destiny and 'direct them to beg from the public' (PR § 245R). He immediately notices that any man who had once begged would soon lose the habit of working and also begin to believe that he is entitled to live without working. It is precisely in this manner that the poor person would become part of the rabble. The rabble is therefore in a first rendering the poor person who has lost more than just his property, that is, also the insight into the necessity of labour and the honour of earning his own subsistence through his own labour. But the individual who belongs to the rabble thereby also loses belief in the legitimacy and functioning of this very principle of civil society (as he or she sees that it is not functioning consistently, but produces contradiction, and also sees that one might be able to live from public begging). Poverty, as a necessary product of the economic dynamic of civil society, provides therefore the constantly given condition of the possibility of the rabble's emergence, of a social existence without honour. Although Hegel characterizes the rabble in terms of a series of losses additional to the material loss that is poverty – the rabble is work-shy, without shame and honour, and lazy – the rabble is at the same time not a necessary consequence of being in poverty. Here one defining feature that Eduard Gans in his additional notes to Hegel's lectures assigns to the rabble needs to be taken absolutely seriously, because it was added in a truly Hegelian spirit, namely, that the rabble 'makes itself' (PR § 244A)[8] – it makes itself precisely through an additional loss, and this is what (onto-)logically distinguishes the individual who is part of the rabble from the poor person. Poverty is a necessary product of the historically self-specifying and self-differentiating movement of modern civil society – and thus not based on individual mistakes or misdeeds, although it may be so with regard to the particular case of an individual destiny. There is necessarily poverty because modern societies function as they do.[9] Fredric

Modern State (Cambridge: Cambridge University Press, 1972). For an extensive exploration of the theme of the rabble in Hegel, see Frank Ruda, *Hegel's Rabble: An Investigation into Hegel's Philosophy of Right* (London: Continuum, 2011).

[8] I have here altered the misleading translation that the rabble 'defines itself automatically …' (PR § 244A). The passage reads as follows: 'The lowest level of subsistence, that of the rabble [*die des Pöbels*], defines itself automatically, but this minimum varies greatly between different peoples'.

[9] This is a consequence that the state of the understanding – civil society – cannot avoid. This Hegelian insight is today obviously still valid.

Jameson has shown that Marx had argued along these lines that *the* problem of capitalism is therefore unemployment,[10] which is in this context just another name for what Hegel describes as poverty. For Marx, there is a problem for any society organized under the capitalist mode of production, which arises from the fact that capitalism cannot ensure the subsistence of all its members through labour, although it officially claims to do so, but in reality thrives on the very contradiction it produces. And, as one can see, this is already Hegel's insight. Civil society functions only by contradicting its own principle, which is why poverty exists.

This is why one should emphasize that, although poverty is a necessary product of society, the rabble is self-generating, *sui generis*. That is to say, the rabble does not necessarily appear (although the social condition of its possibility is necessary), but appears contingently. This also means that the poor and the rabble are distinct – a distinction that finds itself repeated in the distinction between the working class in general and the proletariat in Marx (a distinction which has as often gone unnoticed as the one in Hegel). The rabble emerges only when a contingent attitude supplements the necessary condition, that is, when through the addition of a subjective attitude that entails a further loss (of honour, etc.) the rabble makes itself on the basis of the condition of poverty. For 'poverty in itself does not reduce people to a rabble; a rabble is created only by the disposition associated with poverty, by inward indignation [*Empörung*] against the rich, against society, the government, etc.' (PR § 244A; translation modified). Thus the attitude of the rabble is designated by the name 'indignation'. Why indignation – an attitude or conviction that Hegel also characterizes as a 'conviction without rights' (VPR 3: 703)? One can answer this question by reformulating Hegel's point. If poverty is a necessary product of civil society and does not depend on individual misdeeds, any member of civil society is latently poor. If anyone can become poor, everyone in civil society is latently poor.[11] And if the rabble makes itself contingently by developing an attitude that supplements the fact of being in poverty, one can infer that any poor person can transform him- or herself into

[10] Fredric Jameson, *Representing Capital: A Reading of Volume One* (London and New York: Verso, 2010).

[11] The actuality of Hegel's thesis can be seen at work in the recent diagnosis offered by Jean-Claude Milner that today the bourgeoisie is ultimately nothing but 'salaried bourgeoisie'. This means that the modern market dynamic even overcomes objective – and sociologically describable – class sedimentations. The members of what appears to be the bourgeois class, say bankers, brokers, etc.– even if relatively rich now – can lose their status easily, simply when they lose their jobs. This is due to the fact that, as Milner argues, somehow anyone could actually do their job. See Jean-Claude Milner, *Clartés de tout* (Paris: Verdier, 2011).

part of the rabble. This means that everyone in civil society is latently poor and therefore latently rabble. Or, more precisely, everyone will have been latently rabble. Why this peculiar temporality? One here needs the future anterior because the logical insight into the fact that there is this redoubled kind of latency is an effect of the very emergence of the rabble. But what is the rabble? One can characterize it more precisely by looking at its attitude (*Gesinnung*), that is, its indignation.

The Indignant (and the Corrupt) of the Earth

Hegel further defines the content of the rabble's indignation by stating that the rabble deprives the state and all its institutions of their legitimacy. The rabble thereby devalues the rationality of the existing state of things and denies them the right to exist. Such a devaluation and denial can take two different shapes, but Hegel refers to only one of them in terms of indignation. The distinction between two forms of depreciating the existing institutions also allows Hegel to distinguish between two types of rabble. What are they? The first is, as stated, a possible consequence of poverty and is characterized by its indignation, and I will return to it. To introduce the second type of rabble a short detour will prove instructive. For Hegel civil society is organized into different estates and participation in one of them is necessary for each of its members. Outside these estates one's subsistence cannot be attained in an adequate manner – everyone needs to have a job, so to speak, and anyone standing outside the estates is for Hegel 'merely a private person' (PR § 207A). Private persons can thereby be differentiated into two categories, namely *those who are involuntarily* and *those who are voluntarily* private persons. In short, there are the poor and what Hegel calls the gamblers (PR 1821/22, 230).

Anyone can *involuntarily* become poor, whereas one can become a gambler only if one *voluntarily and arbitrarily* decides to satisfy one's interests solely on one's own and not with others in a corporation. The gambler assumes that he or she alone – even without a job and thus without proper qualification – will nonetheless make a living, and he or she bets on the contingent movement of the existing economy. Such a decision relies on the hope that because of good luck one will contingently – say through winnings gained in the stock market – secure one's subsistence. But this is a highly particular form of reasoning, because a gambler him- or herself needs some stock to start with – and, if it is not earned through the investment of his or her own labour, it is a contingent and particular(izing) condition from the very start. If in the economic game such success is then achieved, the gambler immediately and necessarily assumes an attitude that Hegel calls 'corruptness' (PR 1821/22, 223), which not only depends on objectively contingent events (and is therefore objectively and not subjectively contingent) but also makes him or her into a representative of the second kind of rabble (without making itself) that I call the *luxury rabble*.

Luxury is a name for a specific kind of possession (and not property), namely, the arbitrary form of possession enjoyed by the member of the rich rabble, the former gambler, the now-lucky winner. The luxury rabble also deprives nearly all existing institutions of their right and their legitimacy, but fundamentally does not devalue one of them, namely the one on which its own existence relies, that is, the arbitrary dynamic of the market. The luxury rabble is therefore fundamentally determined by several arbitrary factors: (1) the arbitrary existence of a certain stock it can invest in a type of gambling; (2) the arbitrary decision to gamble and to stand outside the estates; (3) the arbitrary logic of the act of gambling itself; and, therefore, also (4) arbitrary success by means of this act. And this concatenation of arbitrariness is continually repeated, simply because any actual winnings will one day be spent and without a job the luxury rabble can only repeatedly return to gambling and hope to reconstitute itself as a luxury rabble.[12] The rich rabble is corrupted by arbitrariness and particularity.[13] Yet this does not hold for the poor rabble.

The poor rabble is indignant and its indignation is directed at the conditions of its own possibility. That is to say, it is outraged that poverty exists, because poverty marks its own condition of existence. And it infers from this that an ethical–political community which does not prevent the emergence of this condition of existence is therefore itself ultimately an illegitimate accumulation of self-seeking interests without any rational and actual universality. The poor rabble sees the rich rabble everywhere. For it the whole of society assumes the form of the rich rabble, of a corrupted existence that exists in a merely arbitrary fashion, without universality. This explains the rabble's 'inward indignation against the rich, against society, the government, etc.'. The rabble is indignant because it perceives itself to be in a 'state that lacks rights [*Rechtlosigkeit*]' (PR 1821/22, 222), which falsely presents itself as, and appears to be, a state of right. The rabble is indignant because it takes the condition of its own existence

[12] A longer account of the luxury rabble – in which I mainly focus on two aspects of its arbitrariness – can be found in Ruda, *Hegel's Rabble*, 49–74.

[13] As Hegel states, 'One can call this corruptness that the rich person assumes himself to be at liberty to do anything' (PR 1821/22, 223). Also relevant in this context is the claim that 'Everything in the world that has been corrupted, has been corrupted on good grounds' (EL § 121A).

as proof that civil society is a gigantic masquerade. A society that proclaims its own universality without the existence of any actual universality within it is unmasked by the rabble's verdict on it. The rabble unmasks the masquerade of a civil society not simply because it is its 'victim', but rather also because the rabble points towards a dimension that includes potentially everyone and thereby makes it possible to think of a non-exclusive, that is, actual, universality that would be as universal as Hegel's sphere of ethical life within the state (as anyone is latently poor and any poor person is latently rabble). But it is important to remark here that this claim cannot be found in Hegel's text, although it can be derived from it.

Why does one not find this claim in Hegel's *Philosophy of Right*? Here the reader of Hegel's *Philosophy of Right* has three options. Option 1 is that Hegel simply did not see what he himself had excavated conceptually and therefore one can, and therefore should, identify this consequence in a completely Hegelian spirit – this would mean trying to be more Hegelian than Hegel himself was concerning the rabble. Option 2 is that one could argue that, for the concept of the state that he presents, the rabble is no problem at all and that Hegel is therefore completely justified in not inferring anything from its existence. Finally, option 3 is that one could argue that one can and should develop the consequences of the rabble concept that Hegel did not develop, but at the same time one should emphasize that these consequences, although they demonstrate an internal limitation of the concept of the state that Hegel presents, ultimately prove a Hegelian point: namely, they offer a reason why the state that Hegel depicts will at a certain point perish and decay, just as all individuals, all individual states have a life that begins, expands and ends. The rabble could then be taken to be one (and maybe not the only) conceptual explanation of why the withering away of the Hegelian state conceptually has or had to take place. Let me deal with these readings successively.

The First Reading of the Rabble: Hegel against Hegel

The first reading of the rabble can emphasize the following point: Hegel clearly notes that civil society is driven into the contradictory production of poverty but he cannot (or for some reason simply does not) understand the tormenting effects of its contradictory nature as he should have done according to his own dialectical method. In other words, because Hegel does not infer what he should infer from what is implicitly present in the concept of the rabble, paradoxically, in and for Hegel the rabble itself does infer precisely what he himself did not infer. The thought of the rabble thus necessarily implies that one should (and cannot but) be more Hegelian than Hegel. The groundwork for this is provided by a reading of the contradictory nature of civil society as something that will not be dealt with and sublated in or by the state and its internal as well as external ethical institutions. One can rather, as a Hegelian, but against Hegel himself, side with the rabble's judgement that if the production of poverty cannot be avoided this makes the totality of the socio-political system in which it exists into a system of injustice. Although Hegel clearly observes that poverty is a condition in which one lacks the very possibility of realizing one's own freedom, and although he also demonstrates that this deficiency, this *impossibility* (of realizing one's own freedom),[14] is unavoidable, i.e. *necessary* as well as being artificially produced, he does not conceptually understand this deficiency as an injustice. For, if he had drawn this conclusion, civil society, 'the *world of appearance* of the ethical' (PR § 181) in its totality would have turned out to be a gigantic concatenation of injustices, which incessantly produces the impossibility of universally validating (i.e. for all) the very principle on which civil society relies. The rabble, on the other hand, does not hesitate to draw this conclusion, and its indignation at the existing state of things is the very expression of this conclusion. This legitimizes the rabble's claim to a right to subsist without labour, since it cannot, *de facto*, subsist by labouring. But to claim such a right can only appear irrational to Hegel, since he links the very concept of right to the notion of the free will, which can only be what it is, that is, free, when it realizes itself through the activity of labour (which is precisely what the rabble does not perform). To demand a right to subsistence without labour implies for Hegel that one assumes a right which neither has nor is able to have the universality or the objective validity found in the concept of right. This is why he consequentially characterizes the rabble as a particularity which unbinds itself from all relations of right and duty, and thus adheres to mere particularity.[15] Yet the rabble, for the simple reason that everyone is latently poor and latently rabble, is not only a particularity. This means that the right that the rabble claims is not simply a particular right; rather it embodies something like a concrete universality, in that it has a latent universal dimension. In its very expression – in its

[14] Hegel had earlier already defined poverty as the 'impossibility of bringing something in front of oneself [*etwas vor sich zu bringen*]' (JR, 232).

[15] Hegel: 'If a man makes himself to be without rights and also keeps himself unbound from duties … then this is the rabble' (PR 1821/22, 222). One can see here why Gans' addition that the rabble makes itself is in a fully Hegelian spirit simply because it seems to have been used by Hegel himself in the context of the rabble several times.

indignation – it points towards an organization of freedom and equality beyond the existing order – an organization that Hegel is unable to see, although it would represent a genuinely Hegelian insight. Hegel cannot accept such an idea, because he fundamentally seeks to depict the rationality of a stable statist organization that is able to deal with internal contradiction; hence his need to criticize the rabble's claim as a mere particular claim without any true relevance. Against Hegel, the first reading thus insists with Hegel on another end to the conceptual unfolding that Hegel himself presents.

The Second Reading of the Rabble: The State against the Rabble

The second reading of the rabble would seek to oppose the first one on a couple of points. It would emphasize that the rabble is not a problem for Hegel simply because his whole point is that the sphere in which the rabble can emerge, namely civil society, is contradictory (contradiction is implied in its very concept) and the rabble thereby simply manifests and embodies precisely the contradictions that Hegel wanted to present. Therefore Hegel does not shy away from the contradictions of civil society (which are most radically embodied in the rabble); rather, they are precisely what he wanted to depict so as to show the inherent (conceptual) unsustainability of civil society considered by itself. These contradictions make intelligible why Hegel can contend that civil society is driven beyond its own limits (PR § 246), and this is to say (through the contradiction in its concept) that it goes beyond itself into the conceptual realm of the state. What the presentation of the inherent impasses and obstacles faced by civil society is supposed to demonstrate is ultimately nothing but the necessity of the state. Therefore it is precisely the concept of the state that Hegel can derive from these impasses. The rabble is no problem for Hegel because it merely belongs to the sphere of civil society and, as the state overcomes and sublates its inconsistencies, the problem of the rabble is overcome in the very same move. The rabble is the name for a necessary problem, yet not for Hegel but for civil society. He can even hail its existence, since because of it he can infer the move from civil society to the state.

Here a problem arises: this second reading completely holds for the role of poverty in Hegel's conception of civil society. He does not have a conceptual problem with the contradictions of civil society, and one can argue that this is why the state is necessary. But even if the state can be conceptually derived from the contradictions of civil society, if the state is not itself able to solve the problem of poverty and poverty becomes something subjective in the form of indignation (this is what happens with the rabble), the possibility of the claim that the rabble articulates is constantly present even within the state. Therefore, the state does not solve the problem of the rabble. The claim that there is still a contradiction within the state – namely in its appearance as civil society – is not done away with and hence the problematic nature of the rabble remains. One can thus see that there is a twofold logical movement: one that starts from civil society, traverses poverty as the embodiment of its contradictory constitution, and ends in the state; another that starts from civil society and via poverty ends in the rabble. This is to say that the rabble and the state appear on the same logical level and hence the former is not simply a problem of civil society. For it appears conceptually and logically precisely where the state appears and therefore should be discussed on the same level. The rabble is therefore more – and somehow less – than an embodiment of the contradiction of civil society. This is because, precisely as much as the state does, it points to the possibility of resolving the contradiction of civil society, and the rabble-sublation of this contradiction therefore stands in a direct relation to (or maybe even in conceptual competition with) the state.

A proponent of the second reading could here then insist that this reply itself relies on the problematic assumption that the condition of the possibility of the rabble is not done away with by the emergence of the state. Yet this is what Hegel seeks to demonstrate, since, with the conceptual emergence of the state (which for Hegel is 'logically' there from the very beginning, but I have to leave this aside), institutions emerge that deal with and overcome the very conditions of the possibility of the rabble and thus solve the problem. The two institutions that Hegel locates in this transition are the police and the corporation. So what about them? The corporation generates a common property which allows for those of its members who have fallen into poverty to be provided for by it. Yet the problem concerning the corporation is that of the second-generation poor, say, since participation in the corporation implies mastery of one's profession or trade and hence those without one must remain outside it. Those who constantly lack employment and whose children lack education (*Bildung*) and employment are not, and conceptually cannot be, subsidized by any corporation.

The police – a complex notion in which resonates the whole range of the so-called '*Policeywissenschaft*' of Hegel's times[16] – also does not provide

[16] For this concept, see Mark Neocleous, *The Fabrication of Social Order: A Critical Theory of Power* (London: Pluto Press, 2000).

a rigid means of preventing poverty from arising. Why not? Firstly, because it operates according to the determination and on the ground of the dynamic of civil society and can thereby only seek to tame and limit its contradictory effects. And secondly, it is an institution that is inherently determined not only by the arbitrariness of the market but also by the arbitrariness of the judgements of actual policemen. In short, neither of the two state institutions can do what the second reading claims they are able to do.

Ultimately, a proponent of the second reading could seek recourse to a final way out by emphasizing that, even if Hegel's state institutions do not provide a proper way out of the problem of poverty and the rabble, there is the right of necessity (*Notrecht*), the *ius necessitas*. Such an interpretation would then emphasize how in § 127 of his *Philosophy of Right*, where he introduces the right of necessity, Hegel also implicitly demonstrates that an individual who is part of the rabble and suffers injustice does indeed have a right to claim his or her right and that, if it is refused to him or her, he or she is entitled to draw certain practical conclusions from this. The right of necessity thereby turns into a right to have rights,[17] into a right of revolution whose subjects are all those who are excluded from what was promised them (namely, that they could subsist by means of their own labour power). The right of necessity would thereby be a right to transform the present state fundamentally into a new and better one: a right to revolutionize the state within the state that is inscribed into the state. And Hegel certainly does claim that the right of necessity should protect individuals from becoming victims of the existing system of right (an insight that is linked to his critique of Roman Law). The right of necessity is without doubt the right not to be violated by existing right if one has out of necessity committed a wrong. Yet the right of necessity is a positive right that appears within the constitution of the state and it essentially means that if one has violated the existing system of right out of necessity (because, say, one would have otherwise died from hunger) one does *not have to be* punished.[18] But it is also clear that Hegel conceptually links the application of this right only to particular cases within the existing system of rights, that is, to a court of law that decides that someone is not to be punished for something which otherwise would have been a crime.

[17] For this, see Werner Hamacher, 'The Right to Have Rights (Four-and-a-Half-Remarks)', *The South Atlantic Quarterly*, 103(2/3) (2004): 343–356.

[18] This is also the argument made in Domenico Losurdo, *Hegel and the Freedom of the Moderns*, trans. Marella and Jon Morris (Durham, NC: Duke University Press, 2004), 170–171.

The right of necessity is a positive right that depends on the existence of right and its jurisdiction. This is why the right of necessity is *not* a right to revolutionize the state that is part of the state's positive constitution at a certain historical moment. The right of necessity is certainly a right that characterizes the modern conception of right, yet it is not, and cannot be, to my mind a right to abolish or fundamentally transform all coordinates of right. The second reading criticizes the first for not taking into account the means that Hegel proposes to deal with the problem of the rabble. Yet the second reading of the rabble does not offer any convincing arguments that could fundamentally invalidate the first reading. A third reading is therefore needed.

The Third Reading of the Rabble

The third reading can start from the following point: the rabble's indignation does not merely articulate frustration with the existing state of affairs and affairs of the state. It is also not simply a sign of the loss of self-respect, and hence not an expression of melancholia. Rather its indignation entails positive self-assertion. Indignation thereby can be read as an expression of self-respect. The society to which someone who is part of the rabble is supposed to belong denies him or her the right to exist; the rabble asserts a right to exist in a world and against a world in which it is not supposed to exist. The right it claims is rightly depicted by Slavoj Žižek as 'a universal right to have rights, to be in a position to act as free autonomous subject. The demand to be provided for life without working is thus a (possible superficial) form of appearance of the more basic and in no way "irrational" demand to be given a chance to act as an autonomous free subject, to be included in the universe of freedoms and obligations'.[19]

The rabble is indignant at the excessive, unnatural and perverse effects of the economic movement of society, because in and through these effects it becomes clear that the legal claim with regard to the subsistence of all individuals can be upheld only under the condition of constantly depriving large masses of poor individuals of their rights – something that becomes retroactively visible with the emergence of the rabble. The possibility of upholding the right to subsistence of all implies within society at the same time the impossibility of guaranteeing the right to subsistence for all. This insight into the perverted, unnatural essence of society is what

[19] Slavoj Žižek, 'The Politics of Negativity', in Frank Ruda, *Hegel's Rabble: An Investigation into Hegel's Philosophy of Right* (London: Continuum, 2011), xvi.

generates the rabble and its indignation. *Indignation is therefore indignation at indignation*, at the condition of the possibility of being indignant at all. Hence, it is not directed at a concrete object of the world but rather at the world as it is. Indignation is directed at a world in which there is indignation. Indignation thereby can be read as a way in which an injustice, which is not recognized to be one because it results from the very constitution of the world, is subjectivized.

Given its contingent origin, this indignation could be read in terms of what Adorno called the 'addendum' (*das Hinzutretende*).[20] This category describes a subjective attitude that contingently supplements a situation, in which a subject encounters an impossibility (in the rabble's case the impossibility of bringing something before itself, that is, an impossibility of realizing one's own freedom under given conditions) and practically deals with it. Adorno states that 'the subject's decisions do not roll off in a causal chain; what occurs is a jolt, rather'.[21] Hence the subject's decision relies on an addendum, the additional indignation. Indignation also results from a jolt and it is thus the necessary content and the necessary form of a contingent attitude, which is directed against the condition of its own possibility. And it is precisely this interplay of the necessary possibility of indignation, that is, poverty and of the contingent genesis of this attitude that ensures its universality. Indignation is, at least latently, the indignation of everyone. He who is indignant in the rabble sense of the term is therefore a representative of the whole of humanity. Therefore, indignation can become a possible category of political action and the rabble is the latent – not yet active political – subject of it. Indignation is not merely negative, since it has a positive kernel, namely the formulation of a right (without right) to subsist without working. This right thereby

[20] See Theodor W. Adorno, *Negative Dialectics*, trans. E. B. Ashton (London: Continuum, 1973).

[21] Adorno, *Negative Dialectics*, 226–227. In a different context, Adorno gives an example of this kind of 'jolt' (*Ruck*). He reports the following: 'In the first few months after I returned to Germany … from emigration, I had the opportunity to make the acquaintance of one of the few crucial actors of the 20th July and was able to talk to him. I said to him, "Well, you knew very well that the conspiracy's chances of success were minimal, and you must have known that if you were caught you had to expect a fate far more terrible than death … What made it possible for you to take action notwithstanding this?" – Whereupon he said to me … "But there are situations that are so intolerable that one just cannot continue to put up with them, no matter what may happen and no matter what may happen to oneself in the course of the attempt to change them." He said this without any pathos – and I should like to add, without any appeal to theory … – the fact that things may be so intolerable that you feel compelled to make the attempt to change them, regardless of the consequences for yourself, and in circumstances in which you may also predict the possible consequences for other people – is the precise point at which the irrationality, or better, the irrational aspect of moral action is to be sought, the point at which it may be located'. Theodor W. Adorno, *Problems of Moral Philosophy*, trans. Rodney Livingstone (Stanford, CA: Stanford University Press, 2001), 8.

also has a latently universal dimension that, although articulated from a particular position, includes everyone in its address. And it has a reflexive structure in the sense that its negative dimension is directed at the condition of its own possibility (i.e. at the world which allows indignation to exist).

It is important to add here that Hegel employs the word 'indignation' (*Empörung*) in a twofold manner. He uses it not only to mean the affective determination of the attitude of the rabble but also in the (etymologically wrong) sense of rebellion, revolt, turmoil, insurrection. This is why he can write that a 'rebellion … in a province conquered in war … is not the same thing as a revolt [*Empörung*] in a well-organized state' (PR § 281A). The latter is a veritable 'political crime' (PR § 281A): a crime against the consistency of social bonds – duties and rights – which make the state into the state, i.e. an attack on the world as it is. One can link the two uses of indignation here and claim that the rabble is in a state of affective indignation at the state and outraged at the existing order, and this leads it to claim a right to subsist without labouring, which marks a moment of absolute unbinding from the concepts and spheres of right, from the social bond, etc. This leads to the fact that one can claim that one here moves from the condition of the possibility of indignation to the reproduction and perpetuation of it. *The indignation about the world raises itself up – akin to the infamous Baron Münchhausen's famous self-liberation from the marsh – to indignation against the world, which puts the latter in a state of turmoil.*

The indignation is directed at the state, the order, the world, as it is. Indignation is therefore for Hegel an *anti-statist* force, because it is literally an *a-social* subjective attitude. It is an attitude of possible political subjectivization; it is not an attitude indicating political subjectivity already *in actu* – hence the sole dimension that is present in it is a latently universal one (or, in other terms, the rabble is not organized). But it indicates a place for (another kind of) politics, for a form of political action that starts by breaking the social bond and diminishes the evidence of the state (of things). With regard to the rabble one can say that its true revolt is the indignant unbinding from the (alleged) necessity of the world as it is. The rabble asserts, emphasizes and indignantly demonstrates a possibility of politics that must from the perspective of the state seem impossible. This is because indignation expresses the contradiction between concept and reality, that is to say, between the concept of right and the reality of right and the implied deprivation of the rights of the poor; between the concept of the free will and the reality of its realization. Already in his early *Realphilosophie* Hegel had characterized inner indignation as 'highest inner turmoil of the will', which is brought about by 'the inequality of wealth and poverty' (JR, 232–233). Here indignation does not only designate the subjective thinking of the rabble-like poor vis-à-vis the rich; rather it is directed at the very possibility of this splitting, of the split between poverty and wealth as such. Indignation is hence not hatred on the part of the poor directed towards the rich, but rather what is generated when this split between the poor and the rich becomes a principle structuring the world. The rabble's indignation in its latent universal dimension therefore indicates that the social bond is already broken.

This is why Hegel describes indignation as highest turmoil (*höchste Zerrissenheit*) – as a rupture of the social, which at the same time comes with an insight into a fundamental and universal dimension that is no longer founded in the social, but rather in its impossibility (this is what marks the place of possible political action). So, what is one to do with this? One may answer by referring again to Eduard Gans. He once lectured on Hegel's philosophy of right and remarked when elaborating the very concept of the state (in Hegel) that 'states are individuals with a slightly longer life but which also fall in the end, destroyed in the struggle with world history. They are rivers that pour into the ocean of history ...'[22] This means that states will also end when they become internally petrified, ossified and simply positive. Yet one can also link this to the implications inscribed into the concept of the rabble. Robert Pippin rightly remarked that what Hegel states in the infamous preface to the *Philosophy of Right* should be taken absolutely seriously. Namely, 'When philosophy paints its grey in grey, a shape of life has grown old, and it cannot be rejuvenated, but only recognized, by the grey in grey of philosophy; the owl of Minerva begins its flight only with the onset of dusk' (PR *Preface*, 23[28]). Philosophy begins when a shape of life is inevitably declining, when it has grown old and is on the verge of dying. This means that the concept of the state whose concept Hegel depicts as it is (and not as what should be) is a concept that has grown old – and will inevitably die at some point. This means not only, as Pippin has rightly argued,[23] that Hegel does not present any normative account of what a state or a civil society should look like, but also that he rather depicts the status quo of

[22] Eduard Gans, *Naturrecht und Universalgeschichte. Vorlesungen nach G. W. F. Hegel* (Tübingen: Mohr Siebeck, 2005), 204.

[23] See Robert Pippin, 'Back to Hegel?', *Mediations* 26(1–2), at www.mediationsjournal.org/articles/back-to-hegel.

contemporary society because it is 'a shape of life grown old' and thus has come close to its end.[24] Philosophy, especially Hegel's philosophy, which depicts what is and never what ought to be, can therefore never become apologetic. It depicts what is in a state of decline and it can only depict this because it is itself in decline. The end is therefore not only near, but always already here. *If there is philosophy the end has always already taken place.* His *Philosophy of Right* is therefore clearly not an apologetic book, but rather emphasizes that the state he presents in its internal rationality is not here to stay. If the state and the rabble both emerge at the same logical point, might one not assume in full Hegelian spirit that the rabble – and the other kind of politics it points to – may be one of the reasons for the decline of the state that Hegel depicts?

[24] In some sense this implies not only that all states have a history, that they emerge and disappear within it, but also that conceptually any state will have been a failed state at some point.

CHAPTER 9

Practical Necessity and the 'Logic' of Civil Society

David James

In the Preface to the *Elements of the Philosophy of Right*, Hegel offers a statement concerning the relationship between this text and his *Science of Logic*, in which he sets out, and seeks to demonstrate the necessity of, the basic logical determinations that govern rational thought as such and form the object of philosophical knowledge at the level of pure thought. This statement reads as follows:

> Since I have fully developed the nature of speculative knowledge in my *Science of Logic*, I have only occasionally added an explanatory comment on procedure and method in the present outline. Given that the subject-matter is concrete and inherently of so varied a nature, I have of course omitted to demonstrate and bring out the logical progression in each and every detail. But on the one hand, it might have been considered superfluous to do so in view of the fact that I have presupposed a familiarity with scientific method [*mit der wissenschaftlichen Methode*]; and on the other, it will readily be noticed that the work as a whole, like the construction of its parts, is based on the logical spirit. It is also chiefly from this point of view that I would wish this treatise to be understood and judged. For what it deals with is *science* [*Wissenschaft*], and in science, the content is essentially inseparable from the *form*. (PR, *Preface* 10[12–13])

From this statement it appears that the content of the *Elements of the Philosophy of Right*, that is to say, the concept of right, is to be regarded as inseparable from the scientific form in which it is presented. This identity of content and form has to do with the way in which the content exhibits a logically necessary structure. Although this identity is not always fully manifest, the concept of right and its various determinations will to some extent exhibit the same logical structure that forms the content or object of speculative logic. Since Hegel singles out the logical progressions described in the *Elements of the Philosophy of Right*, one would expect to find any appeals to the logical necessity described and demonstrated in his speculative logic especially in some of the key transitions that take place within this work. The necessity of such transitions would, therefore, ultimately have to be explained in terms of the idea of logical necessity.

The claim that anyone conversant with Hegel's speculative logic will be able to recognize, and even to provide, the logical progression which explains a particular transition raises a number of problems. To begin with, the question arises as to how the content of this work, the concept of right, can be classed as 'inseparable' from its form if the latter is the *logical* form that must be supplied in order to explain the necessity of the transition from one moment of the concept of right to another one. In other words, the development that the concept of right undergoes in the course of the *Elements of the Philosophy of Right* will not be purely immanent to that which Hegel calls the 'science of right' (*Rechtswissenschaft*) (PR § 2), even though he himself speaks of 'an *immanent* progression and production of its own determinations' which is 'assumed to be familiar from logic' (PR § 31). If the development that the concept of right undergoes is not a purely immanent one, and thereby does not fully exemplify Hegel's scientific method, it is difficult to see how the science of right can be regarded as a 'science' in the full Hegelian sense of the term. Rather, the development that the concept of right undergoes would be a truly immanent one only in the sense that its development can be explained within Hegel's philosophical system as a whole.

If any of the major transitions within the science of right cannot be viewed as purely immanent to this particular science, an obvious difficulty arises for anyone who wants to understand and to defend this science in purely ethical, social and political terms, so as to avoid any appeal to Hegel's speculative logic, on the grounds that it is highly problematic in itself and is therefore unfit to perform the foundational role which Hegel wishes to assign to it.[1] For it can then be argued that Hegel's *Philosophy of Right* can only be fully understood with reference to its logical grounding and legitimation as developed in his speculative metaphysics, and that any anti- or post-metaphysical interpretation of his practical philosophy is for this reason directly at odds with his own intentions and must ultimately fail to comprehend the actual content of his theory of a modern form of ethical life.[2]

In what follows I draw attention to the way in which one of the key transitions in Hegel's theory of ethical life, namely, the transition from

[1] See Allen W. Wood, *Hegel's Ethical Thought* (Cambridge: Cambridge University Press, 1990), 4–6.
[2] See Klaus Vieweg, *Das Denken der Freiheit. Hegels Grundlinien der Philosophie des Rechts* (Munich: Wilhelm Fink, 2012).

civil society to the state, is nevertheless best explained in terms of practical necessity rather than in terms of logical necessity. This transition is an especially important one because it marks the transition from a partially justified but inadequate way in which individuals conceive of their relation to the greater whole of which they are members to another one which is, for Hegel, the only truly appropriate mode of relation when it comes to the citizen's relation to the state. Although explaining the transition in question in terms of the idea of practical necessity goes a long way towards providing an immanent reading of this transition, it ultimately falls short of explaining the necessity of this transition in a way that fully accords with Hegel's own understanding of a genuinely ethical relation between individuals and the state. I shall begin by identifying a problem with which Hegel must deal if he is to succeed in explaining the immanent necessity of the transition from civil society to the state. This problem is already present in the Introduction to the *Elements of the Philosophy of Right*, in which Hegel clearly does appeal to a logical progression whose necessity he thinks he has demonstrated elsewhere by means of his speculative logic.

The Concept of the Will

In §§ 5–7 of the Introduction to the *Elements of the Philosophy of Right*, Hegel describes the concept of the will in terms of three moments. The concept of the will is the unity of the first two moments, which are universality and particularity, and this unity itself is identified with the moment of individuality (PR § 7). Hegel describes the first moment of the will as 'the limitless infinity of *absolute abstraction* or *universality*, the pure thinking of oneself' (PR § 5). It consists in an act whereby the 'I' adopts a reflective attitude towards itself. The reflective relation to itself that the 'I' thus establishes enables it to conceive of itself as undetermined by, and in this regard independent of, any of the given features that make it into the determinate, particular 'I' that it happens to be. By reflectively abstracting from any given content, the 'I' becomes purely universal, in the sense of being nothing more than the representation of itself as the locus of any possible content of the will whatsoever.

This moment of indeterminacy, in which any content remains a merely possible object of willing, must nevertheless be transcended, because the act of willing by its very nature requires the willing of something. This act of willing something is the will's 'positing of itself as something *determinate*' (PR § 6). Here, for example, an agent wills to act on the basis of desire x rather than desire y or desire z after adopting a reflective relation to these desires which are originally encountered as something given. Since both moments of the will are equally essential to any act of willing, the concept of the will must ultimately be understood as the unity of these two moments. If the will is to be *free*, however, this unity additionally requires that the willing agent be able to identify itself with that which it wills in such a way that it remains 'with itself' (*bei sich*) in its act of willing. This is because, for the act of willing to be an act of genuine *self*-determination, it cannot be determined by some external force or agent. Rather, the willing agent wills something that it can recognize as being its very own in the sense that its source lies entirely within itself.

Hegel explicates the structure of the will in terms of the moments of the logical concept, which are universality, particularity and individuality (or singularity) (EL § 163). The unity of universality and particularity that defines the moment of individuality constitutes the speculative moment in Hegel's theory of the will. He describes the logical as such as having three essential moments with respect to its form (EL § 79). First of all, there is the moment of abstraction performed by the understanding, whereby a determination of thought (in this case, universality or particularity) is fixed, in the sense that it is comprehended as possessing a distinctive character or structure which makes it independent of opposing determinations of thought (EL § 80). In the case of the concept of the will, this moment of non-identity amounts to giving an account of what the universality and the particularity of the will essentially are independently of their relation to each other, as Hegel himself does in §§ 5–6 of the Introduction to the *Elements of the Philosophy of Right*. Next there is the dialectical moment in which the fixed nature and the independence of opposing determinations of thought are undermined, because each determination of thought is shown to be bound up with its other without, however, the ground of the necessary relation that exists between opposing determinations of thought being comprehended by thought itself (EL § 81). Universality and particularity, for example, are essentially related despite their opposition in the minimal sense that one is the opposite of the other, so that by knowing what universality is we also know what particularity is not and vice versa. Finally, there is the speculative moment in which the necessary relation that exists between opposing determinations of thought is fully comprehended without their opposition being denied, by means of their unification in a higher determination of thought (EL § 82). This is the moment of individuality.

The way in which Hegel explains the concept of the will in terms of the moments of his speculative logic does not necessarily signal that he intends to explain the will, insofar as it forms the object of his 'science of right', in terms of something which is more fundamental in a logical sense. For it could be that he is able to show that the logical structure in question already manifests itself sufficiently in the phenomenon of willing. Indeed, this appears to be Hegel's approach in §§ 11–21 of the Introduction to the *Elements of the Philosophy of Right*. Hegel here provides an account of the will which attempts to show how the will exhibits the relevant logical structure in an increasingly adequate way.

He begins with what he calls 'the *immediate* or *natural* will' (PR § 11). Given that its content is encountered as something given by nature (for example, as the natural desire to eat when hungry or to sleep when tired), the only sense in which the will can be thought to be self-determining here is that the content is *its own*, so that, in being determined by this natural content, the will is not determined by something completely other than itself. Nevertheless, the reflective relation to that which is immediately given that characterizes the first moment of the will is absent, and in this respect it is difficult to see how the first moment of the will is present at all in the natural will. This moment becomes more evident in the next form of willing. This is the resolving will which consists in the act of choosing one thing rather than another one, and thereby implies the existence of some degree of reflection, however minimal. The second moment of the will is also clearly present, since the act of choosing one thing rather than another one represents an act through which the will achieves determinacy as a result of an act of willing. At the same time, Hegel describes this act of resolving as 'purely *formal*', and as one in which the content of the will is not yet 'the content and product of its freedom' (PR § 13). Clearly, then, he thinks that genuine self-determination consists in willing not only something determinate but also the right type of content. In other words, it is not simply a matter of *how* one wills but also *what* one wills.

The purely formal nature of the will becomes more explicit in the arbitrary will (*Willkür*). Here the 'self-reflecting *infinite 'I'* which is with itself … *stands above* its content', and this content thereby becomes a merely possible one that the reflecting 'I' regards as 'external' to itself (PR § 14). While the arbitrary will exemplifies the first moment of the will, the question of the grounds that determine the will's act of resolving to adopt one object of willing rather than another one arises, and in this way the second moment of the will comes into play. Hegel points out that, as it stands, these grounds must be regarded as essentially contingent ones because there is no principle governing such acts of free choice (PR § 17). A principle of this kind is provided by the concept of happiness, however, by which Hegel does not mean momentary pleasure or a temporary sense of well-being. Rather, by the term 'happiness' he means a more lasting condition in which various desires and drives are brought into harmony with each other by means of a reflective process which consists in the formation of a general idea of what would make one happy in the long term. This idea is then employed to determine what one should in fact will. This general idea functions as a '*formal universality*', in that it is something to which our particular drives and desires must be subordinated and with which they must be made to harmonize (PR § 20). In short, the idea of happiness provides a higher-order principle for organizing given desires and drives, with the satisfaction of some of them having to be postponed, or foregone altogether, for the sake of the satisfaction of other ones which are held to be of more overall value or importance relative to the general idea of happiness that an individual has formed. This general action-guiding principle goes only so far, however, in ridding the content of the will of its contingency. This is because (1) depriving this content of its contingency would require subjecting the concept of happiness itself to a higher principle, given that there is no reason for choosing to pursue one conception of happiness rather than another one, and (2) the content of happiness itself turns out for this reason to be ultimately determined by given desires and drives, whose satisfaction an individual happens to value more than that of others at a given point in time, but may come to value less so in the future.

These limitations of the idea of happiness as an action-guiding principle are more clearly identified in some of the student transcripts of Hegel's lectures. In his lectures Hegel describes the content of happiness as something that is always 'particular, subjective, and contingent', and he claims that the principle of happiness thereby contradicts the higher principle of freedom because an individual who acts according to this principle alone finds him- or herself in a 'circle of dependency in general, in a condition that is subject to change, change that comes from outside' (VPR 4: 138). In other words, individuals ultimately remain determined by factors that are not products of their own willing and for this reason they cannot be regarded as fully self-determining. A genuine self-determining will, in contrast, would be one that has itself as its content or object without its content or object being reduced to a contingent and particular one, as ultimately happens in the case of happiness. The content or object of such a self-determining will must therefore be in some sense necessary and universal.

Hegel identifies this type of content of the will with the universally valid content provided by 'the principle of right, of morality, and of all ethics' (PR § 21R), that is to say, with the type of principle he seeks to describe and justify in the course of the development of his science of right. This type of principle is necessary and universal in the sense of being unconditionally valid in relation to the wills of each and every relevant moral, social or political agent. In virtue of its necessity and universality, this content accords with the nature of reason as such and thus with the individual's own essential nature as a rational being, a nature that he or she shares with all other such beings.

The necessity of the transition from the stage of the will exemplified by happiness to the stage of the will associated with rational autonomy presupposes, therefore, both the unconditional validity of certain norms and the possibility of such rational autonomy itself. In other words, since it is not self-evident that the content of the will either ought to be or can be more than a contingent and particular one, the transition from happiness to rational autonomy presupposes the validity and reality of a form of free agency which has the type of logical structure identified in §§ 5–7 of the Introduction to the *Elements of the Philosophy of Right*. Here it looks as if Hegel's line of reasoning is as follows: in order for the will to be fully self-determining it must will a type of content which is both unconditionally and universally valid, because only this type of content would not in any way remain external to the will of a rational agent, and there must, therefore, be (both in a normative and in an existential sense) a form of willing that satisfies this demand. Hegel does not, however, attempt to justify this concept of rational agency itself and to explain its possibility within his 'science of right'. Rather, his account of this concept of rational agency in the Introduction simply presupposes the validity of his account of the will provided in the philosophy of subjective spirit of the third part of the *Encyclopaedia of the Philosophical Sciences* (PM §§ 469–480). Yet there are some even more fundamental presuppositions, in that Hegel's employment of logical terms in relation to the concept of the will signals that this concept can be fully understood only with reference to his logic, especially the doctrine or theory of the concept. The development that this concept undergoes can, therefore, at best be classed as a system-immanent one.

If some kind of logical structure ultimately explains the demand to will an object that is compatible with the notion of rational autonomy, the failure to will such an object and the ethical, social or political consequences of this failure would have to be viewed as a failure of judgement.[3] One would also have to say that human willing *ought* to exhibit the same logical structure as that which rational thought exhibits if it is to be classed as a fully rational and self-determining form of agency. In this way, Hegel's logic would be viewed as having normative implications. We might expect, then, a transition found in Hegel's science of right such as the one from civil society to the state to be based on a logical necessity that somehow possesses a normative import. I shall show that Hegel nevertheless attempts to explain this particular transition in terms of practical necessity rather than in terms of logical necessity, so that any appeal to the latter to explain the necessity of this transition must appear arbitrary. Moreover, Hegel makes certain claims that suggest that he himself regards this transition as one that is truly immanent to his science of right, as when he claims that the 'development of immediate ethical life through the division of civil society and on to the state … is the *scientific proof* of the concept of the state, a proof which only a development of this kind can furnish' (PR § 256R). Thus, before explaining the necessity of this transition in logical terms, our attention should first be directed towards Hegel's attempt to explain this transition in terms of practical necessity.

Practical Necessity and the Transition from Civil Society to the State

Civil society is determined by two principles: the principle of particularity and the principle of universality. We are here reminded of two moments of the logical concept and the concept of the will. As we shall see, the third, speculative moment of individuality obtains only towards the end of Hegel's account of civil society, and even here it does so imperfectly. The principle of particularity is associated with the 'concrete person who, as a *particular* person, as a totality of needs and a mixture of natural necessity and arbitrariness, is his own end' (PR § 182). Individuals are, in short, conceived as being self-interested economic and social agents with various natural and artificial needs who are capable of determining and willing the means of satisfying these needs. The principle of universality is associated with what might be called the basic terms of social cooperation and peaceable coexistence. These terms can be adhered to implicitly in the shape of informal social norms or rules that are unconsciously obeyed, or

[3] See Vieweg, *Das Denken der Freiheit*, 95.

they can be explicitly acknowledged and obeyed, as in the case of following clearly prescribed, publicly known institutional rules and procedures. In civil society, the universal is described by Hegel as arising in the first instance spontaneously through individuals seeking to meet their needs in a condition of interdependence by means of acts of production and exchange.

Although the mode of presentation that Hegel adopts suggests that we begin with individual economic and social agents who exist in isolation from other such agents, it is clear that this is only a matter of presentation, and that the principles of particularity and universality are in reality conceptually bound up with each other from the very start, even if the essential relation that exists between them has not yet become manifest. The tendency to think of these principles as existing independently of each other is partly to be explained in terms of the limits of the discursive understanding. Hegel describes civil society as the 'stage of *difference*' (PR § 181), thereby alluding to the Doctrine of Essence of his logic, in which two concepts are posited as standing in an essential relation to each other at the same time as thought itself – in the form of the reflecting understanding – fails to comprehend them as essential moments of a single conceptual whole. In this way, the reflecting understanding 'assumes the distinctions as *independent* and at the same time posits their relationality *as well*' (EL § 114R).

In the section on civil society Hegel appeals to the idea of a *logical* progression when he states that in civil society 'the Idea gives a *distinct existence* to its *moments*' (PR § 184). The 'Idea' is the term Hegel employs to designate the highest form of speculative unity. This unity consists in the unity of the concept and objectivity (EL § 213). In the case of Hegel's science of right, the unity in question is progressively realized through the increasingly adequate objectification of the concept of right in a set of ethical dispositions, institutions and practices. The opposition between particularity and universality in civil society, and the eventual overcoming of this opposition, are said to manifest 'the truly infinite power which resides solely in that unity which allows the *opposition* within reason *to develop to its full strength*, and has overcome it so as to preserve itself within it and *wholly contain it within itself*' (PR § 185R).

Despite these allusions to his speculative logic, Hegel's explanation of the overcoming of the opposition between universality and particularity, and their unity within civil society, appeals far more to the notion of *practical* necessity than to that of *logical* necessity. By practical necessity, I mean the way in which the wills of social agents can be constrained in the sense that these agents are forced to act in certain ways so as to realize certain ends that they have, and not simply the fact of having to act in certain ways so as to avoid something that one considers to be undesirable. Hegel explicitly appeals to the notion of practical necessity when he adopts an 'invisible hand' mode of explanation which involves the claim that I cannot pursue my own interests and welfare without *unintentionally* furthering the interests and welfare of others, or, as he himself puts it:

> In this dependence and reciprocity of work and the satisfaction of needs, *subjective selfishness* turns into a *contribution towards the satisfaction of the needs of everyone else*. By a dialectical movement, the particular is mediated by the universal so that each individual, in earning, producing, and enjoying on his own account, thereby earns and produces for the enjoyment of others. (PR § 199)

This process, through which the principle of particularity and the principle of universality become bound up with each other in a practical sense, involves much more than the satisfaction of natural needs that directly concern the basic conditions of human survival and functioning or the satisfaction of artificial needs that, despite being a product of human society, have come to assume a subjective necessity, in the sense that human beings feel compelled to satisfy them. Rather, through economic and social interaction, individuals also come to develop certain capacities and conceptions of themselves and their relations to others that determine how they think and how they act. What we have is, in fact, a formative process whereby subjectivity *qua* the 'particular' is educated towards a more universal standpoint (PR § 187).

The relevant capacities that individuals develop fall into two main groups. The first group consists of capacities that are developed by means of what Hegel calls 'practical education' (*praktische Bildung*). This type of education fosters the habits of being active, adjusting one's activity to suit the nature of the objects upon which one works or the task in hand, and acting in conformity with norms that are generated by material relations in which one stands with other individuals. This practical education also consists in the production, through repetition, of particular skills that can be applied to a variety of objects and are publicly recognized as belonging to a certain general type of activity (PR § 197). The second group of capacities concerns the ability to exercise the self-constraint required by such modes of behaviour as obedience to social conventions and other norms that spontaneously arise on the basis of the necessity of cooperating with others in order to satisfy one's needs and pursue one's other interests effectively (PR § 187).

This process, whereby individuals are constrained by practical necessity to adopt a more universalistic standpoint, is for Hegel one through which they achieve freedom both in the form of independence of that which is purely natural and in the form of the capacity to determine their activity in accordance with norms and practices that are self-imposed, in the sense of being products of human thought and activity to which one willingly subjects oneself, as when one chooses to enter a particular trade or profession. Hegel accordingly claims that '*Education* [*Bildung*], in its absolute determination, is ... *liberation* and *work* towards a higher liberation; it is the absolute transition to the infinitely subjective substantiality of ethical life, which is no longer immediate and natural, but spiritual and at the same time raised to the shape of universality' (PR § 187R). He makes clear, however, that, since this form of education is a matter of practical necessity, the unity of particularity and universality that is achieved in this way 'is present not as *freedom*, but as the *necessity* whereby the *particular* must rise to the *form of universality* and seek and find its subsistence in this form' (PR § 186). This judgement already points in the direction of a higher stage of right in which individuals are not simply constrained by practical necessity to think and to act in accordance with what is universal. Rather, they consciously and freely adopt the universal itself as their end instead of willing it merely as the means to an end, and in this way that which constrains their wills becomes something with which they can at the same time fully identify themselves. This further stage in the development of freedom helps explain Hegel's claim that, although the type of education described above represents a form of liberation, it is also only a stage on the way towards a 'higher' liberation.

This conception of the relation of individuals to the universal informs Hegel's understanding of how the state essentially differs from civil society. One essential way in which the state differs from civil society is that it transcends the particular interests of individuals and does not, therefore, exist *only* to secure and protect these interests. Rather, individuals make (or ought to make) the common good (or general interest) of the political whole of which they are members the *direct* object of their willing and in so doing they accord this end an intrinsic value. As Hegel puts it, '*Union* as such [*Die* Vereinigung *als solche*] is itself the true content and end, and the destiny [*Bestimmung*] of individuals is to lead a universal life [*ein allgemeines Leben*]' (PR § 258R). The common good or interest is here to be regarded as a universal that is neither an unintended outcome of the activity of individuals nor something that is willed simply as the means to an end.

This direct identification with the political whole of which one is a member represents a way of explaining the unity of particularity and universality which constitutes the speculative moment that Hegel terms 'individuality', because in making the universal into the direct object of their willing, particular individuals through their own willing establish their identity with the end of the state, an end which is by its very nature universal. Yet how is this form of association possible on the basis of the relation between particularity and universality that characterizes Hegel's theory of civil society? Hegel must provide an answer to this question if he is to demonstrate that the transition from civil society to the state is, in accordance with his notion of a genuinely scientific progression, a necessary one that is immanent to his science of right. In order to make clear what it would mean to demonstrate the necessity of this transition, I shall begin with certain features of Hegel's account of civil society that by his own admission fail to explain the type of identity in question.

Hegel views civil society as the sphere of ethical life in which particularity is satisfied in a number of ways, most notably through the legal protection of personal freedom and the satisfaction of particular needs and interests. The satisfaction of their particularity in turn leads individuals to identify themselves more closely with the state and thereby helps to strengthen the state itself: 'The principle of modern states has enormous strength and depth because it allows the principle of subjectivity to attain fulfilment in the *self-sufficient extreme* of personal particularity, while at the same time *bringing it back to substantial unity* and so preserving this unity in the principle of subjectivity itself' (PR § 260). Even if civil society allows human beings to satisfy their needs and to pursue their particular interests effectively, and thereby provides them with good reasons for identifying themselves with the state and willing not only its existence but also its flourishing, it is by no means self-evident that this idea by itself sufficiently explains the 'substantial unity' which must be assumed to involve a strong form of identification with the state that results in the absolute unity of the principle of particularity and the principle of universality. Rather, the unity achieved here can itself be viewed as an example of the kind of instrumental relation that Hegel associates with what he calls the 'state of necessity',[4] because individuals continue to view the state as that

[4] This instrumental relation of the individual to the state is made especially clear in Hegel's lectures. See PR 1821/22, § 187.

which serves to secure the rights of personal freedom and property as well as guaranteeing the social conditions of the effective pursuit of legitimate interests. Thus, '*the interest of individuals as such* becomes the ultimate end for which they are united [*vereinigt*]' (PR § 258R). This statement alone shows that we here have only an indirect mode of identification with the state that cannot simply be equated with the kind of union that Hegel has in mind when he says that *union as such* becomes an individual's end.

Hegel's recognition of how the type of relation between the individual and the state described above cannot sufficiently explain the existence of a mode of identification with the state which represents a practical expression of the unity of universality and particularity that constitutes the speculative moment of individuality is signalled by his description of the police, understood broadly as an institution charged with ensuring social order and the regulation of civil society, as '*an external order and arrangement* for the protection and security of the masses of particular ends and interests which have their subsistence in this universal' (PR § 249). The relation between the particular will of the individual and the legal and institutional arrangements that constitute the universal at this stage of civil society is external in the sense that individuals recognize and will the universal as the means to an end, and it is therefore possible that they would not recognize and will the universal in the form of the state if they could discover alternative means of realizing their ends.[5] Thus the relation between the individual and the state is ultimately a contingent one, or at least can be thought to be so. Even if the state is held to be the necessary ground of civil society, in the sense of a universal that prevents civil society from destroying itself as a result of tensions that it itself generates and which it itself cannot resolve,[6] the relation between the individual and the universal would still be an external one. This is because the constraints would continue to be ones that individuals could accept as being necessary while lacking any other sense of identification with them than that of the form of identification associated with a purely instrumental attitude.

Hegel's remarks on the nature of the transition from civil society to the state are somewhat vague, as when he claims that 'in the very act of developing itself independently to totality, the principle of particularity passes

[5] See David James, *Rousseau and German Idealism: Freedom, Dependence and Necessity* (Cambridge: Cambridge University Press, 2013), 169–171.

[6] For an example of this type of interpretation of the relation between civil society and the state, see Rolf-Peter Horstmann, 'The Role of Civil Society in Hegel's Political Philosophy', in Robert B. Pippin and Otfried Höffe (eds.), *Hegel on Ethics and Politics*, trans. N. Walker (Cambridge: Cambridge University Press, 2004), 208–238.

over into *universality* [*geht … in die* Allgemeinheit *über*]' (PR § 186). The notion of passing over recurs in the final paragraph of the section on civil society when Hegel claims that the 'sphere of civil society thus passes over into the *state* [*geht … in den* Staat *über*]' (PR § 256). This notion of a transition in which civil society 'passes over' into the state implies a spontaneous process, and it thereby accords with Hegel's account of civil society as a sphere of human activity in which the universal is largely unintentionally and unconsciously produced. Although the full development of 'personal individuality and its particular interests' is later said to '*pass over* [*übergehen*] of their own accord into the interest of the universal', Hegel also states that individuals 'knowingly and willingly acknowledge this universal interest even as their own *substantial spirit*, and *actively pursue it* as their *ultimate end*' (PR § 260). Here the universal is taken to be consciously and directly willed as one of the individual's own fundamental ends, as opposed to being regarded merely as the means to such an end. Thus the state is no longer simply 'an *external* necessity' but has instead become an '*immanent* end' (PR § 261). In other words, any remaining element of externality in the relation between the will of the individual and the universal is overcome and a complete identity of the particular and the universal is thereby established. This is the unity of universality and particularity characteristic of citizenship, and it is therefore in the section on the state that we encounter such claims.

I shall now show with reference to a passage from Adam Smith's *The Theory of Moral Sentiments* why Hegel would have been tempted to speak of civil society as passing over spontaneously into the state in such a way as to explain in terms of practical necessity, rather than in terms of logical necessity, how an identity or unity of the particular and the universal that prefigures the one found at the level of the state is established. The passage in question reads as follows:

> Among well-disposed people, the necessity or conveniency of mutual accommodation, very frequently produces a friendship not unlike that which takes place among those who are born to live in the same family. Colleagues in office, partners in trade, call one another brothers; and frequently feel towards one another as if they really were so. Their good agreement is an advantage to all; and, if they are tolerably reasonable people, they are naturally disposed to agree … The Romans expressed this sort of attachment by the word *necessitudo*, which, from the etymology, seems to denote that it was imposed by the necessity of the situation.[7]

[7] Adam Smith, *The Theory of Moral Sentiments*, ed. D. D. Raphael and A. L. Macfie (Oxford: Clarendon Press, 1976), 223–224.

In this passage, Smith describes a process driven by practical necessity whereby individuals end up pursuing consciously the common good embodied in a form of association. This form of association and the ethical disposition connected with it are initially viewed as unintended outcomes of the pursuit of self-interest. The form of association in question corresponds, moreover, to the kind of trade or professional association that Hegel calls a corporation, an institution that is meant to play an essential mediating role between civil society and the state in his *Philosophy of Right*. In the passage quoted above, three distinct stages of this process leading to an ever greater and more direct identification with the universal or whole of which one is a member can be identified.

The first stage consists in a partial and indirect identification with the universal, for it concerns the way in which an institution comes into existence through individuals seeking to further their own ends and interests once they have recognized that the effective pursuit of these ends and interests demands joining forces with others with similar ends and interests. Individuals here accept the constraints that cooperation places on their actions on the grounds of enlightened self-interest, and the emphasis is thereby firmly placed on the idea of practical necessity. This would correspond to the kind of relation between the particular and the universal that is characteristic of that which Hegel calls the 'state of necessity'.

The second stage consists in a fuller identification with the universal demanded by the fact that the common interest embodied in an associative form of life must be consciously willed if the original purpose of the association of which one is a member is to be realized. An association's members must, for example, exhibit such qualities as a sense of commitment and a willingness to sacrifice some of their particular ends and interests for the sake of the ends and interests of the association as a whole. Thus, we have a form of association whose individual members consciously identify themselves with the general will embodied in the association, by regarding this association itself as one of their own fundamental ends, though not necessarily their highest end. This would correspond to the relation between the particular and the universal that is characteristic of the form of association that Hegel finds exemplified in the corporation.

The third stage would consist in an even fuller and more direct identification with the universal, with the result that the social bonds that are generated are even stronger than those found at the previous stage. Smith's appeal to the idea of friendship not only implies the existence of a human good which cannot be attained independently of an individual's membership of a certain form of association, but also concerns a need which might be thought to be first generated through membership of such a whole. This is because full consciousness of the benefits of friendship and of its true value – and thus a desire for friendship based on a genuine understanding of what friendship is – cannot be achieved independently of the act of associating with others in the relevant way. In experiencing the true meaning and value of friendship, individuals may then come to identify themselves more fully with the form of association in which this human good is made truly possible and its nature is made fully manifest. In this way, individuals may also come to experience their membership of such a form of association as a fundamental need and end, to which their original reasons for entering this form of association are subordinated. In other words, membership of the whole has come to possess an intrinsic value that it may have initially lacked for its members. Here we can see how individuals would be motivated to will the universal as such, as opposed to willing it on instrumental grounds alone. The ethical disposition in question is, however, not presupposed as something given; rather, it is viewed as emerging over time as the result of cooperation, not as the cause of cooperation. As we have seen, the cause of cooperation is initially identified with self-interest and the desire to secure the means of satisfying its demands.

This way of explaining the type of unity of universality and particularity that marks the transition from civil society to the state nevertheless takes us only so far. This is because the corporation – or any equivalent form of human association – can be regarded as a form of association with its own ends and interests that cannot simply be assumed to harmonize with those of society as a whole. Hence Hegel's own description of the corporation's end as a 'limited and finite' one that 'has its truth in the *end which is universal* in and for itself and in the absolute actuality of this end' (PR § 256), and as only a 'relatively universal' one (PM § 534).[8] The nature of this problem can be highlighted by comparing the following two passages, the first of which occurs in the remark to the final paragraph of the section on the police and anticipates the unity of universality and particularity achieved through membership of a corporation, while the second directly concerns the corporation:

> In accordance with the Idea, particularity itself makes this universal, which is present in its immanent interests, the end and object of its will

[8] For more on this point, see James, *Rousseau and German Idealism*, 187–192.

> and activity, with the result that *the ethical returns* to civil society as an immanent principle; this constitutes the determination of the *corporation*. (PR § 249)

and

> [I]n the *association*, the *selfish* end which pursues its own particular interest comprehends and expresses itself at the same time as a universal end; and the member of civil society, in accordance with his *particular skill*, is a member of a corporation whose universal end is therefore wholly *concrete*, and no wider in scope than the end inherent in the trade which is the corporation's proper business and interest. (PR § 251)

The speculative nature of the transition is stressed in the first passage, in that the unity of the particular and the universal is described as being established in such a way that individuals directly will the universal. The ethical here 'returns' in the sense that the unity of universality and particularity found at the level of the family, which is an immediate unity based on a naturally determined, emotional identification with the whole of which one is a member, is reconstituted in such a way as to be a result of conscious willing, making the unity in question compatible with the idea of freedom. This return of the ethical is treated, moreover, as the result of a process that is immanent to civil society and culminates in the corporation, in which the 'external' relation between universality and particularity characteristic of the previous moment represented by the police is transcended. In the second passage, in contrast, the willing of the universal by the particular, that is to say, by the individual as the possessor of a particular skill or as the practitioner of a particular trade or profession, is mentioned at the same time as the limited nature of the universal that forms the object of the individual's willing is acknowledged. The way in which Hegel's account of the 'logic' of civil society as a matter of practical necessity cannot fully explain the transition to a universal standpoint, whose direct object is a general good or interest that transcends *all* particular interests, including any corporate ones, can be further illustrated with reference to how he indirectly excludes certain people from membership of a corporation.

For Hegel membership of a corporation depends on the possession of the skills or aptitudes associated with a particular trade or profession. Unskilled workers are therefore by definition excluded from this mediating institution as much as unemployed people are. The members of this social group are thus denied the benefits that membership of a corporation provides, including protection of its members' livelihoods and material support during times of illness or lack of employment. The corporation is also an important source of social recognition or 'honour', in that its members are viewed both by each other and by the wider society as independent, productive members of society (PR § 253). The social exclusion suffered by unskilled workers as well as by the unemployed therefore represents a double problem. Individuals are not only condemned to economic uncertainty and denied an important form of social recognition,[9] but also fall outside the institution which performs the essential mediating function of making them members of a greater whole with which they can identify themselves, thereby preparing them for membership of the even greater whole of the state and fostering a closer identification with it. This double problem invites the following question: would it be possible for unskilled workers to form an alternative type of association based on mutual support in which each of them is able not only to gain the support of others and social recognition, but also to become the member of a greater whole with which he or she fully identifies him- or herself, even if Hegel did not recognize such a possibility?

The fact that Hegel may simply have been wrong to exclude the possibility that such workers might, as a result of practical necessity, come to develop the type of identification of oneself with the whole of which one is a member that is fostered by participation in a corporation is shown by the following description given by the young Marx of the form of associational life enjoyed by communist workers:

> When communist *workmen* gather together [*sich vereinen*], their immediate aim is instruction, propaganda, etc. But at the same time they acquire a new need – the need for society – and what appears as a means has become an end. This practical development can be most strikingly observed when one sees French socialist workers united [*vereinigt*]. Smoking, eating and drinking, etc., are no longer means of creating links between people. Company, association [*Verein*], conversation, which in its turn has society as its goal, is enough for them. The brotherhood of man is not a hollow phrase, with them it is a truth, and the nobility of man shines forth upon us from their work-worn figures.[10]

[9] Hegel himself makes this point in the following way: 'If the individual is not a member of a legally recognized corporation … he is without the *honour of belonging to an estate*, his isolation reduces him to the selfish aspect of his trade, and his livelihood and satisfaction lack *stability*' (PR § 253R).

[10] Karl Marx, 'Ökonomisch-philosophische Manuskripte (1844)', in *Marx-Engels-Werke* (hereafter MEW), ed. Institut für Marxismus-Leninismus beim Zentralkomitee der Sozialistischen Einheitspartei Deutschlands, 43 volumes (Berlin: Dietz Verlag, 1956–1990), Vol. 40, 553–554; *Early Writings*, trans. Rodney Livingstone and Gregor Benton (London: Penguin, 1992), 365; translation modified.

Here we begin with the idea that individuals initially associate with each other as a matter of practical necessity, in the sense that they cannot otherwise realize certain ends that they have both as individuals and as the members of a socio-economic group, ends which in this particular case concern the need to defend and further the interests that they share as workers. Yet this act of association based on individual and collective self-interest in time generates a need to associate with others that has become to some extent independent of the interests that first motivated each individual to associate with others. In this way, the act of associating with others together with the particular social activities that define this act become ends that have assumed an intrinsic value.

Thus, we appear to have the type of unity of universality and particularity that Hegel claims is made possible by membership of a corporation. At the same time, however, the fact that this form of association is made up of workers committed to socialism means that the universal embodied in it can be viewed as particular in relation to society as a whole, just as the corporation's end is particular in relation to the ends of the political state. To avoid this conclusion one would, like Marx, have to assume that, or explain how, the proletariat has the character of a 'universal' class, in the sense that it represents the historical condition of universal human emancipation and the overcoming of all class interests, and thus the overcoming of class society more generally.[11] Indeed, the fact that the examples of the 'logic' of civil society provided by Smith and Marx concern different social groups with different, and potentially conflicting, interests serves to illustrate the problem in question.

On the one hand, Hegel's employment of the idea of practical necessity in his account of the dynamics of civil society has the advantage of being able to explain the formation of group identities and forms of collective social action in a way that is internal or 'immanent' to his 'science of right'. On the other hand, it leaves him, or so I have argued, unable to explain the necessity of the transition from civil society to the state in a way that makes this transition truly internal to this particular science. This is because the identity or unity of universality and particularity achieved in the corporation falls short of the unity which is meant to be achieved at the level of the state. Although there is the required identification with the universal on the part of each individual member of the whole, the whole itself lacks the universality of the state. To argue

[11] Karl Marx, 'Zur Kritik der Hegelschen Rechtsphilosophie. Einleitung', *MEW*, Vol. 1, 390; *Early Writings*, 256.

that the necessity of this transition must therefore be explained in terms of certain logical categories risks, however, introducing what must appear to be a set of external considerations, given the way in which Hegel's own explanation of this transition depends so heavily on the idea of practical necessity.

CHAPTER 10

How Modern is the Hegelian State?

Ludwig Siep

Whether Hegel's political philosophy, as he developed it in the last part of his *Elements of the Philosophy of Right* (1821) in particular, is modern or 'reactionary' has been disputed from the time of his own students up to this day. For Karl Marx, to give one example, Hegel's method was admittedly modern in the sense that every scientific treatment of the constitution and development of society and the state must employ dialectical thinking. The content of Hegel's political philosophy, however, contradicted this modern element. It revealed that Hegel's thinking remained determined by a metaphysical concept of spirit, which represented a hypostatization and projection ultimately derived from religion and philosophical theology. Today the assessment is often reversed: it is widely disputed that Hegel employs a scientific method in Marx's sense, which consists in the development and 'sublation' (*Aufhebung*) of contradictions in concepts and objects of thought, and is 'applied' to norms, social systems and institutions. His concepts of freedom and action, law and the constitution, market society and the welfare state, however, are regarded by many as relevant today, because they at least partly anticipated the problems of modern society. Precisely as a diagnostician of social developments is Hegel to be classed as 'modern'. Jürgen Habermas, for instance, calls him 'the first philosopher to develop a clear concept of modernity', and likewise the first 'for whom modernity became a problem'.[1]

The assessment has also swung in this direction in the Anglo-Saxon philosophical world. Although the image of the metaphysician and reactionary 'Prussian philosopher of the state' was the dominant one after the end of the British and American Hegelianism of the late nineteenth century, Hegel is today regarded by many eminent Anglophone philosophers

[1] Jürgen Habermas, *The Philosophical Discourse of Modernity*, trans. Frederick Lawrence (Cambridge: Polity, 1987), 4 and 43.

as a prominent thinker of modernity. The revival of pragmatic thought and the influence of the later Wittgenstein favour such a viewpoint. Hegel is regarded as a precursor of the notion that consciousness and language, action and society cannot be comprehended on the basis of individualistic premises alone, but must instead be understood on the basis of social and communicative processes. His practical philosophy is said not to proceed from eternal ideas of an *a priori* law of nature or reason but instead to have paved the way for the conception of an open society which finds itself engaged in a continual process of communication and shaping of a common will.[2]

How modern actually is Hegel's *Philosophy of Right*, especially his conception of the state? Any judgement regarding this issue of the kind that will be outlined here naturally depends on the concept of 'modernity' that one employs. Today, however, an abundance of them can be found in disciplines ranging from sociology, through the historical sciences – especially legal history, art history and religious history – to philosophy. The classical 'theories of modernization', especially of sociology – in the tradition that extends from Max Weber to Talcott Parsons and Niklas Luhmann – entered a deep crisis. Now the talk is of levels of modernity – for instance, Ulrich Beck's 'second modernity'[3] – of a plurality of forms of modernity,[4] and naturally of postmodernity or even the post-secular age. In such debates it is often not even clear what meaning is intended: a temporal meaning (the present age of the speaker or the most recent past), a procedural one (modernity as a process of 'modernization'), a qualitative modernity which has particular characteristics or, finally, a normative one (modernity as a value in the light of which any preliminary stages and regressions can be assessed). Disagreement naturally dominates most of all discussions of the qualitative sense: what features of human beings, societies and states mark out an age as 'modern'? There

[2] See, for example, Robert B. Brandom, 'Holism and Idealism in Hegel's *Phenomenology*', in *Tales of the Mighty Dead: Historical Essays in the Metaphysics of Intentionality* (Cambridge, MA: Harvard University Press, 2002), 178–209; 'Some Pragmatist Themes in Hegel's Idealism: Negotiation and Administration in Hegel's Account of the Structure and Content of Conceptual Norms', *European Journal of Philosophy* 7(2) (1999): 164–189; Robert B. Pippin, *Hegel's Practical Philosophy: Rational Agency as Ethical Life* (Cambridge: Cambridge University Press, 2008); Terry Pinkard, 'Reason, Recognition and Historicity', in Barbara Merker, Georg Mohr, Michael Quante and Ludwig Siep (eds.), *Subjektivität und Anerkennung* (Paderborn: Mentis, 2003), 45–66; and Frederick Neuhouser, *Foundations of Hegel's Social Theory: Actualizing Freedom* (Cambridge, MA: Harvard University Press, 2000).

[3] Ulrich Beck, *Risikogesellschaft. Auf dem Weg in eine andere Moderne* (Frankfurt am Main: Suhrkamp, 1986).

[4] Shmuel N. Eisenstadt, *Die Vielfalt der Moderne* (Weilerswist: Velbrück, 2000).

are many candidates: the 'differentiation' of the domains of religion, politics, law, science and so on, 'rationalization' in the sense of the instrumentally rational organization of all social domains and forms of life, 'bureaucratization' in the sense of the 'institutional character' (Weber's *Anstaltscharakter*) of modern states and large firms, the 'secularization' of norms and with it the freeing of the individual from all social constraints, and much more besides. It goes without saying that not all these features were already developed in Hegel's time; industrialization and mechanization especially were still in their infancy.[5]

In what follows, I shall first of all investigate the concept of modernity that Hegel himself employs. My concern will then be the essential features of civil society and the state that are modern from Hegel's perspective. I shall thereby draw attention to the differences between Hegel's concept of modernity and the concepts of modernity that are common today. This will enable me to draw a preliminary conclusion regarding the extent of the Hegelian conception of the state's modernity.

Hegel's Use of the Term 'Modern'

One rarely finds the expression 'modern' in Hegel's published works. It is more often found in fragments and lecture transcripts.[6] He frequently uses expressions such as 'new', 'most recent' and 'our time'. Different meanings that one must distinguish from each other are thereby in play, even if Hegel himself does not always make this explicit.

The *first* meaning concerns the opposition between the ancient world and post-classical Christian Europe. It derives from the scholarly use of concepts which from the Middle Ages to the eighteenth century drew a distinction between the *antiqui* and the *moderni*. This opposition dominated in particular the major intellectual debate in Europe concerning the superiority of one or the other epoch initiated by the Académie Française in the form of the *querelle des Anciens et des Modernes*.[7] For Hegel, there is a crucial reason for preferring the post-Christian world to the ancient world: the significance of free individuality and subjectivity. To this belongs the issue of legal responsibility – as opposed to the

[5] For more on the process of industralization in Europe see Jürgen Osterhammel, *Die Verwandlung der Welt*, 5th edn (Munich: C. H. Beck, 2010), 907–928.

[6] The use of the transcripts of lectures, whose subject matter is also treated in texts that Hegel himself had published, appears to me justified when it seeks to elucidate the published text but not to correct it.

[7] See, for example, the marginal note to PR § 105 (*Werke* 7: 203–204) and PR § 279A.

fateful guilt of ancient tragedy – and the right of personal conviction or conscience. Hegel calls this aspect 'morality'.[8] The final decision of a subjective will within the state embodied in the person of the monarch also belongs here – Hegel distinguishes it from how oracles were consulted in the ancient world (PR § 279). Other forms of differentiation concerning the state and religion or the professionalization of the state administration will be discussed later.

In his philosophy of history, Hegel calls the post-classical age the 'Germanic world'. It is 'modern' mainly in the sense of representing through Christianity an advance in the development of reason that goes beyond anything achieved in the ancient world. Christianity brings the infinite value of the individual to consciousness, because for it every human being is loved by God and through the Incarnation is destined to be identical with God. This religion already contains the principle of individual freedom, which will be unfolded in the whole course of European history, but has been made a reality by means of institutions only since the end of the eighteenth century.

There is, however, another side to this process: the absolute significance accorded to individuality, both as the pursuit of personal interests and as the right to demand that general norms be justified, can also undermine the necessary common ground of moral demands and ends for which individuals must make sacrifices. For Hegel, the realization of the individual's rational 'vocation' requires recognition within a group, extending from the family, through a trade or professional estate, to the state, in which he or she can lead a 'universal life' (PR § 258R). The task of the 'modern' state is therefore to create a political community which offers such forms of life in to which individuals are integrated while safeguarding individual freedom. Its 'task' does not mean, however, a moral or juridical ideal in Kant's sense, but the tendency exhibited by a historical development that can be comprehended and must be justified.

The *second* meaning of the term 'modern' refers to the modern age in opposition to the world of the Middle Ages. It is characterized by the process whereby sovereign states become separate from the claims to power of a universal church and by the distinction between civil society and the state – in today's terminology their 'differentiation'. The Reformation was of decisive importance for Hegel with regard to both of these processes. For one thing freedom of conscience and religious freedom achieved

[8] See, for example, his comment to PR § 118: 'in "modern" guilt a base, evil will' (*Werke* 7: 220). On the right of conscience and the demand for justification, see also PR § 261A.

recognition – in the beginning only 'in principle' but not yet as a historical reality. The institutional guarantee of these freedoms in the long run demanded the confessional neutrality of a state justified in terms of 'worldly' reason. For another thing the Reformation, for Hegel, contributed to the legitimation of a bourgeois acquisitive market society with its own civic virtues.

A *third* meaning is that of the most recent age or 'of our day'. Here the French Revolution marks a breakthrough, because it made 'the restructuring of the state in accordance with the concept of right'[9] into a plan of action – and, what is more, a concept of right developed not on the basis of tradition and privileges but on the basis of rational principles. The decisive principle is freedom, though not only in the form of the subjective rights of the individual. For Hegel, the 'strength' of the modern state consists in how it supports the development of individual interests and rights at the same time as it manages to integrate them within a whole (see PR § 260). By his late lectures on the philosophy of history, however, especially in the light of the revolution of 1830, Hegel's faith in this power to integrate individual interests and rights had been shaken. He therefore claimed that even the modern state needs religion as a basis of its citizens' allegiance.

When Hegel employs the expression 'modern' in so many different senses without being more precise about their essential differences, it may be asked whether he understands by it a single concept at all.[10] Rather, he treats it as what he calls a 'representation' (*Vorstellung*). This term refers not only to images or metaphors, but also to 'condensed' thoughts whose various meanings have not been subjected to analysis and 'comprehended' as necessary moments of one single thought.

The historical order also presents difficulties. The concept of the 'modern state' (PR § 260), or the 'developed' state 'of our day'[11] cannot be historically classified with sufficient precision. The Reformation is an essential precondition of it. Yet its essential principles, freedom of conscience and the separation of state authority from church authority, were at first not

[9] *Werke* 12: 532 ('modern', 535). See Ludwig Siep, 'Das Recht der Revolution – Kant, Fichte und Hegel über 1789 und die Folgen', in Rolf Groeschner and Wolfgang Reinhard (eds.), *Tage der Revolution – Feste der Nation* (Tübingen: Mohr & Siebeck, 2010), 115–144.

[10] The expression 'modern' is otherwise encountered more often in the lecture transcripts and Hegel's marginal notes. In the published texts the expressions 'new', 'more recent [*neuere*] times' etc. are more common. See Ludwig Siep, *Hegels praktische Philosophie und das 'Projekt der Moderne'* (Baden-Baden: Nomos, 2011). The use of 'modern' in the English translation for Hegel's '*neuer*' has been corrected here and in what follows (author).

[11] The formulation of this addition to PR § 258 derives from Griesheim's transcription of the lectures from 1824–25 (VRP 4: 632).

realized at all in the Reformed states, especially not in the territories forming part of the Holy Roman Empire. Hegel had already commented on the principle of *cuius regio, ejus religio* in the early manuscript *The German Constitution*.[12] For him, although the actual separation of church and state is admittedly not recognized in the constitution of the Holy Roman Empire, the compatibility of the same system of government with different confessions and churches is recognized, at least in principle.

In this manuscript Hegel notes other features of the modern state that he explicitly denies are possessed by the Holy Roman Empire. Prominent among these features is the centralization of the means of administration and defence. To a modern administration there also belongs a division of tasks which Hegel compares to the division of labour in the production process.[13] A state of this kind was achieved, however, in Catholic France rather than in areas shaped by the Reformation.

It is likewise difficult to determine the point in time occupied by *economic* modernity, that is, the emergence of markets, freedom of occupation and freedom of trade, as well as competition within a sphere of civil society that is partly independent of the state. Hegel's thinking is here informed by classical political economy, especially Adam Smith, and by the early-industrial forms of the economy found above all in England. This is also a condition of the modern state according to the *Elements of the Philosophy of Right*,[14] but its preconditions were first present only in the late eighteenth century.

A state with a developed civil society belongs to the third concept of modernity, namely, the 'most recent times' that begin in the late eighteenth century. Its defining feature is the realization of the principle of the freedom of the subject in a political and social order: 'The principle of modern states has enormous strength and depth because it allows the principle of subjectivity to attain fulfilment in the *self-sufficient extreme* of personal particularity, while at the same time *bringing it back to substantial*

[12] In his discussion of the Peace of Westphalia (1648), Hegel criticized the restriction of confessional freedom to sovereigns on the grounds that it contradicted the principle of freedom of conscience (GW 5: 98). The epoch of 'confessionalization' in early-modern times is for Hegel, however, that which it is still largely judged to be today, namely, an intermediate stage in the process of secularization. See Michael Stolleis, '"Konfessionalisierung" oder "Säkularisierung" bei der Entstehung des frühmodernen Staates', *Ius Commune. Zeitschrift für europäische Rechtsgeschichte* 20 (1993): 1–23 and Horst Dreier, 'Kanonistik und Konfessionalisierung – Marksteine auf dem Weg zum Staat!', *Juristen-Zeitung* 57(1) (2002): 1–13.

[13] In PR § 290 with the reference back to § 198.

[14] See PR § 189R (the 'political economy' of Smith, Say and Ricardo etc. has 'originated in recent times as their element'). See also Lisa Herzog, *Inventing the Market: Smith, Hegel, and Political Theory* (Oxford: Oxford University Press, 2013).

unity and so preserving this unity in the principle of subjectivity itself' (PR § 260). This praise of the modern state also contains, however, a criticism of modernity, as is shown by the end of the passage. For integration within a substantial unity, which is not only able to act but is a source of meaning as well, is also threatened in the states that have for Hegel developed in most recent times – not only in historical reality but also in theory. Contract theories of the state in particular confuse the state with civil society. They take the 'particular' subject with its private interests to be the exclusive ground of the justification of norms. Remembering the political freedom of the 'ancients' must here serve to correct modernity. To this extent Hegel is also a critic of modernity who seeks to systematize the criticisms developed by Rousseau, Schiller and Hölderlin.

Despite this critical element, the demand remains that the modern subject be allowed to reflect upon every tradition, authority and normative requirement and examine their claims to legitimacy, and Habermas must be said to be right in this respect. Modernity is an age of reflection, including reflection on its own historical position. Hegel does not, however, draw any democratic or egalitarian conclusions from the right of the individual to examine and to assent to norms.[15] From today's perspective, his conception of a constitutional monarchy with significant elements of an estates-based society contains, as we shall see in what follows, modern as well as traditional elements.

The Modern Human Being and Civil Society

It is for Hegel an essential part of the 'principle' of the modern state that the individual can develop him- or herself in his or her natural and cultural 'particularity' (PR § 260). The individual has the right to pursue his or her private plans of life and ideas of happiness. The space for this freedom is provided by civil society, in which there exists the right of particularity 'to develop and express itself in all directions' (PR § 184).

Hegel does not make clear, however, when the 'modern state' achieved this freedom. Since a civil society presupposes freedom of occupation, at the very least relaxation of the privileges enjoyed by the guilds must be presupposed. To the idea of a developed market economy, there belongs

[15] In his later lectures on the philosophy of history Hegel criticizes 'liberalism'. It opposes to the principle that 'those with understanding have influence among the people and trust rules in the people', which he regards as rational, 'the principle of atoms, of singular wills … everything ought to happen by means of their express authority and explicit consent' (*Werke* 12: 534).

a market for property in land – something about which Hegel himself clearly had some reservations.[16] In terms of the history of ideas, his justification of a bourgeois market society is aimed especially at Rousseau, Fichte and other critics of urban and early-industrial society representative of early socialism and Romanticism.

Fichte had deduced the necessity of state economic planning from every individual's right of self-preservation by means of self-determined action.[17] To guarantee the right to work the state must coordinate needs, occupations and jobs and ensure that a stable relationship exists between them. In Hegel's view this makes choice of occupation and with it the unfolding of 'personal particularity' impossible. The pursuit of their interests by individuals as well as their integration into general patterns of behaviour and the promotion of the common good can in principle be facilitated by market processes, or so Hegel, like Adam Smith, assumes. Hegel thereby has in mind not only the 'invisible hand' processes of the market. He is concerned with the manifold ways in which the individual must for the sake of his or her own legitimate 'selfish' ends adapt him- or herself to general processes. These ways range from the implicit conventions associated with fashion and everyday behaviour, through the knowledge and skill required to earn a living successfully together with adaptation to the collective processes of shaping needs and demands, to the legal framework on which the market depends. The 'abstract right' of the first part of the *Elements of the Philosophy of Right*, namely the right of the person to acquire property for his or her own ends and to exchange it in the form of free contracts, becomes 'actual' only in civil society. For one thing this means that practices and institutions through which legal disputes can be decided are discussed ('the Administration of Justice'). For another thing, this actuality of abstract right requires that individuals must also

[16] Hegel approves of the political representation of aristocratic landowners as the moment that mediates the '*changing* element' (PR § 308), that is, civil society, and the constancy of the 'princely' element (see PR §§ 305–308). For more on the incipient liberalization of the economy undertaken by the Prussian reformers, to whom Hegel was otherwise close, see Reinhart Koselleck, *Preußen zwischen Reform und Revolution* (Stuttgart: Klett-Cotta, 1975), 305 and 314–315.

[17] Fichte had already justified this right in his *Foundations of Natural Right* from 1796–97 und set out its conditions in *The Closed Commercial State* from 1800. See Johann Gottlieb Fichte, *Grundlage des Naturrechts nach Prinzipien der Wissenschaftslehre*, in *Gesamtausgabe der Bayerischen Akademie der Wissenschaften*, ed. Reinha rd Lauth, Hans Jacob and Hans Gliwitzky (Stuttgart-Bad Cannstatt: Frommann-Holzboog, 1962–2012), I/3 and I/4 (English translation: *Foundations of Natural Right*, ed. Frederick Neuhouser, trans. Michael Baur [Cambridge: Cambridge University Press, 2000]) and *Der geschloßne Handelsstaat*, in *Gesamtausgabe der Bayerischen Akademie der Wissenschaften*, I/7 (English translation: *The Closed Commercial State*, trans. A. C. Adler [Albany, NY: SUNY Press, 2012]).

be guaranteed the material conditions of attaining and safeguarding their rights. Market processes are not, however, sufficient in relation to this end.

Hegel is no unconditional 'free-market liberal'. What he *also* infers from writings on early-industrial England is the instability of this system, the first signs of which he could have already experienced in Prussia as well. Both contingent factors – such as the distribution of raw materials or the unpredictability of the climate – and law-like economic regularities are responsible for this instability. A 'concentration of wealth' on the one hand and impoverishment caused by sales and wage crises on the other lead to a formation of classes which can result in the dissolution of any allegiance to right on the part of those without hope.[18] It is then shown that 'despite an *excess of wealth*, civil society is *not wealthy enough* … to prevent an excess of poverty and the formation of a rabble' (PR § 245).

Hegel himself calls this process of increasing productivity and wealth, on the one hand, together with class division and the erosion of a communal consciousness and obedience to law, on the other, the 'dialectic' of civil society, through which it is 'driven beyond itself' (PR § 246). Many dialectical and revolutionary social theorists after Hegel have adopted this thesis. However, it is often overlooked that Hegel does not allow any synthesis *at the same level*, namely, at the level of the economic organization of society, to follow from this contradiction of a self-destroying society.

The 'beyond itself' must be understood to possess three different meanings. First of all, a country's civil society must go beyond itself through emigration, colonization and the opening of other markets for its goods (PR §§ 247–249). In this it can be supported by the state by means of a foreign-trade policy that in Hegel's case is restricted neither by international law nor by any supranational organizations. Secondly, civil society must develop within itself forms of conscious activity and arrangements that aim to avoid, moderate and offset the crises that it produces. Although this partly takes place through the family, it is predominantly achieved through trade and professional organizations, and finally through state administration (*Polizei*). Hegel terms this state activity that aims to preserve and stabilize civil society the '*state of necessity* and *of the understanding*' (PR § 183). Thirdly, however, the whole set of ways of thinking and

[18] See PR § 244. This loss of any sense of identification with the state and law is for Hegel characteristic of the 'rabble'. Even in the case of the wealthy, as he had acutely pointed out in his lectures, a 'rabble mentality' arises: 'The rich man regards everything as something he can buy' (PR 1819/20, 196). The 'public begging' (*öffentliche Bettel*), of which Hegel speaks in PR § 244, in contrast clearly has to do with an estate that is recognized and supervised by the state. See also Norbert Waszek, 'Hegels Schottische Bettler', *Hegel-Studien* 19 (1984): 311–316.

behaving, ends, rights and duties must be raised to a new level. This represents the necessity of the transition to the true state as 'the actuality of the ethical Idea' (PR § 257).

For Hegel's conception of the state the second and third senses of the 'transcending' of civil society are especially important. The role of the state is at first to stabilize civil society within the latter's own principle of ethical life. This principle is characterized by the promotion of the individual's interests within a framework of civil law and by the disposition towards rectitude and respectability characteristic of the member of an estate (PR § 207). On account of its 'dialectical' self-destructive structure, civil society already requires within this framework sufficient state support to prevent a large mass of people from sinking into poverty (PR § 244). In addition the state can 'for the protection and security of the masses of particular ends and interests' (PR § 249) even encroach on property rights and intervene in the sphere of trade and industry, though without destroying freedom of trade and without being able to guarantee permanent economic security (PR §§ 236–237). Hegel still attributes these – in modern parlance – 'welfare state' functions to civil society, which they aim to preserve. This does not mean, though, that these are not yet functions of the state. They belong to the functions that must be enforced by means of legal coercive power, that is to say, they belong to the state's monopoly on the use of force.[19]

The measures undertaken by the state that Hegel views as arising in this sphere and seeks to justify include such forward-looking elements as the supervision of trade (PR § 236) and measures relating to welfare and transport policy ('public poorhouses, hospitals, streetlighting', PR § 242R). In the case of 'public poorhouses', the state or 'universal power' is, however, also equipped with disciplinary and coercive powers that do not accord with today's ideas of freedom and fundamental rights: they counteract 'the disposition of laziness, viciousness, and the other vices' (PR § 241). Among the goals that the state promotes by means of this form of 're-education' belong not only civic virtues but also loyalty and patriotism in an 'ethical' state which is more than a mere state of necessity and state of the understanding (*Not- und Verstandesstaat*).

Hegel regards a permanent overcoming of the 'dialectic' of civil society within its own ethical framework, that is, within the framework of its rules, attitudes and motives ('dispositions'), as impossible. He views the

[19] See PR § 259. This does not concern, however, separate administrative bodies, but different tasks of the same 'government' (see PR § 287).

poverty found in civil society as systematic and unavoidable (PR § 244). The state can at most seek to prevent its intensification and the large-scale emergence of a rabble mentality which renounces any allegiance to law (PR § 245). The 'division [*Entzweiung*] of civil society' (PR § 256) is not overcome as society develops; it is just as permanent as its ethical overcoming is constantly necessary. The fact that the one constantly requires the other even constitutes for Hegel the '*scientific proof* of the concept of the state' (PR § 256R).

The political state is not only the strong state that is capable of setting free the 'principle of particularity', that is, the choice of personal plans of life and the pursuit of one's own interests. A state which can endure the 'division of civil society', that is to say, a market untrammelled by morality or religion, for Hegel needs its own 'ethics' (*Sittlichkeit*). It must be able to set against, or place above, the self-interest of market players and the rights upon which they can insist higher ends within the community. As will be shown, the state is a source of meaning and fosters a sense of identity that is equal to the powerful sense of conviction fostered by religion. In order for it not to be dominated by religious claims, Hegel accords the state an ethical content. An ethical state must, as we shall see, be able to lend meaning even to the most extreme of sacrifices. The poor person shares this consciousness of being a '*citoyen*' to the same degree as every other fellow citizen. This view is strange to us today and hardly modern, but it must be thought to have been otherwise for the age ushered in by the French Revolution. Hegel's concept of philosophy aims at comprehending things retrospectively, at most discerning tendencies but never postulating or prophesying future states.

All in all, Hegel's theory of civil society is modern in the sense that it distinguishes from one another the spheres of the economy and the state, and differentiates forms of existence within the family, professional or occupational life and political life. It is modern also in the sense of describing, and partly even anticipating, the abolition of estates-based and political privileges. It does not, however, pursue a project of permanently overcoming economic crises by means of a rationally planned and administered management of the economy. It wants to tame the powers of the markets through the transformation of traditional institutions, through professional virtues,[20] and through the state. The state ought – as the state

[20] See PR § 253. The prestige enjoyed by the member of an estate has less to do with economic success than with respectability and solidarity with the other members of the estate. See Hans-Christoph Schmidt am Busch, *'Anerkennung' als Prinzip der Kritischen Theorie* (Berlin: de Gruyter, 2011), 237–244.

of necessity or state of the understanding – to have a stabilizing effect. Above all else, however, as an ethical state it ought to open up a new dimension with regard to the meaning of life and forms of community.

Sovereignty, Secularism and the *Citoyen*

From all that has been said, how modern is the genuine 'political' or ethical state? With respect to its form of government, Hegel's state is a particular type of constitutional monarchy. He regards this type of constitutional monarchy not only as modern but also as a rational synthesis of the classical forms of government. Only an analysis of the distribution of rights and competences found in this state can show how it should be judged from today's perspective. A strong concept of sovereignty, which without doubt corresponds to the modern concept of sovereignty that begins with Bodin, turns out to be central to this conception of the state. The secular character of this state also appears modern. Hegel believes, however, that a stable modern state must incorporate the religious consciousness. He thereby draws on elements of both ancient political religion and modern enlightened Protestant Christianity.

Constitutional Monarchy

Hegel had begun to develop a determinate conception of constitutional monarchy as the result of a rationally comprehensible constitutional history by the end of his Jena period (1805–6).[21] In his lectures on the philosophy of right given in Heidelberg and during the early part of his Berlin period, Hegel viewed the French Constitution of 1815 as the rationally justified outcome of the development of the French Revolution.[22] In § 273 of the *Elements of the Philosophy of Right*, he describes constitutional monarchy as a result of the 'concrete rationality' of the 'recent world'. In contrast to 'the old world', this form of government contains within itself classical monarchy, aristocracy and democracy 'reduced … to [the status of] moments' (PR § 273R). As moments they are transformed, whereas he characterizes the understanding of them as unmodified 'elements' as a modern ('in recent times') misunderstanding. Hegel's theory of a division of powers aims to deduce these moments from the Idea of a rational state.

[21] GW 8: 263.

[22] See VNS § 134R. Concerning the synthesis of different constitutional forms in a constitutional monarchy, see VNS § 137.

It is decisively aimed against all theories of 'checks and balances', which he criticizes for being mechanical.[23] The fact that he understands his own theory to be 'organic' means that the powers are particular functions that reciprocally support each other and are integrated into a self-conscious whole that is capable of action. This 'horizontal' division of powers has less of a control function of preventing the misuse of state power than does the 'vertical' one existing between the central authorities and local 'corporations', that is, estates-based and communal self-governing bodies. Hegel's position is here close to the reforms of Freiherr vom Stein, which he presented as alternatives to the centralization and bureaucracy characteristic of post-revolutionary France.[24]

Hegel's triad of powers comprises the power of the sovereign ('prince'), the executive power and the legislative power. One can offer a plausible account of these powers with reference to Hegel's logic of the concept, that is, according to the moments of universality, particularity and individuality. If one views them against the background provided by European constitutional history, however, one may doubt their modernity. Hegel rejects popular sovereignty as much as he rejects the primacy of the legislative power, representation of every citizen as much as equal and universal elections. His reasons for doing so are not those of modern critics who point to the fact that in the case of the right to vote in his time only economically independent males, who commonly were graded according to the amount of tax they paid, represented the nation. Rather, he considers elections to be a game of chance and opinion, and he regards shifting majorities as a danger to the unity of the state. His alternative is representation by means of the expert knowledge of professional corporations and areas of business or trade that are socially important. In the upper chamber the land-owning nobility are represented, and in the second chamber one has 'the assembly of the Estates', the deputies of the corporations, who have been 'summoned' by the monarch (PR § 308). The importance of differences between the estates also finds expression in how the administration, at the higher levels at least, ought to be in the hands of a scientifically

[23] Ludwig Siep, 'Hegels Theorie der Gewaltenteilung', in Ludwig Siep, *Praktische Philosophie im Deutschen Idealismus* (Frankfurt am Main: Suhrkamp, 1992), 240–269; and Michael Wolff, 'Hegel's Organicist Theory of the State: On the Concept and Method of Hegel's "Science of the State"', in Robert B. Pippin and Otfried Höffe (eds.), *Hegel on Ethics and Politics*, trans. Nicholas Walker (Cambridge: Cambridge University Press, 2004), 291–322.

[24] See PR § 290A. This addition comes from Griesheim's transcript of the lectures from 1824–25 (VRP 4: 692). Concerning the reforms of Freiherr vom Stein, see also Koselleck, *Preußen zwischen Reform und Revolution*, 163–169 and 560–572.

(especially legally and philosophically) trained civil service whose members' material needs are met by the state.

Hegel's monarchy is by no means based on divine right, nor can it be called absolutism in the traditional sense. The legitimacy of the rights and duties of the monarch, as with those of the citizen, derives from the idea of the rational state and its constitution. We shall later examine the concept of sovereignty that underlies Hegel's account of monarchy. In order to judge the modernity of this constitution, one must examine the way in which responsibilities are distributed. This shows that it is only in a very weak sense that the monarch is constrained by the legislative power of the representatives of the estates. Nor is the government obliged to justify itself before the assembly of the Estates. Legislation concerns only one part of state power and the princely power has as much of a share in it as the government and both chambers. The domain of foreign affairs and the military – the latter especially took a large slice of the state's budget in Hegel's day – is exempted from the right to control the budget enjoyed by the chambers (PR § 329; see also PM § 544R). Decisions concerning war and peace are left to the monarch alone.[25] One can say that Hegel's form of constitutional monarchy is closer to the 'German type' of the nineteenth century, according to which representatives of the people and the monarch share legislative power, than to the Western European or American ones in which, despite many differences, popular sovereignty manifests itself primarily in parliamentary legislation. Despite the restrictions placed on the right to vote, they represent from today's perspective a 'more modern' form of the division of powers and 'civic involvement' than does Hegel's type of constitutional monarchy.

Sovereignty

Hegel is a philosopher of state sovereignty ('sovereignty belongs to the *state*', PR § 279).[26] He rejects a sovereignty of the people that stands above the constitution as much as Kant does. He distinguishes between *populus*, understood as a unified whole made up of citizens with their rights and

[25] In PR § 329 and more explicitly in the *Encyclopaedia* of 1830 decisions concerning war and peace contrary to the republican tradition are expressly assigned to the princely power of the sovereign to the exclusion of the assembly of Estates (PM § 544).

[26] Dieter Grimm sees in Hegel's idea of state sovereignty and its manifestation in the monarch a precursor of the 'German' theory of state sovereignty in the late nineteenth century. See Dieter Grimm, *Souveränität. Herkunft und Zukunft eines Schlüsselbegriffs* (Berlin: Berlin University Press, 2009), 52.

duties who are bound together by the constitution, and *vulgus*, understood as an 'aggregate of private persons' (PM § 544R). In the third edition of the *Encyclopaedia* he describes 'the sole aim of the state' as being 'that a people should *not* come to existence, to power and action, *as such an aggregate*' (PM § 544R). This corresponds to the classical rejection of ochlocracy and also to the modern rejection of lawless mob rule. Hegel, however, rejects along with this any idea of a transfer of sovereignty and authority on the part of individuals to a representative assembly and a government appointed by it in the tradition of Locke or Rousseau. Social contract theory makes the state dependent on individual interests and 'confuses' it with civil society (PR § 258R). The act of unification that constitutes a state and a 'public life' within it has to be understood instead as the end and 'vocation' of the citizens (PR § 258R). Only as a 'member' of the objective spirit of the state does the individual have 'objectivity, truth, and ethical life' (PR § 258R). Since his Jena period, Hegel had interpreted the Aristotelian concept of the *polis* ontologically by means of a Spinozist concept of substance.[27]

Although constitutions arise from the 'spirit of a people', that is, from its history and political culture, a founding act on the part of the people is not necessary. At most the people can represent the sovereignty of the state together with its monarch. The modern ('in recent times') view that opposes popular sovereignty to the sovereignty of the monarch belongs to 'those confused thoughts which are based on a *garbled* notion of the *people*' (PR § 279R). For Hegel, the monarchy is necessarily connected with the '*articulation* of the whole' (PR § 279R). To this '*internally organized* whole' belong the constitution and the 'organic' working together of the various powers and estates, on the one hand, and the 'absolute beginning' of governmental action by the monarch, on the other. The latter encompasses a series of rights, such as the right to pardon, the appointment of officials, putting laws into effect and supreme command of the 'armed forces' (see PR § 329) that have been linked with the idea of sovereignty since Bodin. The sovereignty of the state is represented by the person of the monarch, however, only in unity with the rational constitution and insofar as the monarch is the expression of this unity.

What is problematic about the Hegelian concept of sovereignty in the light of further developments that the modern age has undergone is

[27] See Karl-Heinz Ilting, 'Hegels Auseinandersetzung mit der aristotelischen Politik', *Philosophisches Jahrbuch* 71 (1963/1964): 38–48.

that Hegel does not comprehend the fundamental rights of individuals as being essentially connected with a limitation of sovereignty.[28] On the contrary, the highest expression of sovereignty, with which it also comes closest to Hegel's philosophical concept of the absolute (absolute spirit, absolute idea), is precisely the negation of all the individual's rights in war. War is admittedly an exceptional, extreme condition, but it is not exclusively imposed upon the state by the necessity of defending itself. Rather, states must sometimes bring it about so as to prevent the ossification of public life and the reduction of society to an 'aggregate' of private interests (PR §§ 278, 323–324).

One can certainly claim that fundamental rights play a central role in Hegel's philosophy of right.[29] He accorded high value to the significance of various declarations of them, but he wants to see them made concrete and given the form of positive law in the various domains of right. Hegel did not accord fundamental rights a constitutional status that would allow one to appeal to them *in opposition to* positive laws and the actions of the government. He holds the idea of tracing them back to historical agreements made by the estates with the monarch to be pre-modern and inappropriate in relation to the demands of a rational development of right. This claim, however, leads him to neglect their function as fundamental limits to state sovereignty in modern developments in international law. Hegel not only neglects this, but consciously places the rights of sovereignty above all others and regards the sovereign state as an absolute end in itself (PR §§ 257–258).

This is not simply a time-bound 'conservatism' on Hegel's part. It has instead to do with his theory of subjectivity, according to which not only individual but also institutional subjects constitute a 'simple self', which, although it has an inner 'organism' made up of functions and aims – in the case of the state its 'particular powers and functions' (PR § 276) – equally 'idealizes' them, that is, negates their independence and reduces them to

[28] Concerning the essential – and historical – connection between fundamental rights and restrictions on sovereignty, see Martin Kriele, 'Zur Geschichte der Grund- und Menschenrechte', in Norbert Achterberg (ed.), *Öffentliches Recht und Politik* (Berlin: Duncker & Humblot, 1973), 187–211.

[29] See Gertrude Lübbe-Wolff, 'Über das Fehlen von Grundrechten in Hegels Rechtsphilosophie. Zugleich ein Beitrag zum Verständnis der historischen Grundlagen des Hegelschen Staatsbegriffs', in H.-C. Lucas and O. Pöggeler (eds.), *Hegels Rechtsphilosophie im Zusammenhang der europäischen Verfassungsgeschichte* (Stuttgart-Bad Cannstatt: Frommann-Holzboog, 1986), 421–446; and Ludwig Siep, 'Constitution, Fundamental Rights and Social Welfare', in Pippin and Höffe, *Hegel on Ethics and Politics*, 268–290. I here part company with Herbert Schnädelbach, whose judgement concerning Hegel's modernity I share in most regards. See Herbert Schnädelbach, 'Die Verfassung der Freiheit', in Ludwig Siep (ed.), *G. W. F. Hegel. Grundlinien der Philosophie des Rechts*, 3rd edn (Berlin: Akademie Verlag, 2014), 260.

their functionality for the whole. This can happen either 'unconsciously' or in an explicit manner. The unconscious aspect concerns 'times of peace' characterized by the normal functioning of the political organism and the market society in which the 'selfishness' of the citizens not only finds free play in the 'unconscious necessity' of socio-economic processes, but is also '*transformed* into a contribution to mutual preservation, and to the preservation of the whole' (PR § 278R). To this normal, largely unconscious process, however, the conscious aspect of integration must be added. This happens already through the 'direct influence' of the 'executive power', which collects taxes and punishes violations of law (PR § 278R). The 'making ideal' or suspension of the tendency of self-interest to become independent first becomes manifest, however, in 'situation[s] of crisis', whether in the internal one of rebellion or in the external one of war. The state engages in wars not only to defend itself against insurrections and external attacks. Rather, it must occasionally bring about wars for the sake of internal discipline – or, to put it more nicely, to activate moral energies that are directed towards the whole. Only then does the process of making ideal occur and 'idealism … attains its distinct actuality' (PR § 278R).

This is made very clear when Hegel comes to discuss 'external sovereignty'. The negation of the particular now appears to be for the state not merely an emergency but its '*own* highest moment – its actual infinity as the ideality of everything finite within it. It is that aspect whereby the substance, as the state's absolute power over everything individual and particular, over life, property, and the latter's rights, and over the wider circles within it, gives the nullity of such things an existence and makes it present to the consciousness' (PR § 323). The negation of right, life and property is therefore not merely an accepted means of preserving the state, but the explicit manifestation of the state's sovereignty. According to Hegel, this negation fulfils the individual's highest right, highest duty and ethical vocation. It even provides the individual with the only possible form of immortality, in which death is turned from a chance natural occurrence into an ethically '*willed* evanescence' of life (§ 324R). The individual even has a right to the general *possibility* of sacrificing his or her life, if not to the actual act of offering up his or her own life – 'ethical war' must be consciously brought about by the state when there is disunity or an ossification of the 'particular' (PR § 324).

This sounds highly 'unmodern' when viewed from the perspective of a sovereignty that is restricted to the 'responsibility to protect' and the limitation of war to the *ultima ratio* of defence against attack. One must, however, bear in mind the debates concerning patriotism, enthusiasm for the republic and the immortality gained from posthumous glory within a republic that took place in the period of the French Revolution.[30] For Hegel it is not, however, a 'republic' for which it is worth dying, and it is also not a matter of posthumous glory. Hegel grants 'immortal glory' only to individuals who are of world-historical significance because they have unconsciously anticipated new epochs of world history and helped to bring them about through their actions (PR § 348). The willingness to die concerns the state that is demanded by reason and has been increasingly realized in the course of history, and which finds its highest expression in constitutional monarchy. This willingness or disposition does not, however, have the preservation of the rights of present and future generations of citizens as its supreme object. Rather, it relates to the spirit of the citizens embodied in the state as their 'own *substantial spirit*', and which they '*actively pursue* ... as their *ultimate end*' (PR § 260). This spirit is an absolute, traditionally divine one, even though in the state it is still bound up in manifold ways with that which is 'external', natural and contingent. Therefore, the state cannot be reduced to an instrument either of the market (society) or of religion, the latter having used it for centuries as a means of enforcing truth and bringing about the eternal salvation of its citizens.

Secularism

A defining feature of the modern state is its independence of religion, and how it guarantees freedom from religion and the freedom to belong to a religion. Is Hegel's state a secular state? This question has also been a matter of dispute from the time of Hegel's students up to this day.

To answer this question, two aspects of it must be distinguished. First of all, (a) does Hegel justify the order and validity of the norms and institutions of his philosophy of right with arguments that are somehow linked to religion? Secondly, (b) is conviction of a religious or theistic kind on the part of the modern state's citizens for him a precondition of obedience to law?

[30] See Elisabeth Fehrenbach, 'Nation', in Rolf Reichardt and Eberhard Schmitt (eds.), *Handbuch politisch-sozialer Grundbegriffe in Frankreich 1680–1820*, Vol. 7 (Munich: Oldenbourg Wissenschaftsverlag, 1986), 75–107; and Martin Papenheim, *Erinnerung und Unsterblichkeit. Semantische Studien zum Totenkult in Frankreich 1715–1794* (Stuttgart: Klett-Cotta, 1992).

(a) Hegel does not make use of arguments drawn from religion or theology in his philosophy of right. He does, though, employ predicates that are applied to God in philosophical theology ('absolute unmoved end in itself', 'infinite', 'eternal' etc.). In the philosophy of right, however, only legal and 'ethical' relations existing between the state and its citizens, estates, institutions etc., but not anything transcendent, are characterized in this way. The state itself is not, moreover, a conscious person, apart from how it manifests itself in the monarch, who is himself, however, bound by the constitution.

In his famous remark on the relationship between the state and religion (PR § 270R), Hegel nevertheless claims that the rational state agrees in terms of its content with the concepts of a rational religion. The development of objective spirit in his system necessarily results, moreover, in an absolute spirit which finds expression in narrative form ('in the element of representational thought') in the truths of Christianity. Philosophy can, as Hegel says in the final paragraph of the *Elements of the Philosophy of Right* (§ 360), recognize nature, the state and the 'ideal world' of art, religion and science to be equally justified manifestations of this absolute. With respect to ethical obligations and their necessary grounds of justification, the state does not, however, require this further development. In terms of right the state is placed above all religious communities; it exercises legal 'supervision' (PR § 270R) of them and it must prevent anything from this direction undermining its authority. The foundations of his philosophy of right are 'secular' ones that are not dependent on any particular religious tradition or revelation. Viewed from this angle, the justification Hegel provides can be called a secular one despite the 'divine' predicates that he attaches to the state.

(b) Hegel, however, in another respect calls religion the 'foundation' of the state (PR § 270, PM § 552). Like the majority of his predecessors since Plato, he believes that the state must be supported by a religious 'disposition' or the religious conscience of its members.[31] What this means is a difficult topic and Hegel himself, judging from the transcripts of his lectures, occasionally vacillated between the views that the religious disposition was a useful, desirable or necessary condition of stable loyalty to the state and obedience to law.[32]

[31] In a similar way, Kant regards the 'moral church' as being in the long run the only means of the moral improvement of its members and guaranteeing their firm obedience to law. He therefore considers even the still superstitious faith of the people to be less dangerous than atheism (R, 109).

[32] See Ludwig Siep, *Der Staat als irdischer Gott. Genesis und Relevanz einer Hegelschen Idee* (Tübingen: Mohr & Siebeck, 2015).

In some relevant passages in his works he assumes, however, the dependence of the state on the religious disposition which supports it.[33] In the *Elements of the Philosophy of Right* he therefore even attributes to the state the duty 'to require that all its citizens ... belong to a religious community' (PR § 270R; translation modified). Here it is not a matter of fear of punishment after death for undetected violations of right, as it is in traditional political philosophy. The state must rather, like religion, be sustained by a profound enthusiasm that even allows the interest in preserving one's own life to be overcome. This is something that social contract theory cannot do. An accord between religious feeling and conviction and a 'worldly' ethical life, which sees something absolute in the family, working life and the state itself, is instead needed. In his final years Hegel thought that only a liberal-minded, philosophically 'enlightened' Protestantism was capable of this.[34]

If this interpretation is right, Hegel cannot accord to citizens without religion a form of recognition within the state equal to that accorded to those citizens who are religious. The state admittedly should not compel citizens to be religious but only 'require' them to join a church, and it should support their religious activities. Both things set limits to the neutrality and secularity of the state. This corresponds, moreover, to the legal position of atheism in Europe until at least the middle of the nineteenth century. Even today there are states that privilege one religion in particular. When such a state does not legally discriminate against other religious communities or against people with no religion, legal scholars, for instance, speak of a (Christian or Muslim) 'tolerant state'.[35] It is questionable, however, whether this suffices for genuine religious freedom,

[33] In § 270R of the *Elements of the Philosophy of Right* and § 552 of the 1830 edition of the *Encyclopaedia*. It seems that Hegel's criticism of the 'error of our times' of characterizing religion only as something 'desirable' for the 'strengthening' of the state in the *Encyclopaedia* refers to an expression found in Kant's *Religion within the Boundaries of Mere Reason* (R, 95).

[34] Hegel criticizes forms of Protestantism that focus on a feeling that seeks to escape the real world (see *Werke* 17: 329–332) as well as the combining of religious and political feeling (see PR *Preface*, 15[18] and 16–17[20]). Regarding the criticisms of Schleiermacher and Fries in the Preface to the *Elements of the Philosophy of Right*, see Ludwig Siep, 'Vernunftrecht und Rechtsgeschichte. Kontext und Konzept der "Grundlinien" im Blick auf die "Vorrede"', in Ludwig Siep, *Aktualität und Grenzen der praktischen Philosophie Hegels* (Munich: Wilhelm Fink, 2010), 26–29. Regarding the connection between pietism and patriotism in Germany, see Gerhard Kaiser, *Pietismus und Patriotismus im literarischen Deutschland. Ein Beitrag zum Problem der Säkularisation* (Frankfurt am Main: Athenäum, 1973).

[35] Hans-Martin Pawlowski, 'Zur Aufgabe der Rechtsdogmatik im Staat der Glaubensfreiheit', *Rechtstheorie* 19(4) (1988): 409–441.

including religious freedom in the sense of the equal opportunity to engage in public activity and to participate in political life. Such a state can surely be called 'secular' only in a restricted sense.

Hegel's Modernity and Its Limits

Hegel's conception of the state can undoubtedly in some important respects be regarded as what one would today call 'modern'. The state has the legal task of protecting individual rights and promoting its citizens' welfare. It ought to leave room for freedom of conscience, the critical examination of norms and the pursuit of personal plans of life. It must be as free of religious paternalism, especially when exercised by a church, as it is free from the domination of economic interests. The administration of it ought to be rationally and professionally organized.

Features that from the standpoint of later constitutional history and political philosophy *cannot* be called 'modern' are, however, equally evident. They are often not superficially 'time-bound' features but ones whose validity Hegel has consciously asserted in opposition to tendencies of the modern age that have for him led to the loss of ethical life and state sovereignty. Hegel shares with the revolutions in the United States, and above all in France, the appeal to antiquity, not just the ideal of the free citizen, but also that of the state (*polis*), to live in which and to live – and possibly die – for which constitutes the human being's political and rational nature. He does not combine this, however, with revolutionary demands for popular sovereignty, republicanism or a strong elected parliament. The significance of fundamental rights is, moreover, severely restricted by his concept of sovereignty. This concept corresponds to Hegel's concept of a subjectivity which divides itself into 'moments' and functions, while at the same time 'sublating' them into a simple unity. This is the foundational structure of reality which is also developed in the other parts of the system and itself becomes an object of reflection (*Science of Logic*). The context provided by constitutional history and the function of subjectivity and idealism in Hegel's system as a whole ought to discourage hasty attempts to bring Hegel's political philosophy up to date.

The basic concept of Hegel's philosophy of right, the concept of freedom, is certainly modern. Hegel called freedom an 'abstract' idea, however, so long as it had not differentiated itself into a system of forms of freedom – to be precise, into the rights, duties and responsibilities found in a constitution (PM § 482). The term 'constitution' must thereby be understood to mean both an order of strict rights and a political and social 'culture'.[36] Hegel attempts in the most varied ways to combine in this system of freedom the willing of rational law and the welfare of the whole with the pursuit of particular interests without generating open conflict or forms of oppression. When one examines this system more closely, however, the sovereignty of the state turns out to be in decisive respects too powerful and the individual's right of political participation – though in extreme cases also to resistance – too weak. This is the case not only when viewed from today's perspective but also in comparison with the political philosophies and the constitutional history of his time. A comparison of this kind would allow one to see with more precision in what ways Hegel is 'more modern' than his contemporaries and in what ways he is not so. In comparison with Kant, for example, his concept of a 'welfare state' is more modern, whereas his theory of war and international law is not. One can doubt whether modernity is a criterion of truth at all. Certainly, though, it is a criterion of that which promises to be relevant to discussions of present-day problems. We should not, however, ignore the historical gap.[37]

[36] See Ludwig Siep, '"Gesinnung" und "Verfassung". Bemerkungen zu einem nicht nur Hegelschen Problem', in Siep, *Praktische Philosophie im Deutschen Idealismus*, 270–283.

[37] Translated from the German by the editor, who would like to thank the author for his help in improving the translation.

Bibliography

Adorno, Theodor W., *Negative Dialectics*, trans. E. B. Ashton (London: Continuum, 1973).

Hegel: Three Studies, trans. Shierry Weber Nicholsen (Cambridge, MA: MIT Press, 1993).

Problems of Moral Philosophy, trans. Rodney Livingstone (Stanford, CA: Stanford University Press, 2001).

Negative Dialektik (Frankfurt am Main: Suhrkamp, 2003).

Arthur, Christopher J., 'Hegel on Political Economy', in David Lamb (ed.), *Hegel and Modern Philosophy* (London: Croom Helm, 1987), 102–118.

Avineri, Shlomo, *Hegel's Theory of the Modern State* (Cambridge: Cambridge University Press, 1972).

Beck, Ulrich, *Risikogesellschaft. Auf dem Weg in eine andere Moderne* (Frankfurt am Main: Suhrkamp, 1986).

Benhabib, Seyla, 'On Hegel, Women, and Irony', in Patricia Jagentowicz Mills (ed.), *Feminist Interpretations of G. W. F. Hegel* (University Park, PA: Pennsylvania University Press, 1996), 25–43.

Benjamin, Jessica, *The Bonds of Love: Psychoanalysis, Feminism and the Problem of Domination* (London: Virago Press, 1988).

Berlin, Isaiah, *Two Concepts of Liberty* (Oxford: Clarendon Press, 1958).

Blasche, Siegfried, 'Natural Ethical Life and Civil Society: Hegel's Construction of the Family', in Robert B. Pippin and Otfried Höffe (eds.), *Hegel on Ethics and Politics*, trans. N. Walker (Cambridge: Cambridge University Press, 2004), 183–207.

Brandom, Robert, 'Some Pragmatist Themes in Hegel's Idealism: Negotiation and Administration in Hegel's Account of the Structure and Content of Conceptual Norms', *European Journal of Philosophy* 7(2) (1999): 164–189.

'Holism and idealism in Hegel's *Phenomenology*', in *Tales of the Mighty Dead: Historical Essays in the Metaphysics of Intentionality* (Cambridge, MA: Harvard University Press, 2002), 178–209.

Brod, Harry, *Hegel's Philosophy of Politics: Idealism, Identity, & Modernity* (Boulder, CO: Westview Press, 1992).

Bubner, Rüdiger, 'Hegel's Concept of Phenomenology', in *The Innovations of Idealism*, trans. Nicholas Walker (Cambridge: Cambridge University Press, 2003), 119–144.

Buchwalter, Andrew, *Dialectics, Politics, and the Contemporary Value of Hegel's Practical Philosophy* (New York and London: Routledge, 2011).

'Hegel, Human Rights, and Political Membership', *Hegel Bulletin* 34(1) (2013): 98–119.

(ed.), *Hegel and Capitalism* (Albany, NY: SUNY Press, 2015).

'The Concept of Normative Reconstruction: Honneth, Hegel, and the Aims of Critical Social Theory', in *Reconstructing Social Theory, History and Practice: Current Perspectives in Social Theory* 35 (2016): 57–88.

Carré, Louis, 'Populace, multitude, *populus*. Figures du peuple dans la *Philosophie du droit* de Hegel', *Tumultes* 40 (2013): 89–107.

Ciavatta, David V., *Spirit, the Family, and the Unconscious in Hegel's Philosophy* (Albany, NY: SUNY Press, 2009).

'The Family and the Bonds of Recognition', *Emotion, Space and Society* 13(1) (2014): 71–79.

Comay, Rebecca, *Mourning Sickness: Hegel and the French Revolution* (Stanford, CA: Stanford University Press, 2010).

Deranty, Jean-Philippe, 'Hegel's Social Theory of Value', *The Philosophical Forum* 36(3) (2005): 307–331.

Dreier, Horst, 'Kanonistik und Konfessionalisierung – Marksteine auf dem Weg zum Staat!', *Juristen-Zeitung* 57(1) (2002): 1–13.

Eisenstadt, Shmuel N., *Die Vielfalt der Moderne* (Weilerswist: Velbrück, 2000).

Ellmers, Sven, *Freiheit und Wirtschaft. Theorie der bürgerlichen Gesellschaft nach Hegel* (Bielefeld: Transcript, 2015).

Fehrenbach, Elisabeth, 'Nation', in Rolf Reichardt and Eberhard Schmitt (eds.), *Handbuch politisch-sozialer Grundbegriffe in Frankreich 1680–1820*, Vol. 7 (Munich: Oldenbourg Wissenschaftsverlag, 1986): 75–107.

Fichte, Johann Gottlieb, *Gesamtausgabe der Bayerischen Akademie der Wissenschaften*, eds. Reinhard Lauth, Hans Jacob and Hans Gliwitzky (Stuttgart-Bad Cannstatt: Frommann-Holzboog, 1962–2012).

Foundations of Natural Right, ed. Frederick Neuhouser, trans. Michael Baur (Cambridge: Cambridge University Press, 2000).

The Closed Commercial State, trans. A. C. Adler (Albany, NY: SUNY Press, 2012).

Forster, Michael, *Hegel's Idea of a Phenomenology of Spirit* (Chicago, IL: University of Chicago Press, 1998).

Förster, Eckart, *The Twenty-Five Years of Philosophy*, trans. Brady Bowman (Cambridge, MA: Harvard University Press, 2012).

Franco, Paul, *Hegel's Philosophy of Freedom* (New Haven, CT: Yale University Press, 1999).

Gans, Eduard, *Naturrecht und Universalgeschichte. Vorlesungen nach G. W. F. Hegel* (Tübingen: Mohr Siebeck, 2005).

Gillespie, Robert, 'Progeny and Property', *Women and Politics* 15(2) (1995): 37–51.

Goodfield, Eric Lee, *Hegel and the Metaphysical Frontiers of Political Theory* (London: Routledge, 2014).

Grimm, Dieter, *Souveränität. Herkunft und Zukunft eines Schlüsselbegriffs* (Berlin: Berlin University Press, 2009).

Geuss, Raymond, *Outside Ethics* (Princeton, NJ: Princeton University Press, 2005).

Habermas, Jürgen, *The Philosophical Discourse of Modernity*, trans. Frederick Lawrence (Cambridge: Polity, 1987).

The Theory of Communicative Action, Volume 2: Life World and System: A Critique of Functionalist Reason, trans. Thomas McCarthy (Boston, MA: Beacon Press, 1987).

Halper, Edward C., 'Hegel's Family Values', *The Review of Metaphysics* 54(4) (2001): 815–858.

Hamacher, Werner, 'The Right to Have Rights (Four-and-a-Half-Remarks)', *The South Atlantic Quarterly* 103(2/3) (2004): 343–356.

Hardimon, Michael O., *Hegel's Social Philosophy: The Project of Reconciliation* (Cambridge: Cambridge University Press, 1994).

Hart, H. L. A., *The Concept of Law*, 2nd edn (Oxford: Oxford University Press, 1997).

Haym, Rudolf, *Hegel und seine Zeit. Vorlesungen über Entstehung und Entwicklung, Wesen und Wert der Hegelschen Philosophie* (Leipzig: Heims, 1973).

Haym, Rudolf, 'Extract from *Hegel and his Times* (1857)', in Robert Stern (ed.), *G. W. F. Hegel Critical Assessments*, Vol. I, trans. Julius Kraft, (London: Routledge, 1993), 217–240.

Herzog, Lisa, *Inventing the Market: Smith, Hegel, and Political Theory* (Oxford: Oxford University Press, 2013).

Honneth, Axel, *The Struggle for Recognition: The Moral Grammar of Social Conflicts*, trans. Joel Anderson (Cambridge, MA: MIT Press, 1995).

Suffering from Indeterminacy: An Attempt at a Reactualization of Hegel's Philosophy of Right, trans. J. Ben-Levi (Amsterdam: Van Gorcum, 2007).

The Pathologies of Individual Freedom: Hegel's Social Theory, trans. Ladislaus Löb (Princeton, NJ: Princeton University Press, 2010).

'Labour and Recognition: A Redefinition', in *The I in We: Studies in the Theory of Recognition*, trans. Joseph Ganahl (Cambridge: Polity, 2012), 56–74.

Freedom's Right: The Social Foundations of Democratic Life, trans. Joseph Ganahl (New York: Columbia University Press, 2014).

Horstmann, Rolf-Peter, 'The Role of Civil Society in Hegel's Political Philosophy', in Robert B. Pippin and Otfried Höffe (eds.), *Hegel on Ethics and Politics*, trans. N. Walker (Cambridge: Cambridge University Press, 2004), 208–238.

Houlgate, Stephen, *An Introduction to Hegel: Freedom, Truth and History*, 2nd edn (Oxford: Blackwell, 2005).

'Recht und Zutrauen in Hegels Philosophie des Rechts', in Gunnar Hindrichs and Axel Honneth (eds.), *Freiheit. Stuttgarter Hegel-Kongress 2011* (Frankfurt am Main: Vittorio Klostermann, 2013), 613–626.

Hutchings, Kimberly, *Hegel and Feminist Philosophy* (Cambridge: Polity Press, 2003).

'Hard Work: Hegel and the Meaning of the State in his Philosophy of Right', in Thom Brooks (ed.), *Hegel's Philosophy of Right* (Oxford: Blackwell, 2012), 124–142.

Ikäheimo, Heikki, *Anerkennung* (Berlin and Boston, MA: de Gruyter, 2014).

Ilting, Karl-Heinz, 'Hegels Auseinandersetzung mit der aristotelischen Politik', *Philosophisches Jahrbuch* 71 (1963/1964): 38–48.

Irigaray, Luce, *Speculum of the Other Woman*, trans. G. C. Gill (Ithaca, NY: Cornell University Press, 1985).

Jagentowicz Mills, Patricia, *Woman, Nature, and Psyche* (New Haven, CT: Yale University Press, 1987).

'Hegel's *Antigone*', in Patricia Jagentowicz Mills (ed.), *Feminist Interpretations of G. W. F. Hegel* (University Park, PA: Pennsylvania University Press, 1996), 59–88.

James, David, *Rousseau and German Idealism: Freedom, Dependence and Necessity* (Cambridge: Cambridge University Press, 2013).

Jameson, Fredric, *Representing Capital: A Reading of Volume One* (London and New York: Verso, 2010).

Jarvis, Douglas E., 'The Family as the Foundation of Political Rule in Western Philosophy: A Comparative Analysis of Aristotle's Politics and Hegel's Philosophy of Right', *Journal of Family History* 36(4) (2011): 440–463.

Kaiser, Gerhard, *Pietismus und Patriotismus im literarischen Deutschland. Ein Beitrag zum Problem der Säkularisation* (Frankfurt am Main: Athenäum,1973).

Klikauer, Thomas, *Hegel's Moral Corporation* (Basingstoke: Palgrave Macmillan, 2015).

Knowles, Dudley, *Hegel and the Philosophy of Right* (London: Routledge, 2002).

Kosch, Michelle, 'Fichtean Kantianism in Nineteenth-Century Ethics', *Journal of the History of Philosophy* 53(1) (2015): 111–132.

Koselleck, Reinhart, *Preußen zwischen Reform und Revolution* (Stuttgart: Klett-Cotta, 1975).

Kriele, Martin, 'Zur Geschichte der Grund- und Menschenrechte', in Norbert Achterberg (ed.), *Öffentliches Recht und Politik* (Berlin: Duncker & Humblot, 1973), 187–211.

Ladwig, Bernd, 'Moderne Sittlichkeit. Grundzüge einer "hegelianischen" Gesellschaftstheorie des Politischen', in Hubertus Buchstein and Rainer Schmalz-Bruns (eds.), *Politik der Integration. Symbole, Repräsentation, Institution* (Baden-Baden: Nomos Verlagsgesellschaft, 2006), 111–135.

Losurdo, Domenico, *Zwischen Hegel und Bismarck. Die achtundvierziger Revolution und die Krise der deutschen Kultur* (Berlin: Akademie Verlag, 1993).

Hegel and the Freedom of the Moderns, trans. Marella and Jon Morris (Durham, NC: Duke University Press, 2004).

Lübbe-Wolff, Gertrude, 'Über das Fehlen von Grundrechten in Hegels Rechtsphilosophie. Zugleich ein Beitrag zum Verständnis der historischen Grundlagen des Hegelschen Staatsbegriffs', in H.-C. Lucas and O. Pöggeler (eds.), *Hegels Rechtsphilosophie im Zusammenhang der europäischen*

Verfassungsgeschichte (Stuttgart-Bad Cannstatt: Frommann-Holzboog, 1986), 421–446.

Lucas, Hans-Christian and Rameil, Udo, 'Furcht vor der Zensur? Zur Entstehungs- und Druckgeschichte von Hegels Grundlinien der Philosophie des Rechts', *Hegel-Studien* 15 (1980): 63–93.

Marx, Karl, *Marx-Engels-Werke*, ed. Institut für Marxismus-Leninismus beim Zentralkomitee der Sozialistischen Einheitspartei Deutschlands, 43 volumes. (Berlin: Dietz Verlag, 1956–1990).

Capital: Volume 1, trans. B. Fowkes (London: Penguin Books, 1976).

Early Writings, trans. Rodney Livingstone and Gregor Benton (London: Penguin, 1992).

Selected Writings, ed. D. McLellan, 2nd edn (Oxford: Oxford University Press, 2000).

Matsumoto, Naoko, *Polizeibegriff im Umbruch. Staatszwecklehre und Gewaltenteilungspraxis in der Reichs- und Rheinbundpublizistik* (Frankfurt am Main: Klostermann, 1999).

Milner, Jean-Claude, *Clartés de tout* (Paris: Verdier, 2011).

Mohseni, Amir, *Abstrakte Freiheit. Zum Begriff des Eigentums bei Hegel* (Hamburg: Felix Meiner, 2014).

Moyar, Dean, *Hegel's Conscience* (Oxford: Oxford University Press, 2011).

'Consequentialism and Deontology in the *Philosophy of Right*', in Thom Brooks, (ed.), *Hegel's Philosophy of Right: Essays on Ethics, Politics and Law* (Oxford: Blackwell, 2012), 9–42.

'Fichte's Organic Unification: Recognition and the Self-overcoming of Social Contract Theory', in Gabriel Gottlieb (ed.), *Fichte's Foundations of Natural Right: A Critical Guide* (Cambridge: Cambridge University Press, 2016).

Murray, Patrick, 'Value, Money and Capital in Hegel and Marx', in Andrew Chitty and Martin McIvor (eds.), *Karl Marx and Contemporary Philosophy* (Basingstoke: Palgrave Macmillan, 2009), 174–187.

Neocleous, Mark, *The Fabrication of Social Order: A Critical Theory of Power* (London: Pluto Press, 2000).

Neuhouser, Frederick, *Foundations of Hegel's Social Theory: Actualizing Freedom* (Cambridge, MA: Harvard University Press, 2000).

Nicolacopolous, Toula and Vassilacopolous, George, *Hegel and the Logical Structure of Love: An Essay on Sexualities, Family and Law* (Aldershot: Ashgate, 1999).

Osterhammel, Jürgen, *Die Verwandlung der Welt*, 5th edn (Munich: C. H. Beck, 2010).

Papenheim, Martin, *Erinnerung und Unsterblichkeit. Semantische Studien zum Totenkult in Frankreich 1715–1794* (Stuttgart: Klett-Cotta, 1992).

Patten, Alan, *Hegel's Idea of Freedom* (Oxford: Oxford University Press, 1999).

Pateman, Carole, 'Hegel, Marriage and the Standpoint of Contract', in Patricia Jagentowicz Mills (ed.), *Feminist Interpretations of G. W. F. Hegel* (University Park, PA: Pennsylvania University Press, 1996), 209–233.

Pawlowski, Hans-Martin, 'Zur Aufgabe der Rechtsdogmatik im Staat der Glaubensfreiheit', *Rechtstheorie* 19(4) (1988): 409–441.

Pinkard, Terry, 'Reason, Recognition and Historicity', in Barbara Merker, Georg Mohr, Michael Quante and Ludwig Siep (eds.), *Subjektivität und Anerkennung* (Paderborn: Mentis, 2003), 45–66.

Pippin, Robert, 'Hegel's Political Argument and the Role of "Verwirklichung"', *Political Theory* 9 (1981): 509–532.

'Hegel, Freedom, the Will', in Ludwig Siep (ed.), *Grundlinien der Philosophie des Rechts* (Berlin: Akademie Verlag, 1997), 31–54.

Hegel's Practical Philosophy: Rational Agency as Ethical Life (Cambridge: Cambridge University Press, 2008).

'Back to Hegel?', *Mediations* 26(1–2) (2013), at www.mediationsjournal.org/articles/back-to-hegel.

Popper, K. R., *The Open Society and Its Enemies, Volume II, The High Tide of Prophecy: Hegel, Marx, and the Aftermath* (London: Routledge & Kegan Paul, 1945).

Priddat, Birger, *Hegel als Ökonom* (Berlin: Duncker & Humblot, 1990).

Quante, Michael, *Die Wirklichkeit des Geistes. Studien zu Hegel* (Berlin: Suhrkamp, 2011).

Quante, Michael and Mohseni, Amir (eds.), *Die linken Hegelianer. Studien zum Verhältnis von Religion und Politik im Vormärz* (Paderborn: Wilhelm Fink, 2015).

Rawls, John, *A Theory of Justice*, Revised Edition (Cambridge, MA: Belknap Press, 1999).

Ritter, Joachim, *Hegel and the French Revolution: Essays on the 'Philosophy of Right'*, trans. Richard Dien Winfield (Cambridge, MA: MIT Press, 1982).

Metaphysik und Politik. Studien zu Aristoteles und Hegel (Frankfurt am Main: Suhrkamp, 2003).

Rózsa, Erzsébet, 'Das Prinzip der Besonderheit in Hegels Wirtschaftsphilosophie', in *Hegels Konzeption praktischer Individualität* (Paderborn: Mentis, 2007): 182–213.

Ruda, Frank, *Hegel's Rabble: An Investigation into Hegel's Philosophy of Right* (London: Continuum, 2011).

Schmidt am Busch, Hans-Christoph, 'Personal Respect, Private Property, and Market Economy: What Critical Theory Can Learn from Hegel', *Ethical Theory and Moral Practice* 11(5) (2008): 573–586.

'Anerkennung' als Prinzip der Kritischen Theorie (Berlin and New York: de Gruyter, 2011).

'Personal Freedom without Private Property? Hegel, Marx, and the Frankfurt School', *International Critical Thought* 5(4) (2015): 473–485.

Schnädelbach, Herbert, 'Die Verfassung der Freiheit', in Ludwig Siep (ed.), *G. W. F. Hegel. Grundlinien der Philosophie des Rechts*, 3rd edn (Berlin: Akademie Verlag, 2014), 243–266.

Sennett, Richard, *The Corrosion of Character* (New York: W. W. Norton, 1998).

Siep, Ludwig, *Praktische Philosophie im Deutschen Idealismus* (Frankfurt am Main: Suhrkamp, 1992).

'Constitution, Fundamental Rights and Social Welfare', in Robert B. Pippin and Otfried Höffe (eds.), *Hegel on Ethics and Politics*, trans. Nicholas Walker (Cambridge: Cambridge University Press, 2004), 268–290.

'Das Recht der Revolution – Kant, Fichte und Hegel über 1789 und die Folgen', in Rolf Groeschner and Wolfgang Reinhard (eds.), *Tage der Revolution – Feste der Nation* (Tübingen: Mohr & Siebeck, 2010), 115–144.

'Vernunftrecht und Rechtsgeschichte: Kontext und Konzept der "Grundlinien" im Blick auf die "Vorrede"', in Ludwig Siep (ed.), *Aktualität und Grenzen der praktischen Philosophie Hegels* (Munich: Wilhelm Fink, 2010), 5–30.

Hegels praktische Philosophie und das 'Projekt der Moderne' (Baden-Baden: Nomos, 2011).

Anerkennung als Prinzip der praktischen Philosophie. Untersuchungen zu Hegels Jenaer Philosophie des Geistes, 2nd edn (Hamburg: Felix Meiner, 2014).

Der Staat als irdischer Gott. Genesis und Relevanz einer Hegelschen Idee (Tübingen: Mohr & Siebeck, 2015).

Smith, Adam, *The Theory of Moral Sentiments*, eds. D. D. Raphael and A. L. Macfie (Oxford: Clarendon Press, 1976).

Steinberger, Peter, *Logic and Politics: Hegel's Philosophy of Right* (New Haven, CT: Yale University Press, 1988).

Stillman, Peter G., 'Property, Contract, and Ethical Life in Hegel's *Philosophy of Right*', in Drucilla Cornell, Michel Rosenfeld and David Gray Carlson (eds.), *Hegel and Legal Theory* (London: Routledge, 1991), 205–227.

Stolleis, Michael, '"Konfessionalisierung" oder "Säkularisierung" bei der Entstehung des frühmodernen Staates', *Ius Commune. Zeitschrift für europäische Rechtsgeschichte* 20 (1993): 1–23.

Stone, Alison, 'Matter and Form: Hegel, Organicism, and the Difference between Women and Men', in Kimberly Hutchings and Tuija Pulkkinen (eds.), *Hegel's Philosophy and Feminist Thought* (New York: Palgrave Macmillan, 2010), 211–232.

'Gender, the Family, and the Organic State in Hegel's Political Thought', in Thom Brooks (ed.), *Hegel's Philosophy of Right: Essays on Ethics, Politics and Law* (Oxford: Blackwell, 2012), 143–164.

Tugendhat, Ernst, *Self-Consciousness and Self-Determination*, trans. Paul Stern (Cambridge, MA: MIT Press, 1989).

Vieweg, Klaus, *Das Denken der Freiheit. Hegels Grundlinien der Philosophie des Rechts* (Munich: Wilhelm Fink, 2012).

Waszek, Norbert, 'Hegels Schottische Bettler', *Hegel-Studien* 19 (1984): 311–316.

The Scottish Enlightenment and Hegel's Account of 'Civil Society' (Dordrecht: Kluwer, 1988).

Weisser-Lohmann, Elisabeth, *Rechtsphilosophie als praktische Philosophie. Hegels 'Grundlinien der Philosophie des Rechts' und die Grundlegung der praktischen Philosophie* (Munich: Wilhelm Fink, 2011).

Wellmer, Albrecht, 'Models of Freedom in the Modern World', in *Endgames: The Irreconcilable Nature of Modernity: Essays and Lectures*, trans. David Midgley (Cambridge, MA: MIT Press, 1998), 3–37.

Werner, Laura, *The Restless Love of Thinking: The Concept of Liebe in G. W. F. Hegel's Philosophy* (Helsinki: Helsinki University Press, 2007).

Westphal, Kenneth, 'The Basic Context and Structure of Hegel's "Philosophy of Right"', in Frederick C. Beiser (ed.), *The Cambridge Companion to Hegel* (Cambridge: Cambridge University Press, 1993), 234–269.
Wildt, Andreas, *Autonomie und Anerkennung. Hegels Moralitätskritik im Lichte seiner Fichte-Rezeption* (Stuttgart: Klett-Cotta, 1982).
Williams, Robert R., *Hegel's Ethics of Recognition* (Berkeley, CA: University of California Press, 1997).
Winfield, Richard D., *The Just Family* (Albany, NY: SUNY Press, 1998).
Wolff, Michael, 'Hegel's Organicist Theory of the State: On the Concept and Method of Hegel's "Science of the State"', in Robert B. Pippin and Otfried Höffe (eds.), *Hegel on Ethics and Politics*, trans. Nicholas Walker (Cambridge: Cambridge University Press, 2004), 291–322.
Wood, Allen, *Hegel's Ethical Thought* (Cambridge: Cambridge University Press, 1990).
'Evil in Classical German Philosophy: Evil, Selfhood and Despair', in Andrew Chignell and Scott MacDonald (eds.), *Evil* (Oxford: Oxford University Press, Forthcoming).
Žižek, Slavoj, 'The Politics of Negativity', preface in Frank Ruda, *Hegel's Rabble: An Investigation into Hegel's Philosophy of Right* (London: Continuum, 2011).

Index

Lightning Source UK Ltd.
Milton Keynes UK
UKHW022156010319
338316UK00020B/433/P